PLEASANT BAY

INGONISH

CHETICAMP

CAPE BRETON I.

MARGAREE FORKS

ST. ANN

E EDWARD I.

INVERNESS

BADDECK

SYDNEY

PORT HOOD

LOUISBOURG

MONASTERY

HAWKESBURY

NGOUCHE

PICTOU

ANTIGONISH

ALMA

NEW GLASGOW

MULGRAVE

HOLME

GUYSBOROUGH

CANSO

TRURO

CROSS ROADS COUNTRY HARBOUR

MELROSE

SHERBROOKE

STORMONT

OCEAN

LA

MARIE JOSEPH

TANGIER

RTMOUTH

TIC

THIS is NOVA SCOTIA

AUTHOR'S ROUTE

STEVEN

A. P. Dunn.

Xmas. 1950.

THIS IS NOVA SCOTIA

Will R. Bird

ENTRANCE TO PORT ROYAL HABITATION

THIS IS
NOVA
SCOTIA

WILL R. BIRD, Litt.D.

THE RYERSON PRESS ~ TORONTO

Published April, 1950

ACKNOWLEDGMENT

Every effort has been made to trace
ownership of copyrighted material that
has been quoted. Information will be
welcome which will enable the pub-
lishers to rectify any reference or credit.

PRINTED AND BOUND IN CANADA
BY THE RYERSON PRESS, TORONTO

Contents

List of Illustrations

1

The Overland Gateway

First Romance. The wide marshes. Beaubassin. Fort Lawrence. The ship railway. Standfast Billings. The Saxby Tide. The Maiden's Cave. The whale. Bass River. Truro. Grand Lake.

A GLANCE at the map of Canada will show that Nova Scotia is like a long lobster claw jutting out into the Atlantic, stretching 300 miles from tip to tip, and anchored to the mainland by a seventeen-mile-wide isthmus that constitutes the overland gateway to this sea-haunted province. The sea is all around it; the turbulent tides of Fundy, the pounding Atlantic and the warm and comparatively calm waters of Northumberland Strait.

Generations of Nova Scotians have been aware of a sense of isolation, and it has had a certain influence in their lives. Daily existence seems to have a different tempo from the rest of Canada, and there is that inexplicable strength of character that comes to those who live largely by themselves. Average Nova Scotians are quite content to feel apart; in fact, they might feel that way if there were no geographical arrangement keeping them from the mainland, for they hold a tremendous pride in the history of the province, and in its sea environment.

We motored into the peninsula as if we were strangers, trying to view it as a visitor who had not been there before, and made our resolve to make a complete encirclement of the province, avoiding side roads and telling only of what we saw and encountered as we made the tour.

1

The entry point is the bridge over the Missiquash River, dividing line between Nova Scotia and New Brunswick, once claimed to be the boundary of British Acadia, and named in a strange manner.

Over to the right, on the New Brunswick side, is a rising in the marsh that is known as "Tonge's Island." It is the exact centre of the Maritime Provinces and it was the capital of Nova Scotia seventy years before Halifax was founded. There Michel Le Neuf, Sieur de La Vallière, a son of one of the four families of noble blood in Canada during the middle of the 17th century, established himself in 1676. He lived in feudal style, enclosing his possessions and the homes of himself and his retinue with a stockade of timbers. He had a vessel which he sailed up and down the coast to collect tribute from foreign fishermen, and to trade with Indians.

His daughter, Marguerite, was the beauty of the family, and it is related that her royal breeding showed in her graceful carriage and manners. She was soon in love with the marshes and neighbouring upland, riding everywhere on a favourite horse. Her father adored her, and named the river on the marsh "Le Marguerite" in her honour. The stream is so marked on all old French maps of Acadia. He planned that she would marry a nobleman of Montreal when it was convenient to visit that area again, but the romance of Acadia began to stir in Marguerite's veins and she could not wait the pleasure of a titled dandy whom she had never seen. So love had its way. One dark night she eloped with a widower from a tiny settlement up the ridge, a man who already had six children and no more than a rude log cabin for a home.

There was nothing the proud father could do about the romance, but he did something about the river. He issued a proclamation, changing its name from "Marguerite" to the most dreadful word he could imagine, "Missiquash," and the Missiquash it has remained to this day.

The vast Tantramar marshes lend an impressive setting to the overland gateway. The ribbon of paved highway—

Trans-Canada Highway 2—is the only definite marking running through a sea of grass tops. The huge marshes stretch on
either side, their green expanse broken only by occasional
hay barns, most of them weathered to a dull grayness, the odd
one having wide doors painted red. For nine miles the
marshes extend, interrupted by three ridges and four tide-
ruled rivers that appear channels of ugly redness at ebb.
Ragged dykes rim the river channels, and all the dyke banks
are covered with wild roses. Above them hover low-flying
marsh hawks, incessantly in search of field mice.

The marshes always rouse the interest of visitors, whether
it be spring after the first warm rains have laid a mist of green
over them and pussy willows by the dykes are warming their
silvery fur in the sun, or mid-summer when thousands of acres
of grass tops shimmer beneath tiny heat waves. Visitors will
stop on the ridges and gaze for an hour as if they are fascinated
and watching the waves of a real ocean. The waves are there,
too, for the wind is funnelled up Fundy Bay to Cumberland
Basin, and summer, winter, fall or spring that restless little
breeze is there, waving the grass, wafting the scent of wild
roses for miles, tossing the gulls and crows that haunt the
flats when the tide goes out.

Across the Missiquash and up the ridge leads to the
Nova Scotia Government Information Bureau. In the Bureau
a courteous staff hands out booklets and maps and information on almost every subject. Across the way is "Windy Mere,"
a handcraft shop. All around are fields that once formed a
part of the village of Beaubassin, and two centuries of farming
have not removed traces of the old roadway and various
Acadian cellars.

Beaubassin was founded in 1672, and soon became a
prosperous settlement. The Acadians found the marshes the
haunts of thousands of wildfowl, and the instinct for dyking
was with them. Soon they reclaimed the land from the ducks
and geese, and cleared the fertile marsh slopes. They had a
tannery, a brickyard, a chapel and thirty acres of apple trees.
The Indians were friendly and the world seemed a kind place,

for they knew nothing of troubles elsewhere, and had a document from an English officer promising them protection at all times.

In New England, however, the Indian raids had become bitter, and there was insistent demand for retaliation. So an armed force was raised and sent in whale boats, under command of Ben Church, to do what damage might be done to Acadian settlements. Ill-luck guided them to peaceful Beaubassin in 1696. The villagers met Church and his men in friendly fashion, taking care, however, to show them the document they had from high British authority. Church took the missive and put it in his pocket. Then his men killed sheep and cattle, tore down the dykes and fences, burned the chapel and many buildings. After which Church drew up a new allegiance to King William and forced the Acadians to sign it.

The fences and dykes were mended, the homes re-built, but the Indian atrocities in New England continued. So once more revenge was requested and Church returned to the restored Beaubassin, his instructions being "to have prayers on ship daily, to sanctify the Sabbath, and to forbid all profane swearing and drunkenness, to burn and destroy all French holdings." The people of Beaubassin took to the woods, and from there watched their homes being plundered and destroyed. No doubt they wondered what made the British such brutal folk. Then, when the boats and raiders were gone, the Acadians came from their hiding and started to build once more.

Their village grew larger than ever. But French and English forces were warring for possession elsewhere in Nova Scotia, and there came a time when the French decided that the Missiquash would be the boundary between them and the English. The people of Beaubassin were asked to move across, with all their possessions. This they refused to do, so Le Loutre, a fanatical priest who headed a band of Indians, burned every building in the settlement and so forced the issue. That was the finish for Beaubassin.

Never has an Acadian returned to the ridge in the two hundred years since that burning, but today you can stand and see where their village existed. At the foot of the ridge by some hemlock groves we dug in the soft earth and, at a depth of no more than four feet, uncovered old brick and knew we were near where the kiln had been. We dug at another location, using an old map for reference, and discovered layer upon layer of hemlock bark still in fair condition—the site of the old Acadian tannery. A farmer came from a nearby house with a toasting fork he had unearthed. Its handle was three feet long. Every now and then, on that ridge, the plow uncovers some rusted implement used by the folk of Beaubassin. When the railway cutting went through it uncovered the forgotten little Acadian cemetery, and many graves had to be removed.

Standing near the Bureau and looking far to the left, one can see the top of an old brick house, a substantial old Yorkshire dwelling dating back to 1776 and built of honest brick burned there on the marsh. There are six fireplaces to heat it. There was a cheese press in the cellar, a loom in the attic, a sun-dial in the garden, an old oaken bucket in the sweep well. There it stands, staunch and four-square, a last link with the eleven shiploads of Yorkshiremen who came and settled in the Isthmus area.

This ridge settlement on which the Bureau stands is Fort Lawrence. A road leading to the right passes a cairn of field stone that marks the site of the old British fort, and a farmhouse there uses a closed-in portion of the fort trench as its cellar. Near the garden there used to be a few rusted cannon balls that the plow had routed from the fields. The inscription on the cairn reads:

Fort Lawrence. Erected in 1750 by Major Charles Lawrence, afterwards lieutenant-governor of Nova Scotia, for the defence of the Isthmus of Chignecto; garrisoned by British troops until after the capture of Fort Beausejour in 1755, when it was abandoned.

French prisoners were kept in Fort Lawrence after their stronghold had fallen, but one dark night in October eighty-six of them dug their way through the earthworks and escaped. The location overlooks the surrounding marsh on three sides, showing why it was chosen, and visitors who gaze around find it easy to visualize the grassy slopes as they looked in April, 1750, when Major Lawrence arrived with his men and lumber to erect the fort. As they waited a tide they saw the houses of Beaubassin burning fiercely, so they landed an Acadian deputy by boat and told him to hurry and tell the people of the village that the British force would do them no harm, but representatives from among them were desired to come to the vessel for instructions.

None came, nor did the deputy return, and when the troops had landed and located some Acadians, they found them planting a French flag on the marsh, and the excuse was that officers from the French fort had sent the flag and ordered it so set up. Lawrence interviewed the French commandant, De la Corne, and was told that he was acting under instructions from Quebec. Soldiers and Indians were lying behind the dykes in readiness for hostilities, so Lawrence decided it was best to sail away and return when he was better prepared for fighting. He returned in September, with a stronger force, and landed despite the opposition of French soldiers and Indians who were led by two priests. The fort was built, and soon some of the Acadians who had been forced, by the destruction of their dwellings, to move to the east side of the river, began slipping back by night, and were well treated by the Fort Lawrence garrison. Foremost among those who had dealings with them was Edward How, a man who spoke French fluently and who held the regard of both the Acadians and the Indians. The fanatical priest, Le Loutre, was fearful of such influence, and planned How's murder.

One October morning a French soldier carrying a white flag appeared on the far side of the Missiquash river and asked for an interview with How, pointing out that he was entirely unarmed and came peacefully. How at once went down to the river's edge to talk with him, when Indians lying hidden in the curves of the dykes opened fire and killed him. Some historians have written that it was Le Loutre himself who wore the French uniform, while others think it was an Indian. At any rate it was an act of treachery that brought Le Loutre scathing condemnation from the French officers in command at Beauséjour.

Then came a morning early in June, 1755, when forty-four vessels sailed into view on Cumberland Basin and bore down toward Fort Lawrence, arriving at a landing in the afternoon. The fort was quadrilateral, consisting of four bastions connected at the corners by curtains. The wall consisted of a palisade of heavy timbers, outside of which was a deep fosse. Timber platforms supported the cannon. There were two magazines within the fort, and blockhouses in the northwest and southeast bastions. Barracks, guardrooms, the Commandant's house, a storehouse and well completed the interior, while outside was a large woodyard, and the one gateway was in the middle of the south curtain. The troops landed and had no opposition. They slept in barns and sheds, and the next day brought their tents and provisions from the ship. It must have been a fine sight to see two thousand men moving about busily, with their tents making a small town outside the fort, and anchored vessels reaching like a strong sea barricade all along the Basin shore.

On June 4th the march up the marsh started, and as the visitor surveys the wide area of green he can imagine how the advance guard of sixty men was spread from ridge to river bank. Then came the soldiers, and the gunners pulling with ropes their short brass field guns, six-pounders. Gulls and crows flapped and sailed overhead, excited by the invasion, and the mouse hawks, angered by the intrusion, flung squawked defiance, and fled. The soldiers, finding it heavy going on the spongy marsh, perspired and swore, no doubt, slapping at mosquitoes, and wondering where the Frenchies would appear. What a sight it must have been?

A few hundred yards along the highway from the Bureau stands a signboard pointing to the "Ship Railway." A great wide road bed leads out on the right to the Basin, and on the left disappears in wooded land leading up the ridge. Here four thousand men toiled to build a railway that would transport ships up to one thousand tons across the seventeen and one-half miles of Isthmus, from Tidnish on the Northumberland Strait to Amherst Docks on Cumberland Basin. It was named the "Chignecto Ship Railway," and H. G. C. Ketchum was the man who had the vision. His object was to save shipping in the Bay of Fundy the long voyage around the peninsula to the Gulf of St. Lawrence. Vessels using the railway would save 500 miles between Saint John and Quebec.

Much money for the project was raised in England, but the Government of Canada also made a generous subsidy that was to extend over a period of twenty years. The cost of the railway and all equipment was estimated to be about four million dollars. There were two tracks laid, with rails of 110 pounds each to the yard. The basin at Amherst Dock was excavated forty feet deep, 500 feet long and 300 feet wide. Walls of massive masonry were erected on the sides to retain the water. A gate thirty feet high and sixty feet wide opened at high water to admit shipping. When admitted, the vessel was to float over a gridiron, a movable part of the track, which, with the cradle upon it, was immersed to the bottom of the dock to receive the vessel for transportation. The cradle was 230 feet long and forty feet wide. It was carried on 192 wheels, and consisted of three sections. Ten hydraulic rams and presses on each side of the track lifted the vessels.

Special masons were imported from Scotland to build the dock walls and the bridges along the way. The hoisting machinery was installed at the Amherst end, and all but three miles of the track had been laid when shipping companies, fearful of a great loss of revenue to be suffered when their sea mileages were so curtailed, rushed to Ottawa to make protest. They were numerous and their lobbying was successful. The Canadian Government withdrew all financial support. Work ceased and Ketchum, so near success, worried to such an extent that he died suddenly, and there was no one else with his courage to try to complete the task. The old dock buildings are gone now. The dock itself is filled with silt from the Fundy, but the old masonry is there as solid as when built, and so are the bridges along the railway. Curious visitors sometimes leave their cars by the roadside and go tramping where the great ties were laid, trying to guess what the dark objects are that are heaped in grotesque manner by the Amherst dock. The piles are countless barrels of cement that were left there. The wood has long since rotted away, but the strange pillars remain in position, roosting places for gulls that haunt the old workings.

Amherst is two and one-half miles away across the marsh, and the approach to the town is not eye-pleasing. An old factory is down at marsh level and seems to be sagging into the mud. It was built too far out on the marsh, and was not completed before its troubles began. The builders dug desperately to find solid ground, sinking steel casings to the depth of nearly thirty feet through the mud. Then they came upon traces of an ancient forest, and realized that some time all the great marsh areas was a forest. Something had caused the sea to break through and rush over the country, uprooting the trees and burying all under the silt of Fundy that, in time, became rich marsh mud.

The town has something about it that reminds one of Kipling's story of "The Man Who Was." Dr. Rand's delving into Micmac history brought forth the fact that the Indians had a large village on the site for centuries, they liking the spot because it was easy to kill wildfowl by the hundreds there in the spring, while the small tidal river at the foot of the slope was literally filled with fish in the spring—the easily-taken gaspereau.

When the Acadians came the Micmacs complained that their settlement at Beaubassin was driving the wildfowl away. But the Frenchmen remained, making no argument, and in time the Indians moved. When they were gone the Acadians occupied the village site, reaching it by a trail across the marsh they had dyked. Some great hewn planks were placed to serve as a bridge over the stream, and so the settlement became known as "La Planche," a name now given to the river.

When Le Loutre destroyed Beaubassin, La Planche was not spared. Years later New England settlers came into the district. British military engineers from the fort garrison laid out a town two miles westward and there the village began. But when the first coaching road came through, it passed near the original La Planche, and so the New Englanders little town, which they had called "Amherst," was moved to where the Acadian cellars were waiting.

Amherst prospered during the work at the ship railway. Several industries came to the town, for it has an excellent central location in the Maritimes, and by 1910 the sign at the railway station bore the name "Busy Amherst." All went well for a time, but the markets in central Canada gradually dried up as far as Nova Scotians were concerned, and the industries were taken over, one by one, by central Canada firms, until there was little left of the "town that was." Its citizens, however, were of the finest stock and they hung grimly on through hard times, developing a fine citizenship. Their courage has been rewarded. Slowly but surely Amherst is regaining its name of being one of the better towns of the province.

The town ridge flattens out toward the westward, and just beyond the town limits is an interesting wild fowl sanctuary. An old ferry at the foot of the ridge once carried many passengers over to Minudie on the other side of the water. Few go there now, but a most unusual sight awaits the visitor who does such exploring, for it is at Minudie that the fat shad run and the fishing is unique. The farmers build tall weirs on the flats, and when the tide, which is high there, has ebbed, they drive out with their carts and stand in them to *fork down* from the nets the shad caught in the net meshes, a "believe it or not" that must be seen to be appreciated.

The Isthmus folk are largely descended from Yorkshire stock. The Yorkshiremen came with money in their breeches and pride in their hearts. They found land cheap and taxes almost nil, so they were happy indeed and their settlements became prosperous. Many a home possesses grandfather clocks and warming pans and spinning wheels that came with one or another of the eleven shiploads arriving in the 1770's. These Yorkshiremen were a practical, hard-headed type, thrifty, working long hours, loyal to each other, proud of their farming methods. Many a tale of those first-comers is re-told yet in the marsh districts.

One deals with Standfast Billings, an industrious cobbler who lived near the fort gate. In October, 1780, Mrs. Billings suffered from the "flux" and the general opinion was that she would not recover. Standfast thought matters over as he pegged stiff leather, and finally made a remarkable decision. He took a quill pen in hand and inscribed an epistle which was addressed "To Any Capable Healthy Middle-aged Female Willing to Wed an Honest Cobbler." He had four small children and visioned with horror his circumstances if left without a wife. The letter, unsealed to save a shilling, was given to the postman who walked fifty miles by blazed trail to Partridge Island, and there caught a ferry to Windsor. From Windsor he walked to Halifax, another forty-odd miles. Being a normal human, the postman had peeped at the contents of the missive before he left, and whispered about what he read. The result was that Mrs. Billings finally heard the whisperings, and was so indignant that she recovered.

Meanwhile the postman was on his way, and at Halifax delivered the letter to a healthy female who worked at a coffee house, and deplored her lack of opportunity to wed. The letter offering immediate marriage and a good home with a "kind and sober affectionate husband" was all that was needed to make her quit her position. She arrayed herself for a long journey on foot and accompanied the postman as he began his return to the fort. They were eleven days making the journey, and when they arrived at the fort cold winter had set in. Mrs. Billings had her hour, and Mr. Billings had a bad time of it indeed, but the lady from Halifax had no desire to return to the town and she obtained work with a farmer in the vicinity. There she laboured four years when Mrs. Billings sickened again and "died on ye Friday without saying a word against ye woman at Bangs farm." Mr. Billings waited a decent period of five weeks, then he and the woman who had answered his letter were properly married and, as far as the records show, lived happily ever after.

Highway 2 winds over the Amherst ridge to the marsh again at Nappan. To the right is a salt plant that is pumping up gallons of brine per minute and will do so endlessly, they say, for the whole underground is a bed of salt. This Nappan marsh has numerous little coves edged in against the upland, and it was here that farmers had great trouble after the Saxby Tide.

In 1869 an officer named Saxby predicted there would be a tremendous tide on the night of October 5th. He was laughed at by the majority, but as the stated time drew near many wondered what would happen. It was hot and still throughout the afternoon, but a great wind came up at night and swept in the highest tide ever known along the upper reaches of Fundy Bay. The sea rolled in over the marshes and simply lifted barns and hay stacks from their foundations. The buildings were swirled about and left shapeless wrecks. Cattle and sheep and horses caught on the flats were carried away and drowned. The hay stacks swept inland on the crest of the tide. Two men, caught out on the marshes, were drowned. Three others escaped by riding on barn timbers until washed onto upland. On a house near the marsh the family went to the upper room and the father took out the window so they might escape if the house should become submerged. The water poured in and the family stood on the bed and chairs, but the tide had reached its height and thereafter subsided, though the water drew out from the bedroom a trunk containing the family savings and it was not seen again.

When the sea had drained back to normal the swollen

bodies of drowned sheep and cattle were stranded over the marsh. In the little coves were countless hay stacks. Some trick of current had carried them there, and for weeks after there were endless arguments about ownership. As there was no means of identifying hay the arguments ended in an agreement to draw lots. One farmer, however, was very definite about his claims. He found a stack miles from his holding but declared the hay was his and that he could prove it as his daughter had lost a scarf in the stack while building it. Many scoffed at him but none stopped him as he came with a cart and began to pitch the hay on it. Soon the bright red scarf was revealed, and the dubious ones were completely dumbfounded. A considerable amount of Nappan history dates to before or after "the Saxby tide."

The Yorkshiremen acquired a goodly portion of the Nappan area. One of these was a young farmer who had left the girl of his choice with the promise that if he found things as good as pictured in Nova Scotia he would send for her at once. His anticipations were more than realized, so he at once wrote the promised letter, not thinking, however, that unless he paid a bounty above the rate made legal, his letter would be slow in moving. He told his neighbours that Mary, his promised lass, was more comely than any in the province, her beautiful blonde hair being a glory beyond compare. Throughout the winter when any social gatherings in kitchens occurred he needed little urging to hold forth on his Mary and her tresses. The winter passed, spring came and went, so did summer and fall, and no Mary arrived. This for the very good reason that the letter was lying in Halifax for many months before someone troubled to hand it to a sea captain proceeding to Liverpool. At Liverpool the letter rested again until the second year, when it was sent on its way.

In late July of that second year a horseman thundered up the lane to the young Yorkshireman's house in the dead of night, hammered at the door and shouted to the awakened man that Mary had arrived, her schooner coming in on the midnight tide, and that she was waiting to see him and could not retire until he had come. She had just received his letter dated two years before and had caught the next ship over. Now she could not wait a single hour but must see him. The young farmer tried to rub sleep from his eyes and in a daze dragged a nag from the stable, mounted and rode with the messenger. But as he rode he began to think of his personal appearance, and of his house. Lack of news from Mary had discouraged him so that he had let things take care of themselves, until his house was like a pig sty and he looked little better than a tramp. He decided to turn back and try to correct matters as much as possible, but the messenger insisted that if he went back to the fort alone Mary would surely ride to the farm. Why not, persuaded the messenger glibly, get married to the girl before she sees your house? It seemed a shady trick, but the young man was desperate. So as he came to the fort he stopped at the parson's house and roused the good man, demanding that he come at once and perform a marriage ceremony by the fort gate. After much protest, the parson agreed, a gold coin having much to do with the agreement.

The anxious Mary was confronted with her man and a parson. She began to explain her reason for wanting him, but the gallant young Yorkie hushed up her every attempt to talk. "After we're wed, lass," he said, "we have all our lives to talk things over." He smothered every protest she made and so the wedding took place, with the messenger a witness. "Now," bragged the new husband to the messenger, "I've the handsomest wife in the country. Show him thy hair, lass." Mary, sobbing, tugged off her bonnet. She was bald. Scarlet fever had made her so, and it was this tragedy she had been trying to tell the young man before the parson tied the knot.

Highway 2 leaves the marshes at Nappan and climbs the Fenwick hills on a long curving grade. At the summit many motorists pause and look back over an unusual panorama of marsh and upland. Then the road enters a wide stretch of sugar maple groves, careens down through a long tract of young hardwood growth and then climbs again, beyond Springhill Junction, to the town of Springhill, atop the deepest coal mines in the Dominion, a hill 652 feet above sea level. This situation provides the town with wonderful views, the long unbroken horizon from west to north showing ridge upon ridge of blue hills extending to New Brunswick, and, against these, the nearer forests show the changing colours of the season. There are many brooks around the foot of the slopes of Springhill, and all bear two or three different local names.

First settlers to Springhill came about 1790, and were Loyalists who received grants in the unclaimed wilderness. They found so many springs around the hill that they called the place "Spring Hill." Later the two words became one, and by 1825 there was quite a settlement. Some of these people found an outcropping of coal. They had no idea of the wealth existing. In winter they sometimes dug out a load or so and sledded it through forest trails to Amherst where they exchanged the fuel for commodities. By 1834 a man named Hunter was selling coal to blacksmiths, and some coal was being hauled as far away as Londonderry. It was 1870, however, before the "Springhill Mining Company" was formed and work commenced on the known seams, while experts searched for others. Finally these had definite knowledge of six workable seams, from eight to fourteen feet in thickness, underlying each other, separated by strata from thirty to three hundred feet.

The Great Springhill Explosion occurred on February 21, 1891. In the morning six hundred men and boys had gone down to their work. They had just finished their noon-day meal when a terrific blast took the lives of one hundred and twenty-five of them and tore out an area of two thousand feet, carrying away doors and stoppings, allowing the fire damp to escape into the workings. This was followed by flame which swept through to the west slope. Those not instantly killed ran for their lives in the terrible darkness, with the din of falling roof and crashing timbers about them. Many gained safety, but others were overcome by the chokedamp following in the wake of the flame. The tragedy shook the town emotionally and all business was suspended while the task of finding and bringing up the dead went on for nearly a week. A monument to the men and boys who lost their lives was unveiled September 11, 1894, by Lord Aberdeen. The gray marble shaft stands on the highest point of Main Street, its four sides being covered with the names of those lost in the disaster, and the whole is surmounted by the figure of a miner in white marble.

From Springhill the Highway turns toward the Parrsboro Shore, passing through the pretty village of Leamington to Mapleton, so called because of the fine groves of sugar maple. These trees produce maple products of the highest quality known anywhere, so superior to products from other parts of America that many accusations have been made about the use of granulated sugar. Tests have shown, however, that these maple products are absolutely pure. The sugar is extremely light in colour and its flavour beyond compare. It is generally said that the abundance of iron ore in the maple hills has something to do with the unusual quality of the maple sap.

The road crosses the Maccan River in the village of Southampton, where once a woollen mill prospered and goes along the West Brook district to Halfway River. The banks of the highway lead to pastures covered with what the people call "sheep laurel," a purple flower that brightens the landscape. Here and there hackmatack takes the place of the usual hardwood grove. The highway surface is smooth as a floor, and away here in the country gay youngsters shoot around on roller skates, playing "follow the leader." Elm trees dot the intervals through West Brook and berry pickers in the distance look like grubs inching their way up a slope. A Baptist church on one corner and a Methodist on the other face each other with grim blockiness of stature, and it is easy to imagine the rival congregations gazing with equal grimness across the highway as they enter their respective places of worship. The road stretches straight for four miles, a rarity in Nova Scotia, and there are swampy areas on either side before Newville Lake is reached. The water glimmers like a mirror, reflecting a high hill with great beauty.

We gulped lungfuls of fresh sea air as we drove into Parrsboro and glimpsed the salt water. Back of the post office there is a parking place, and a lane leads out over a waterway with ancient pilings here and there like the teeth of an old hag that had chewed out the blackened timbers. Gulls settle lazily on derelict posts and chat in querulous notes about the lack of fish offal. An old-timer by his boat was complaining in a thin voice that some evil-minded person had drowned a sack of kittens at his mooring place and the culprits should be fined. We drew him into conversation by listening to his crankiness, and then he pointed out "the Beach," where summer visitors swim: "Them as likes cold water, that is." He told of the fine halibut often taken there and urged us to stroll on beyond main street to "the first Partridge Island, from where this here place moved."

It is but a short distance, and worth the effort. An old building, now the "Ottawa House," is there, and we were told that it was the summer home of one of Canada's best-known statesmen—Sir Charles Tupper. Back of it is a stone building in use as an icehouse, and this is described as the first school house in the Parrsboro district. A climb up a steep hill put us among tangled brush, but we found stone foundations of the Parrsboro blockhouse that commanded the port. In the old days an American invader sailed in to the docks. Her men landed and were terrifying the little village when the lieutenant in command of the blockhouse led his men down and into battle. The fight was a fierce one, but short. The invaders were from Machias, Maine, and they were stout enough lads, but when their leader was killed and two of his best men fell with him, the others gave up. All of them were taken prisoners, and the privateer was a rich prize. Only the stones on Blockhouse Hill remain to tell of that skirmish, but there is another story well preserved of a place beyond the Island.

It is called Black Point, and few Parrsboro visitors venture to the place by car for the trail is a rough one. Along the rocky wall of the Point is a small cavern, being gradually erased by heavy tides. It is known as "The Maiden's Cave," and any fisherman along the shore will tell you it is haunted and offer to take you out at night to hear the despairing cries of the trapped girl. Over two centuries ago, Deno, an Italian pirate, captured a British vessel carrying a rich cargo and made all but the captain's daughter, who was extremely beautiful, "walk the plank." The girl was retained for the pleasure of Deno, but he found her a regular wildcat, one he could not tame. A great storm arose and drove the pirate vessel far off course until it arrived in the Bay of Fundy and Deno sailed without knowing where he was until he landed at Black Point. The beach was littered with jewels, and the amazed freebooters gathered a hefty treasure of amethyst. The captain found the cave on the shore and had his fair captive placed in it. He then walled up the entrance with stone, threw in a number of salted pollock as food, and sailed away. Some time later Indians passing that way heard strange cries. They fled, and told another tribe. Bolder braves went to the place, explored and found the skeleton of the girl. The French named it "Pollock Cave," and kept clear of the spot. Now it is the "Maiden's Cave," and few there are who have not heard the cries when the wind is right at night.

In early days amethyst was plentiful in the Parrsboro district, as were agates and other attractive trap minerals. Footprints of prehistoric animals were found, so well preserved that over one hundred were photographed and plaster casts made for the National Museum at Ottawa. Legend has it that one of the first "lonely hearts" in Nova Scotia was a Parrsboro bachelor whose physical appearance was not in his favour. He inserted a paragraph in a Boston paper, after being induced to do so by a ship's captain he knew. A letter came in reply, was answered and finally the lady from Massachusetts packed her bag and came to the Nova Scotia town. She was not daunted by the sight of the bachelor as she had not much to offer in the way of physical charms herself. They were married the next day, but the man who had stayed single until he was forty-six became nervous when he realized that his bride was acquainted with practically every ship captain who came to port. He had his money in the house and dreaded that his wife would one day take it and vanish. So he purchased a molasses cask and changed every pound he had into pennies. They almost filled the big barrel, and thereafter the husband was more content. He knew his wife could not carry a cask from the house without his knowledge. Finding him so careful of his money, the Boston lady decided life would be too dull for her, so she did go away by schooner one night, taking with her the three pairs of breeches the husband owned. This as a fair precaution to prevent pursuit. History relates that it was late the next day before the poor fellow emerged, wrapped in a blanket, begging the first man he encountered to obtain a pair of breeches for him.

It is in Parrsboro that the visitor will first meet up with some old-timer who still cherishes ballads of the good old days. They are to be found along the coast, down Eastern Shore and South Shore and along Northumberland Strait. In the last century ballad singing was common in every shore community of Nova Scotia. Endless verses would be written about any person who was murdered or came to an untimely end. And there were ballads about brave men in shipwrecks, killing bears and fighting bulls. One favourite in Parrsboro has to do with the final taming of "Slugger" Dunkerson, a tough lad who came from Advocate and looked for fights all along the way. One night in Parrsboro he ran up against a hardrock from Spencer's Island, and when the fracas ended he had been completely thrashed for the first time in his life. The first verse went something like this:

T'was in the town of Parrsboro one dark and stormy night,
When the gallant Slugger Dunkerson got ready for a fight.
He was full of rotten whisky and was feeling very spry,
And he said he'd lick McLellan or know the reason why.

It's a fine drive down along the Parrsboro Shore. The road first follows a brook ravine a considerable distance, winding in and out, and here porcupines in more or less flattened degrees are common sights. Just before Moose River—one of the three in Nova Scotia—there are sharp hairpin turns known as "the devil's elbow," then a second lot before Five Islands. This territory is steeped in Micmac legend. It was along the Parrsboro Shore the Indian man-god, Glooscap, reigned. Before he left he overturned his cooking kettle in the sea and today it forms Spencers's Island. Glooscap became angry with the Beaver that had its dam off the Bay of Fundy, so he tore out a wide section and created Minas Channel. Where the dam had been is today Minas Basin. Then Glooscap wrenched up great handfuls of clods and hurled them after the Beaver. Five giant clods alighted in the water just off shore and formed Five Islands—Moose, Diamond, Long, Egg and Pinnacle. They rise abruptly from the sea, and one has an opening through the centre of the rock. Moose Island was used by pirates as a hiding place for treasure, according to local tales, and dozens of parties have gone there at night and made hurried diggings in search of the buried gold. Each community has tales of Glooscap's adventures, each one varying according to the teller's imagination.

Economy Hill is high and at its crest there is a spring of cold water by the roadside. Hundreds of motorists stop there for a refreshing drink, and to look over the coastal area they have left behind and far below them. Along the Carsbrook district the tides are high and ebb over miles of red sands extending toward the Chimney Rocks, a natural bird sanctuary. A grizzled old-timer swinging a scythe near the road looked up at us as we asked if they caught shad in his country. "Did when I were a boy," he said, removing a cud of chewing large as a hen's egg and nestling it in his hand. "Every house had its smoke-shed out back far enough to be safe from fire. We burnt green wood to smoke 'em. Had a barrel of smoked shad and a barrel of salted shad put down each fall." He stood and put his head back as if he were trying to smell the

evening's weather before it came down. "You ever hear tell
the time we had a whale here, back around forty-odd years
ago. No? Well, it's a fact, for I were the one who seen it first.
It were out on the beach there, threshin' something fearful
as the tide went. Then it got down to no more'n some
quiverin', and time a few of us got out nearby the thing was
dead. There were four of us, so we shook hands on a
'greement and got all the canvas we had, drove stakes and
fenced in that carcass up nigh the meadow. Took eight teams
of horse and high tide to do the movin'. Word went 'round
like a bush fire, and we charged a quarter each to git into the
canvas 'closure. Sunday we had such an almighty crowd we
had to line folks up to take turns goin' in. We made over
fifty dollars that one day. Then it come fearful hot and that
whale begun to stink. Nothin' we could do about it, but
somebody put a piece in the paper, and a constable come
and said we'd have to move it. There weren't any way we
could. It was just a hill of rot by that time, and we told him
so. He come back the next day and took us all to the town
afore a magistrate and we were fined ten dollars each for
makin' a nuisance. Had to pay, of course, but we each had
more'n thirty dollars clear at that. Only thing was, the stink
was terrible and near folks had to move out. You couldn't as
much as git cattle near there. There wasn't no hay cut that
year along them six acres you see by the meadow. Some feller
along a'tween here and Truro has the jaw bones of that whale
yet, if you want to look him up. Anyhow, I'm tellin' you it
was a prime stink."

The old-timer gazed around and sniffed, then replaced his
plug, wiped his chin, took another look at the sky and belched.
We drove on, and reached Bass River, where many signs told
of cottages to rent at the shore nearby, and the principal
feature is a chair factory.

A broth of an Irish boy, James Fulton, was born near
Londonderry, Ireland, in 1740. By the time he was twenty
he had qualified himself as a land surveyor, so he moved to
New England and for five years followed his profession there.

Then he was sent to Nova Scotia to help survey the province, and the chief portion of his compensation was to be a grant of land in some area of his own choosing. That area was the land surrounding Bass River. He cleared a farm and built a stout home, courted a girl with a Scottish name—Margaret Campbell—and was successful. It might have been a placid wooing, or otherwise. In any event young Fulton was stirred to formulate his philosophy of life in twelve stanzas of verse, which he illustrated cleverly with his quill pen as he copied the lines in a parchment folder. The lines are still legible today, and the last verse reads:

> Oh, Man, now see thou art but dust;
> Thy Gold and Silver are but rust;
> Thy time is come, thy glass is spent;
> No worldly care can death prevent.

Fulton may have had his moods as a poet, but history relates that he was a cheerful man. He was married on November 1, 1770, and took his bride to his fine house. There fifteen children were born, thirteen of them living to ripe age, marrying and producing one hundred and seven boys and girls. James Fulton died in 1826, but none save a Fulton has occupied the old homestead, and there are few citizens of Bass River who cannot claim that Fulton blood flows in their veins, for four of James's brothers came to the district and reared families there. One of these was a huge man, named Samuel, possessed of unusual strength and courage. His adventures with three bears are ample proof of his character. One came to his sheep pen early in the morning and Samuel rushed out to see what was the matter. He picked up a short wagon pole and charged bruin, routing him to frenzied flight. Another bear, weighing four hundred on mill scales, disputed his passage in the woods nearby and Samuel grabbed for a length of birch cordwood. One blow caved in the bear's skull, and legend has it that Samuel carried the bear out to the clearing. On a Sabbath afternoon two of Samuel's boys went to visit a neighbour, taking a short cut through the bush.

They did not return at the appointed time, and the father set out to learn the reason why. He came upon them, perched in a spruce tree, while a year-old bear regarded them from below. One of Samuel's huge boots caught the small bruin in the rear, bowling it over. Before it could recover it was caught by the hind feet and dragged ignominiously to the farm, where it was thrown into a strong stall and the door barred. The day was the Sabbath, and Samuel's conscience told him it was not a day for killing. Monday morning he went out early and put an end to the bear without ceremony.

James Fulton became a Judge of the Court of Common Pleas, then represented his County in the Legislative Assembly at Halifax. In 1860 two of the Fulton men built a sawmill near the mouth of Bass River, utilizing the stream to operate a home-made jack-knife saw which moved upward and downward as the log was fed to it by a low-geared ratchet. Soon a lathe was installed and they began making furniture. A chair factory in a nearby settlement was sold by the sheriff and George Fulton bought it and moved the machinery to Bass River, and there the manufacture of chairs was begun on what was then regarded as a large scale. But in 1885 the factory was destroyed by fire, and there was no insurance.

It was a testing time for the little company, but before the year was out another factory had been built and was ready for business, turning out nothing but chairs. Much of the new capital used in reconstruction was subscribed by employees of the company, and that circumstance, in itself, goes far to explain the enduring character of the Bass River Chair Company. In 1892 there was another bad fire, but this time some of the machinery was saved, and there was $4,000 insurance to soften the loss. The older Fulton had died, but his son carried on with the same determination, and the old records show that he worked all hours with all energy for the princely stipend of nine dollars per week.

There have been nine managers in the factory, all descendants of some original Fulton, and all have learned to dread the possibility of fires. Yet in spite of all precautions

taken there was another disaster in 1909, when the plant
was burned to the ground. Again there was the work of
building and importing new machinery, and soon everything
was as before, except the factory was a bit bigger and better
than the previous one. There have been many employees
who gave fifty or more years of service to the company, and
some were outstanding mechanics who simply invented ways
and means of overcoming manufacturing problems. One such
genius was a man named Isaac Munro, and the joiner he
invented is still used. Bass River residents have chairs that
have been in use for half a century and are as good as ever.
Munro made a violin, using a butcher knife and a few pieces
of glass, and it is still in good form.

We admired Bass River. It is a clean place, with the
houses painted white, the lawns spacious, the flowers and
shrubs assorted in good taste. The man we talked with had
worked from boyhood in "the factory," and his father still
worked there, while his son was also on the payroll—three
generations of "chair makers."

Portaupique proved a small place, and so did Highland
Village, but Great Village was pretty beyond words, with tall
elms and other shade trees almost forming a green canopy
overhead as we entered the place. It was evening now and
very still. The aroma of newly-baked bread came from a
kitchen and made us hungry. Some children sat on the steps
of a house eating slabs of bread and jam. Not a word was
being spoken. Two boys lay on grass with their hats pulled
down over their eyes, a dog sprawled between them, while a
cat sat on the verandah rail and surveyed the trio.

We rolled down a gentle grade without a sound being
made by our tires on the pavement, and on our right, in the
shade of a small porch, saw a woman sitting upright in a stiff-
backed chair, sound asleep, with white cotton gloves on her
hands that were clasped loosely over her thick knees. Her
feathered hat was tilted straight back against the wall. On the
walk in front stood a boy of five or six years, staring as if
fascinated.

There was not another car on the road. No one moved anywhere. More kitchen aromas reached us, and we stopped at a small place selling ice cream, according to its sign, and had delicious cups of tea and sandwiches. We were the only customers, and there was no juke box in sight. A delightful lady was in charge and quite willing to talk. She told us about Acadian dykes still to be seen on the Great Village marshes, and of French gardens that were rich ground yet after two hundred years of use.

Glenholme is a small community, the junction of highways 2 and 4. Then the paved road goes through some of the finest farming areas of the province, Lower Debert and Onslow and Masstown. Masstown was once an Acadian village called "Cobequid," and the Acadians had a large place of worship there, the Church of St. Peter and St. Paul. It was burned at the time of the Expulsion but its site can still be traced, and on the lowland the old French dykes are doing service as they did in 1755. Rich expanses of dyked salt marsh adjoin the upland districts and produce heavy crops of hay year after year. Masstown is noted for its strawberries, and huge shipments go from there each season.

This territory was settled by the Irish after the Expulsion, people from northern Ireland and from New Hampshire. During their first year the settlers lived together in blockhouses as much as possible. Legend has it that one of the young men who had a promised girl back in New Hampshire caused his mother great anxiety when he wrote her a letter in the late fall. After his mention of the crops and general prospects he stated that he had given up trying to keep Nellie out of his house, and had taken her in. He would, of course, he wrote, get clear of her before his bride-to-be came in the spring. The mother wrote to friends in Truro and begged them to go to her son and show him the error of his ways and take any needed methods to rid his house of Nellie. The friends came gingerly, and were mightily relieved to find

that Nellie was only a small pig that squealed all night if left
in the pen but slept quietly in the kitchen.

Highway 2 goes past Belmont and into Truro, skirting two
cabin colonies and a large cemetery. Truro is the hub of
Nova Scotia, a town of fine residential streets, shady elms,
busy factories, enterprising citizens. One of these, well up in
his eighties, has a huge collection of scrap books dealing with
almost any subject. His name is Frank A. Doane, and he is a
historian of note, delighting in talking over old times with
anyone.

Truro was a busy place in wartime. The Federal Government established a huge training camp at Debert Station, just
a few miles out, and there tens of thousands of men of the
army and air force received their final instructions before
going overseas. When the day was ended the men entered
Truro by the hundred, being eager to walk about the town
though they had the finest in movie theatres at the camp.
The Truro restaurants did a tremendous business, as did the
theatres. A "Y" was fitted up by Truro residents, and operated
by volunteer workers. The people of the town organized into
groups that did everything possible to give the soldiers a touch
of home while in the locality. Many citizens opened their
homes to the men as they became acquainted, and it is a fine
record to be able to say, as a Truro citizen can, that never at
any time during the war years was there trouble with the men
from the camp.

The town was Irish in the beginning, but early boasted a
fine inn that was described by a traveller of the day as nearly
ideal. He wrote:

We came at night to the pretty village of Truro where we
were put up at a comfortable English inn which served as fine
a dinner as we had had since Boston. Everything about the
place was as clean as soap and water could make it, and the
hostess was a motherly woman of the kindly apple-cheeked
sort whom one likes at first acquaintance. I would that we
could have tarried there a week, for when we walked out in

the morning we were kindly greeted by all we met and especially a group by the local smithy where a troublesome workhorse was being shod while a ring of onlookers cheered the stalwart smith for his courage and efficiency.

Truro had a Normal School by 1855. The first oatmeal ground in Nova Scotia came from the mill of Thomas Dickenson, of Truro, and the first model farm in Canada was established at Truro in 1857. There is also record of the fine wagon that was built in Truro in 1814, a vehicle strong enough to withstand the roads of that time, and heavy enough to require five horses to haul it to Halifax.

The young folk of Truro have a fine place to go in the evenings—Victoria Park—a natural playground of one thousand acres, with alluring footpaths, numerous springs, wishing wells, arbors, lovers lanes and kissing bridges. All very romantic. The young ladies are attending the Normal College, and the young gentlemen attend the Nova Scotia Agricultural College. These, added to the youth of the town, provide plenty of customers for all the romantic spots.

Outside of Truro a short distance is Millbrook, where three different "basket shops" display their wares, made by Micmac Indians. There are over two thousand of the redmen in Nova Scotia and, though there are reservations for them, many prefer to live in settlements of their choosing and to earn their own living. They make baskets of every type, from delicate fancies to large hampers, and they specialize in making strong fishing creels. They also create cunning novelties such as toy birchen canoes, bows and arrows and carved items.

We drove on through Hilden and Brookfield and Brentwood and Alton into Stewiacke, a lumbering centre with two large general stores. Then on again to Shubenacadie, an Indian name meaning "where the wild potatoes grow." This small town is near the point that is headquarters of the Micmacs. A large residential school is there, sited near the original spot of one of the largest encampments in the province. The first French missionary sent by the Society of

Foreign Missions established himself there in 1737, and described it as a large Indian village. In 1754 an English officer reported Shubenacadie as having the finest Mass House in the country "adorned with a fine lofty steeple and a weather cock."

A fine seam of fire clay runs through this district, and the redmen made their pottery there before the white man came. Today the Indian students at the School use the clay to make pottery far more ambitious than that their ancestors formed. There is an old walled well that the missionary had dug, and several markings of ancient Indian workings. Investigations are being carried on, and the place will soon be marked as an historic site.

Milford and Elmsdale and Enfield—we read the names on signboards as we drove along, saw them above schoolhouse doors and on small postoffices. Then Grand Lake. The well-known American columnist, George Matthew Adams, has a summer home on an island of Grand Lake, and has many neighbours who love the peace and quiet of the place. Returning there after World War II, Mr. Adams wrote:

For some sixteen years I have had an island summer retreat on Grand Lake in Nova Scotia. It has been some years since I have been privileged to drive there, but this year I did, and more than ever I was fascinated by the beautiful unspoiled countrysides in New Brunswick and Nova Scotia. They are ideal summer vacation provinces, for their summer weather is about as perfect as it comes. Cool and invigorating. The main roads are excellent, and the prosperous and beautiful farm sights are inspiring. You pass lakes and rivers and gentle rolling country. My favourite drive, for many years, is the one from Moncton, New Brunswick, to my island home by way of Parrsboro, Nova Scotia. It is one of the most beautiful scenic drives I have ever taken anywhere. There are others just as unique, but with a different setting. I have driven both shores of the United States from boundary to boundary. The great Redwood drive out of San Francisco to Portland, Oregon, that magnificent drive along the Columbia highway, those through the Catskills. All have their beauty and their especial attractions, but you have much of them all, in miniature, in the drive into Nova Scotia.

We parked by the roadside. A wizened little man was coming to the shore, rowing easily, and his companion was an Indian of the ageless type so common in the province. Each wore a broad felt hat decorated with flies. They landed without a word being spoken, then the Indian held up three fine striped bass. "Good dinner," he grinned. "One dollar take 'em."

"Okay." We gave him the dollar and accepted the fish. He turned and walked away without a glance at his companion who gazed after him reflectively and spat.

"I reckon," he drawled, "that makes us even. Yes'day I sold the fish and walked off. Clean forgot to divvy with Ike." He shrugged. "You lookin' for anything special?"

"Not much. We were wondering if the Indians used to camp here in their day."

"Reckon they did." The oldster spat again and wiped his chin. "Used to be a reg'lar camp of them in at what's Gay's River. I've heard my old grandfather say that way back they was two tribes in there, and they kep' raisin' hell with the settlers one way and another. One tribe had carved a stump by the brook crossin' into a squaw's head. Mighty good carvin', they said it were. After one settler had his pig stole he was so mad he took a pigskin he had and pulled it down over the stump so the rear was top up. It beat all, but the Indians never thought of blamin' him. 'Stead of that, they blamed each other, and started a reg'lar war atween 'em. Got so hot they each moved away, and they tell that the pigskin was so tough it stayed stretched over that pine stump for over ten years."

He paused and gazed over the lake as if seeing into the past, and began talking. The lazy intonation of his voice seemed as physical as the touch of his hand, but when he paused, now and then, his mouth had the immobility of lips that can guard secrets. He'd sooner go fishing than eat, he said, on account he led a dull life, his wife being both virtuous and without curiosity. He wished he had been born a hundred years sooner when the land was full of game and plenty of fish were in the water. His eyes brightened as he talked until it seemed that his shrivelled body was like a leathery coat of flesh and bones covering the spirit of a venturesome youngster. He'd been born in Brookfield, he said, and could remember his father telling of catching a marten in a trap in the fireplace, when it came down the chimney in summer. He suddenly tugged a dirty creased newspaper clipping from his pocket. "Read that," he piped.

It was an extract from a Creamery Bulletin, regarding working conditions, offering rules that prevailed in a Nova Scotia store during the last century.

Store must be open from six in the morning until nine at night the year around. Store must be swept; counters, base shelves and show cases dusted; lamps trimmed, filled and chimneys cleaned; pens made; windows and doors opened; a pail of water and a bucket of coal brought in before breakfast, and attend to the customers who call. The employee who is in the habit of smoking cigars, getting shaved at the barber shop, going to dances and other places of amusement, will surely give his employer reason to be suspicious of his integrity and honesty. Each employee must pay not less than $5.00 per year to the Church and must attend Sunday School regularly. Men employees are given one evening a week for courting and two if they attend prayer meeting. After fourteen hours of work in the store the leisure hours should be spent mostly in reading.

"How'd you like to live in them days?" he chuckled, watching us read. "I take it you're from around these parts anyhow. That's a Nova Scotia car you're using."

We admitted to being a bluenose, whereupon our amazing entertainer shifted his broad hat, struck a pose and recited:

> God gives all men all earth to love,
> But, since man's heart is small.
> Ordains for each one spot shall prove
> Beloved over all.

He bowed slightly, and spat once more. "Here," we said uneasily. "You take these fish. We didn't really want them."

"Figgered that myself," he acknowledged. "Thanks kindly.

Don't go thinkin' I'm crazy. It's likely I won't talk none for a week now, and my wife won't either."

We drove away, after handing back the clipping, and wondered why the fellow had alarmed us.

There was a quaint old church by the roadside, and more road signs—Wellington, then Fall River. An old road to the left was once a great project, a highway that was to split the eastern part of the province and lead two hundred miles to Guysborough. It was cut through the length by axemen, and bridges placed over several streams. Then a great wind blew so many trees across the way that it was never cleared in the interior and only a comparatively few miles of the highway remained in use. Two miles along its way is a Game Sanctuary, and we can remember a Welshman with a camera sitting day after day at the opening to a bear's den. A New York paper had offered one hundred dollars for a photograph of the bears emerging, this to settle an old argument as to whether or not bears lose their fat during the winter. The photograph was secured without trouble as both bears walked past the man without so much as a grunt, and in a few days the check was received. Beaver invaded the sanctuary in numbers, and it used to be a common thing to see people tramping in the two miles in order to secure pictures of the animals at work on their dams. Now beaver are fairly common throughout the province, and there are a hundred places where they may be seen.

Waverley is next, named by a romantic settler who admired the novels of Sir Walter Scott. Sea planes, almost small as water fowl, take off and light here in Lake William. A road to the left follows the lake shore closely, with trees making a canopy overhead, until a canteen is reached where a bear and monkey and fox on display furnish entertainment for youngsters out for a Sunday car ride.

A few miles more and Highway 2 slopes down to the head of Bedford Basin, and Bedford itself. An ancient house in a high field looks enormous, with its chimney even too large for the house. This building dates far back to the time of a stronghold to guard the Basin. In war years there are signs posted all along the Highway forbidding anyone to use a camera, for it is in Bedford Basin that the great convoys are made up, and it is then a usual thing to see so many ships at anchor that they cannot be counted. The Highway curves in and out, following the Basin shore exactly and two items catch the eye as one reaches Rockingham. The first is an odd-shaped building with a round roof on the left side of the road. The place is known as Prince's Lodge, but this one building was simply the place where the band would play in the days when Prince Edward, later father of Queen Victoria, lived in a fine villa nearby. The estate covered a considerable area and was landscaped by imported experts. Paths led everywhere. There was a heart-shaped pond. Little arbors represented Chinese temples. Chinese bells hung on fine wires tinkled when the breeze stirred them. The kitchen was built apart from the main dwelling and was reached by an underground passage. Here many social functions were held, the chief gallants being officers of the army and navy, while the élite of Halifax drove out by coach and horseback to attend. Gay parties and famous banquets were held nearly every week, and there is record of one officer being killed in a duel fought in the moonlight. Prince Edward had his own French lady at this Lodge, and all Halifax paid her due homage. It is sad indeed to think that such an unusual establishment of such note should have been allowed to fall to ruin and be obliterated.

Farther on a cairn of field stone marks one of the usual National Historic Sites, but any who read the story of the happenings at the spot beside the Basin will pause a long time for there is no other story quite like it in our history. Astounding news reached Nova Scotia in 1746, news which startled New England like a thunderclap. It was reported that a French fleet of over fifty ships of the line, frigates, transports, etc., were enroute across the Atlantic to capture the province. Duc d'Anville was in command and had an abundance of soldiers, arms and ammunition. This fleet left Brest on June

22nd, but a storm struck it soon after and five ships were so damaged that they had to put back. There were more storms, and when d'Anville reached Chebucto on September 10th he had but eight ships with him, five of them transports. Disease struck the men as soon as they landed, and the waiting for the rest of the fleet was an agony. d'Anville, worried and sick, died suddenly on the 27th, the day his Vice-Admiral arrived with a few survivors. The situation appeared desperate to the new commander, and he proposed that they return to France. His officers over-ruled him, and he killed himself with his sword. Sickness spread so that five ships were used as hospitals. The Acadians who brought them provisions died of the sickness. Three out of four Indians in the tribes of the area sickened and died. Bodies were flung from the ships or deposited in the bush. Then the remnant of the once proud fleet set sail and were badly buffeted again by storm before reaching home.

When the settlers who founded Halifax arrived, they found countless skeletons among the trees along the Basin. French muskets were leaned against the trees and French uniforms were mouldering on the moss. In the Basin they could see the blackened hulls of ships the luckless Frenchmen had burned because there were not men enough to form crews for them. Small wonder, then, that there are tales of French ghosts along the Rockingham shore or that residents there move about nervously in their gardens at dusk, dreading they may see a grinning skull beneath one of the trees on the hillside.

2

The Road to the Valley

Mount Uniacke. Ellershouse. Canada's First Fair.
The Improvement Society. No more molasses. William
Hall, V.C. Grand Pré Memorial Park. The Church of
the Covenanters.

WE turned at Rockingham and went back to Bedford to
take the paved highway that leads to "the Valley," through
the Land of Evangeline and Annapolis Royal and down the
St. Mary's Bay Shore to Yarmouth. It is Highway 1, Nova
Scotia's oldest road and most travelled. We would turn at
Yarmouth and return to Halifax by way of the South Shore,
thus making a great loop around the western end of the
peninsula. We had a new glimpse of the huge old house at
Bedford as we returned, and asked an old gentleman by a
drugstore if he knew anything about it.

"I should do—I were born here." He examined critically
a bottle of medicine he had purchased, then placed it in his
pocket. "Fort Sackville was right over there." He pointed to
his left along the highway. "Colonel Joe Scott had a grant of
850 acres here and he put in a sawmill, the first in these parts.
But he died in 1800, and that big house was built the same
year. The sheriff of Halifax came out and built it, and he
brought every stick of the frame from Norway, sound oak.
After a time he got tired of living so far out of town and sold
the place. The new owner hired a cook and run it as a small
hotel. He called it the "Mansion House." Business wasn't too
good with him and he sold out. The next owner planted a
lot of flowers around and had row-boats down at a pier.
He called the place the "Willow Park Summer Hotel," and

did fair business for a time. The name was a bit fancy, but it suited all right for the sheriff had planted willow trees about and they grew to tremendous size. One of them was eight feet around. I remember, too, that there was a log house of heavy timbers right alongside it. I don't know who used it, but it lasted to within my time. The old guard house of the fort was over on the Windsor road, and its chimney was so big that some prisoners went up it when the guard was asleep and escaped."

We thanked him for his information and he followed us to the car. "If you'd asked about the old house anywhere along here you'd been sent to me," he stated. "That's most I do this summer. Tell the history round here." He was neatly dressed and had an easy way of speaking, but we risked offence and handed him half a dollar. He accepted it with dignity and strolled away, swung about and came back.

"That's the Sackville River you'll cross, and that's the fish hatchery along. Back in 1782 they put up a toll gate on the bridge, and the folks that lived beyond put up a real protest. But the gov'ment paid no attention, so one fall a party of masked men on horseback come with axes and smashed the gate to bits and heaved the bits into the river. There was a big reward offered for information about the party, but no one tried to collect. Next year they put up another gate, and it went like the first one. After that they quit trying to take money from them unfortunate enough to live the other side of the River. About nine miles on from here is where paper from wood was invented. You look for a plaque. If you don't see one, ask at some house."

He tipped his hat politely and went away, making it obvious that he had now delivered to us a full fifty cents' worth of information.

We drove slowly on a very curving road with pretty little farms on either side, and when we had gone nine miles there was no sign of any kind, so we rapped at the door of a house and made inquiries. A cheery looking woman answered our summons, untying her apron and dropping it on a chair beside her as she stood.

"Yes, indeed there was a plaque," she nodded. "The Nova Scotia Historical Society put it up and I copied the inscription. Then one night some of them kind that'll take anything for a souvenir stopped their car and tore the plaque down. Wait half a minute and I'll get my copy."

She whisked away to a cupboard and returned with a black-covered note book, moistened a finger and turned pages. "Here it is. It read: 'Here in January, 1821, was born Charles Fenerty, who, after experimenting from about 1839, produced paper from spruce wood pulp, which invention he made public in 1844. He died at Lower Sackville, June 1892'." She closed the book. "I wish I knew more about it," she sighed, "but I don't. I'm from the South Shore and I don't know much about this district, which is a pity, for it's full of history, and nobody knows it."

We drove on, regretting the souvenir hunters that had taken away the plaque. Springfield Lake was on our right, according to a sign, and there was a small lake on the left, and a pretty hillside cemetery where some people walked slowly in file between graves, as if looking for some identification. The homes along the road became fewer. A car nine or ten years old was parked in front of one house. Beside it a small sapling supported a crude cardboard sign: "Car may be sold." Then we saw a great flock of geese on a slope, blotching it gray with themselves, lost feathers and their droppings. Next a huge sign said "Bathing Beach." It was another lake, and on its surface a monster wooden swan, perfect in detail, floated idly.

The highway turned around the end of a small railway station. "Mount Uniacke," the sign said. A short distance beyond we saw an unusual building on our left, with very sharp roof and narrow pointed windows. A man was passing, and we asked him if it were a residence.

"Nope, that was a tea room," he answered. "First off, it was the boat-house back at Uniacke Lake, and some people named Murphy brought it down here for a tea room, but it didn't do good business. It's a pity they ever moved it."

"Where," we asked, "is Uniacke Lake?"

"You mean to say you don't know the Uniacke place!" The man shook his head. "I figgered everybody in this country knowed all about it. Go along half a mile, not quite, till you see a sign on a gate 'Private' and another 'No Trespassing.' Go in there. There's a keeper will show you everything."

We soon saw the gate, and it opened easily. We drove through and closed it after us. Immediately we were in a thick grove of spruce and fir, but the opening was not more than three hundred yards ahead, and we emerged before two huge old wooden gate posts supporting a gate rather the worse for its age. Beyond it, looking between lines of oak and cedar, we could see an enormous house.

A dog barked and a man came from a small cottage to the right. We asked if we might see the Uniacke place, and he seemed to welcome the intrusion. In there, away from the highway and settlement, company had its value. "This where you are parked was the old stage road between Halifax and Windsor," he said. "Come along a bit and I'll show you something." So we followed him over weeds and grass and small bushes until on the upper grade he pointed to a stone. Cut in were figures and letters. "27 miles." It was an old mile-stone, still where it was placed in the 18th century.

Great oaks were everywhere, and as our guide talked it was easy to visualize the place in its heyday. A cask of Irish acorns had been brought across the sea, and the master had planted for the future so that fine Irish oaks ringed his yard and garden, lined the driveway and spread out over the estate. A garden had once existed in grand style at the front, and it was easy to trace the old flower beds and hedges, to note the post that had held a sun dial, and another bird bath column of dark stone carved around and around with a life-like serpent. The Indians had helped plan the garden, our guide said, and for years and years it was a perfect sea of colour. Huge stables were there, and we saw in one the rim of a carriage wheel used in 1815. The coach house was at another angle, and we saw where the horse block had been, and the long greenhouse. Bull's-eye glass was used in those early days and much of it is still there, in windows of a small workshop.

The house is majestic in appearance, at the top of a slope leading from a lovely lake, the site said to be 520 feet above sea level. Across the front is a very wide verandah, its roof supported by four great pillars that rise two stories in height. The Uniacke Arms are on the wide door, and a full head in beautiful brass makes an unusual door-knocker. We walked around and saw knockers on both the back door and cellar door. Our guide showed us the deep stone-lined well that supplied water for the household. A great iron kettle in the yard was once used to boil potatoes for a fine breed of pigs. A path led down to the lake, and a tiny rustic bridge crossed a small ditch. We saw what appeared to be a miniature chapel back of lilac bushes and were told it was the ladies' privy as it was through the 19th century, a most elaborate affair, plastered beautifully and without a crack showing yet in wall or ceiling, with curtains still shredded to the windows. Two high seats for adults and one low seat for children were of artistic design. A high board fence had surrounded the building, but a peephole in the door of the ladies' side prevented any possible surprise. Another apartment at the far side was plainer in design and was for the maids and cook. Nearby a path ran toward a high fence of solid character and a wide trough, green with age, was there. The servants were not allowed to throw out dish water even at the back door, the guide said, but had to cross the ground and empty all into the trough. This prevented flies from becoming a nuisance around the house. The privy for gentlemen had been just as elaborate, and was at one end of the stable.

The main hall was impressive, so large and so well designed. Cabinets were there, twelve Adams chairs as they had been placed in 1815, when Mr. Uniacke had morning prayers for his twelve children. A great clock ticked solemnly, as it had for one hundred and thirty years. Onyx-and-brass oil lamps hung from the ceiling. On the wall was an otter head, and feet, swords, pistols, an old-time carriage whip, and brass roasting forks. To our left was the drawing room, also huge, so that a grand piano seemed to take no space at all. The house is fifty-two feet long and thirty-eight feet wide, and the ceilings very high. There were elaborate lamp stands, rich oil paintings, desks, tables, French arm-chairs, a mahogany music Canterbury. On the left of the hall was the dining-room, with a magnificent dining-table, chairs, china cabinets, a liquor cabinet, an oak chest of knives, silver coasters on the table, cut glass, crystal candlesticks, brass hand bells and other rich pieces. The entire breakfast set purchased in 1815 was there, a tribute to the one who had had charge of the dish washers and dining-room girls.

A portrait of the original Uniacke was there, and what a man! Richard John Uniacke was born in County Cork, Ireland, on November 22, 1753, filled with a zest for life, a love of adventure, a pride in his race and the decent instincts that make a great man. His family was a proud one, and his grandfather had commanded a troop of cavalry for William of Orange at the Battle of the Boyne. Richard John was articled to a Dublin attorney when he was sixteen, agreeing to live with the man, to keep his secrets, not marry without his permission and to refrain from card-playing and dice. Four years later he had a dispute with his father and left for America, going first to the West Indies, then to New York.

A Swiss who had lived in Nova Scotia for many years, Moses Delesdernier, was in the American city looking for settlers when he spied Uniacke, who stood six feet two inches in height and "had a back like a barn door." He asked Uniacke to go to Nova Scotia and work for him at his place near Fort Lawrence, and Uniacke agreed. He not only worked there two years, but married Martha Maria Delesdernier, who was not quite thirteen years old. Then came the American Revolution, and Uniacke rested his sympathies with the Thirteen Colonies. He cared not who heard him and so was arrested, with some others, and taken to Halifax for trial.

His escort took him by way of ferry from Parrsboro to Windsor, and then they walked the bridle path toward Halifax. By a small brook they rested a time, and Uniacke saw a scene so similar to his old home in Ireland that he made silent resolve to possess the land some day.

There was delay in his trial, and an aunt of his bride had given him property in Halifax. So Uniacke sold the gift and had funds enough to take himself and wife back to Ireland to finish his studies in law. In April, 1781, he was admitted to the bar in Nova Scotia, and soon made his presence known. In December of that year he was commissioned as Solicitor-General for the province, and the next year was elected to the House of Assembly as a member for Sackville township. Soon he became Attorney-General, and a member of His Majesty's Council. Then Advocate-General for the Vice-Admiralty Court of Nova Scotia. It was this latter appointment that made him wealthy, for during the war of 1812-1815 numbers of captured ships were brought to Halifax to be auctioned, and their cargoes. It is legend that Uniacke made over fifty thousand pounds in such fees alone.

He was twelve times president of the Charitable Irish Society of Halifax, and was famed for his wit and fluency as a speaker. So he made a vast number of friends, and when he was getting on in years wanted some ease and time to himself. The result was the building of the big house at Mount Uniacke, named after him, above the lake he named after his wife, "Lake Martha." He entertained royally during the summer months. There were seven great bedrooms, furnished with tables and chairs and sofas and stoves. There was a huge kitchen in the basement, with a seven-foot ceiling, and fireplace large enough to hold a dozen kettles. Here the cook and her helpers reigned supreme, and food went up to the dining-room via a mahogany dumb waiter. There was a dairy next the kitchen, a laundry and store room. Everything was on a large scale. The best of woods had been used in the house and Uniacke wanted no carpets to hide his floors. There was no paper on the walls until his son, the Rev. Fitzgerald

Uniacke, had it done in the 1830's, and the paper put on the dining-room walls then is still there.

The entire walls of Uniacke's study are lined with books, one and two centuries old, of all sorts. There is a fine medicine chest, a unique reading glass, a grand desk, a rosewood and brass inkstand, and comfortable chairs. At the back porch, roomy enough, with a great fish in brass as a door knocker, we saw a fine Windsor chair, a spinning-wheel, a copper lantern, carders and the branding-iron Uniacke used to mark all his cattle. He brought over several farm hands from Ireland and built small cottages for them around the estate, which contained five thousand acres. A great bell hung in a tall birch tree called the hands to the dinner-table.

We roamed through the spacious upstairs, seeing garments a century old still hanging in closets, a baby crib made up ready for use, gigantic four-posters, Hepplewaite side chairs, silver water jugs, a bonnet top highboy worth thousands of dollars, a military chest, grand mirrors, Samplers on the wall, braided rugs on the floor. Everything as if the Uniacke family had been called away the previous week.

"People would pay a fortune for some things here," said our guide, "but I've never left the place and no one has a chance to get anything. Now the entire place, grounds, house and furnishings have been sold to the Nova Scotia Government, and when they get it ready it's going to be the best show place of its kind in this part of Canada. The sixth generation of the Uniackes are around now, and interested. One thing, there's always a James Boyle among them. Richard John's grandson, James Boyle, named his first son the same, but the lad died. Later on another son was born, and he was given the same name and is still alive, an old soldier who saw long service in India, he being an officer in a British regiment."

It was hard to leave the place, for any imagination at all could people the spacious verandah and lawn with the élite of Halifax, gay officers of army and navy, judges, doctors, clergy and prominent merchants, chatting and escorting their ladies to the boat-house for afternoon tea. Summer long the gaiety was at its height, and the ambition of the "social climbers" of Halifax was an invitation to Mount Uniacke.

"Don't rush it on this road to Windsor," advised our guide. "Drive in where you see the Ellershouse sign. There's another good story for you."

Anyone can see the sign, and the side road, but few who pass along can imagine what is to be gained by driving a few minutes to what was a great dream of Francis von Ellershausen.

Ellershausen was a German engineer who went to Pittsburgh from southern Germany to be in charge of smelting operations. While there he heard of gold being discovered at Waverley, Nova Scotia, and came to investigate. The mining did not look promising to him, but he was intrigued to see so much virgin forest and decided to lumber on a large scale. He was able to get some German and London financiers interested in his project and, with loans, acquired about sixty thousand acres of rich woodland extending from the Windsor road across the province to the South Shore. He brought over seventy countrymen to work for him, established three sawmills and soon was shipping lumber to many markets. Everything prospered. He paid back his loans. He built homes for his workers. He built a fine place for himself, a small mansion with richest furnishings. Fifteen acres were cleared and landscaped by experts, making a round park consisting of lawns, flower beds, ornamental trees, shrubs, paths and driveway. His White House fronted it. Exquisite crystal, silver and linen made the dining-room superior to anything else in the county. There was a Lodge at the park gate for the head gardener. Madame Ellershausen and her two daughters lived like royalty, a coachman, fine coach and thoroughbred horses being at their disposal. When she walked around the grounds and saw a weed she would blow on a silver whistle and a servant would come running to remove the obnoxious intruder. Alfred Shoeck, a famous Swiss artist, was brought to Nova Scotia to paint a picture five by eight feet of the lake scene near the house. Full-length French mirrors were established in the front rooms, and a beautiful velvet pile carpet covered the floor.

The German workers cleared 200 acres for farming. Ellershausen built a schoolhouse for their children. He built a church for Lutheran service, having a front square pew for his family, and a door at the side for their private use. Colchester House was built for his daughter, and was another masterpiece in the community. A pulp mill was built, but after operating two years was burned. Then Ellershausen heard of copperite being found in Switzerland where the Rhone River vanishes underground, and decided to investigate. He was shipwrecked and landed in Newfoundland, where he heard of copper mines. Later investigation led him to raise all the money he could on his Nova Scotia property and invest it in Newfoundland. For a time all went well, and it seemed that he would soon be a millionaire. A Welsh firm offered him a million pounds for his holding, and the sale was almost complete when the ore ran out. The deal was called off, but Ellershausen persisted in chasing the lode until he had ruined himself financially. He died in Germany during the first World War, and his family were scattered over the earth, while strangers lived in Ellershouse.

The German workers moved away as the lumbering eased off, but today many of the houses built by Ellershausen are still occupied, and twenty-five wells remain beside old cellars to mark other holdings of that era. The two fine homes have lost much of their grandeur, and the park has not been maintained, but there is yet enough beauty of landscape and influence of the past to permit one to visualize the place during its heyday. The great painting is now in a Windsor home, as are some of the French mirrors. Other items are in various parts of the province, and a granddaughter of the engineer, living in England, is now writing the Ellershausen story. She remembers well the quantities of roses that were grown in the garden, the conservatory that adjoined the great house, the separate greenhouse, the elegant croquet lawn.

Old-timers say that the ability of Ellershausen was shown in his first survey of the land, when he laid out logging roads that missed the hills and circumvented swamps so cleverly that they were kept free of windfalls and used for half a century. The mills were located so that the majority of logs cut could be hauled to them down grade and the pulp mill was built beside the St. Croix River at a spot where the utmost water power was available. Every workman chosen by him was of the best, and it is remarkable that during a period of thirty years he had trouble with only one employee—the man supposed to have fired the pulp mill.

We drove on, wondering why there were no modern Uniackes and Ellershausens, and saw Cameron Lake, with cars parked by a canteen, in the fields and on field roads. Then great masts of a naval wireless station were spidery against the sky. It was a lovely part of the day, early evening, as we drove under the elms that line the highway through St. Croix, a picture postcard village around a dam and bridge and high water tower. A boy was picking cherries from a small tree, and his mother, an attractive woman in shorts, appeared from a bungalow as we asked a question about the dam. It was to generate power for a company that supplied all that part of Nova Scotia with electricity, she said, adding that although she was now a summer visitor she had been born in the village and knew its history, which went back to the days of the Acadians. Old French dykes were still in service on the marshes, and at the foot of the upland arrow heads had been discovered.

Our chat extended until darkness had come, for the woman was entertaining with her tales. One concerned a farmer who had an unruly cow that broke out of pasture regularly, kicked the milk pail when it was full, and gored other cattle. Finally the farmer's patience was exhausted. He wanted to punish her severely, and bears were plentiful that summer so he took the cow to a glade in the forest and there tied her firmly to a tree, a helpless victim for the first bruin that came along. It might have been that bears were suspicious of such easy prey. At any rate none molested the cow, and her bawlings reached the ear of a passing Indian who released her. She returned to the farmer's barn that night, bellowing to be milked. The farmer's wife obliged, and not a kick was registered. There was no goring of sister cows that night or after. No breaking out of pasture. The cow, pondering things over as she waited by the tree, evidently decided to lead a better life.

The other account was of two sisters, unmarried, who lived together until the elder, aged eighty-eight, died in her sleep. Friends went to express their sympathy to the survivor, aged eighty-four. She shrugged. "I'm not mournin'," she said. "It's my first chance to have my tea made right. It always had to be her way till this week."

We live in an age of autograph hounds, but our St. Croix informant told us that long ago in that village there were several ladies who sought autographs of friends and famous people. These were written on silk, and then were embroidered cleverly, and became precious possessions. Some of the ladies went visiting across to Boston or up "to Canada" and returned with a fine assortment of names, some inscribed with flourishing characters. One lady had a prize—her own name in Chinese characters—done by a Boston laundryman.

Windsor was a glimmer of lights. We were lucky to obtain a room at the Victoria Hotel, an ancient place that was the country's best fifty years ago, with spacious rooms and lobby and halls. The ceilings are very high. The food was plain but good and our host was a gracious old-timer. Our bedroom would make two of the present-day hotel rooms. We sat in the lobby a time, watching the town people stroll by, and by ten o'clock the street was quiet.

The town was founded in 1703 by the French, and called Piziquid. The British built Fort Edward during their régime, and also a blockhouse. After breakfast we drove back the way we had entered and turned so we could view the place as a stranger sees it. Hills dominate, two hills that look out on the reddish, tide-roiled waters of the Avon River, or upon its dark red flats when the Minas surge has subsided. Both are green hills, attractive hills, though one is of grass alone and the other set with fine old trees. One hill has known blood and sweat and grim discipline; the other is a hill of laughter and echoes of social Windsor a century ago.

Highway 1 winds into Windsor leisurely, an old tree-lined road that turns from one of homes to one of business as it reaches the heart of the town. Here, when it almost reaches the river, it meets the waterfront street, where you find a few docks above and below and behind some of the shops. In-landers love to stop at Windsor and watch the tides. The Avon and St. Croix Rivers help form a natural harbour that can float ocean-going steamers at high tide, and which one could cross with rubber boots at low tide. Vessels can be unloading at the wharf when the stranger parks and views a sea of reddish water almost reaching the floor of the long bridge. He goes shopping and has lunch. Then he returns and stands, amazed. The sea has gone, vanished. Thirty feet below are flats of red mud. The vessels that were being unloaded are now settled on the mud like bedraggled water-fowl, the wharf timbers dripping darkly above them.

It's a comparatively short walk from the docks to the top of one of those Windsor hills, and near the top are the cattle sheds and the judging fields of the Agricultural Society's grounds. Canada's first agricultural fair was held on this hill away back in 1765, and the inscription on a cut stone monument in the town reads:

Commemorating the first agricultural fair in Canada, authorized on the creation of the township of Windsor in 1764, and held at Fort Edward Hill, 21st May, 1765. Prizes were awarded for creditable exhibits of cattle, horses, sheep, hogs, grain, butter, cheese, and homespun cloth.

In 1766 the trustees of the fair received a royal charter which was renewed in 1815. Since that date the fair has had an uninterrupted existence.

On the very top of the hill is an old blockhouse, the last survivor of its kind in Nova Scotia, erected by Major Charles Lawrence in 1750 in an earthworks known as Fort Edward. A cairn bears a tablet reading:

Fort Edward. Erected in 1750 by Major Charles Lawrence for the protection of Piziquid (Windsor) and the surrounding district, and as a Symbol of British sovereignty in western Nova Scotia. Of special importance during the war with France 1755-1762, and the American Wars of 1775-1782 and 1812-1815. Was closely associated with the tragic incidents of the deportation of the Acadians in 1755. Garrisoned by Imperial troops for about a century. A rallying point and training ground for Canadian and Newfoundland forces during the Great War 1914-1918.

The old earthworks are lowered by the passing of years until they no more than suggest the former height of the walls, and the old moat is now a shallow depression. All about is the Windsor Golf Course, and the cairn marking the spot is at the edge of the ninth green, while the seventh is on what was one of Fort Edward's seaward bastions. The view is fine from this hill, town homes and gardens and highway and the sea pouring upstream from Minas Basin or draining out again. Across the river are the green slopes of Falmouth and, far away, the Hantsport Shore, where ship-building once reigned.

It is hard to think of soldiers and harshness in such a setting, but the blockhouse and its memories are there and so we thought of a late August day in 1755 when Colonel John Winslow, of Marshfield, Massachusetts, came riding to the fort from Grand Pré, where his regiment was resting, stout New England militiamen. Captain Murray was in command of Fort Edward, and we can see, in fancy, the two officers meeting. They enter the officers' quarters, and there they will draw up the proclamation of forfeiture of Acadian homes and cattle, the warrant of deportation for all Acadian people. It was supposed to be His Majesty's orders they formulated, but Governor Lawrence of Nova Scotia and Governor Shirley of

Massachusetts were the "King" during that fateful autumn. Historians may not agree on the right or wrong of these proceedings, but the two officers in Fort Edward that pleasant afternoon were, no doubt, heavy hearted, and apprehensive of final results. They could look over miles of Acadian diked lands, Acadian homes and fields and orchards, for it is calculated that more than two thousand Acadians lived in the old Piziquid area.

Another hill of Windsor leads up to a fine entrance of an estate that was the Judge Thomas Chandler Haliburton home a century ago. There are fine gate posts, and a plaque with the inscription:

Clifton, the home of Thomas Chandler Haliburton. Born 1796. Died 1865. The Father of American Humour and Creator of 'Sam Slick', Historian, Jurist, Legislator.

The driveway winds up under a canopy of greenery, and there are great trim lawns and flower beds and then the fine old house itself, filled with furnishings of one hundred years ago. Miss Florence Anslow, the curator, is so steeped in Haliburton lore that she can answer any question about the man and his life at Windsor. She is immensely proud of his place in Nova Scotia history, and enjoys showing visitors around, upstairs to the old fourposters and "sleigh beds," or down to the basement and its great fireplace. Miss Anslow has been gathering relics for years, and has a regular museum of old household implements. Each year more and more people come to spend a quiet morning or afternoon absorbing the atmosphere of this grand old home and admiring its beautiful setting.

Not far away, on this old hill, King's Collegiate School for Boys has its boast about being the oldest educational institution in the British Empire overseas. A tablet affixed to the chapel reads:

King's College. Upon this hill for many years stood King's College, the oldest University in the King's overseas Dominions, from whose halls have gone forth many distinguished men, leaders in Church and State. Founded in 1789 by the Rt. Rev. Charles Inglis, D.D., First Bishop of Nova Scotia, and other United Empire Loyalists. Granted a Royal Charter by King George III in 1802.

King's College is now in Halifax, on the Dalhousie University grounds.

Walking about the site of the buildings that were the original King's we thought of the old days in Windsor when it was the centre of culture. Thomas Chandler Haliburton was born there December 17, 1796. He was descended from a famous Border family quite closely related to Sir Walter Scott, and always had a clever remark about his birthplace. "My father and I," he would say, "were born in the same house, but 20 miles apart." The apparent impossibility was explained by saying that the house was first built at Douglas, on the St. Croix River, where Haliburton senior was born. Later the house was floated down the river on logs and placed on a foundation along the Avon, and there Thomas Chandler was born. He was educated at King's, and though he showed no remarkable aptitude for a legal career, he was a power in the land from early youth.

Sprung from Loyalist stock, born into the official class, educated at King's in the days of its most unpopular exclusiveness, and representing Annapolis, a constituency that prided itself on its romantic history, living and moving as a judge among stiff-necked New Englanders one generation away from transplanting, it is little wonder that he caught a glimpse of the need of reform in government and a cure for the social and economic ills of that period. Haliburton rode around the province by horseback, shay and coach, gathering a vast store of experiences that he used in writing "Sam Slick, the Clockmaker." He served as a member for Annapolis County for three years, then returned to Windsor and about 1835 established his home at "Clifton," the beautiful estate now known as the Memorial Museum. It was easy, walking about the grounds of King's, to visualize young Haliburton and his fellow students, the "upper crust" of which he wrote with much irony, gathered on the brow of the hill to gaze with some superiority upon the village below or to watch, on Fair days, the yokels bringing fat cattle and fowl to exhibit.

There is another picture that also comes clearly. It is the period 1885 to 1895, and an energetic young professor leads the football team in rousing competition, sings in the chapel choir or strolls down to the dykelands on an off-afternoon. The young professor is Charles G. D. Roberts, and often there strolls with him a huge, gray-clad figure who is interested in nature and the river and clouds over the marshes —Bliss Carman. No one can read *The Forge in the Forest* or *A Sister to Evangeline,* without knowing how much Roberts loved those Acadian marshlands. Carman, the dreamer, loved them too, and spent many vacations with his cousin, at "Kingscroft," on the hill. The Avon's flow may have inspired him to write:

> Tides of Fundy—Tides of Fundy
> What is this you bring to me?
> News from nowhere—vague and haunting,
> As the white fog from the sea.
> Night and day I hear fresh rumours,
> From an unknown fabled shore,
> Of new orders soon to reach me,
> And a summons at my door.

Roberts was almost worshipped by the students at King's and it was he who did so much to build the Haliburton Society that still carries on today. Haliburton and Howe and Roberts and Carman were names that entered conversations for half a century at King's, and there must be many whisperings there on the hill when twilight closes in and "gives the mystic hour." Nova Scotia has produced many men of culture, poets and writers and artists, and much of the first cultural glory shone from the old college hill in Windsor.

Old Reports in the Archives at Halifax make plausible the statement that used to be made about the Halifax-Windsor road. "Enough has been spent on it to pave it with silver dollars." For more than a century large amounts, for the times, were expended on it. Some called it the "molasses road." This for the reason that a first account records that the building of the road was "mostly paid out of a sum of money appropriated from a seizure of molasses."

In the early days of Windsor some of its citizens had definite ideas about behaviour. They formed an "Improvement Society," with one Mrs. Longmire as the president, and the local preacher her assistant. A law was passed that no person might use profane language in the town, and anyone not attending divine service regularly was to be fined. These and other restrictions were not too popular with the majority. It was strange, too, that the first person reported for using forbidden language was her husband, and an old diary states the matter quaintly:

Ye president confronted Abraham Longmire, her husband, with the charge of using profane words when he did spill scalding water on his foot while butchering pigs, and he being found guilty was required to pay a fine of three shillings. Whereupon said Abraham Longmire, resenting the action, did repair to ye tavern and there imbided to such an extent that as he returned home he fell asleep in ye cemetery and, being discovered, was fined a further three shillings for such conduct. Whereupon ye said Abraham Longmire did depart ye settlement and has not since been seen nor is his whereabouts known.

Later, came a period when the people met and decided there were too many imports for general prosperity. Several items commonly used were to be banned, but opinion varied when it came to West Indies molasses, and the matter was left for further debate in the autumn. One who wanted to be rid of molasses was Grandfather Coolens. But his good wife said molasses was necessary for her cooking. More than that, some person told them that a quart of molasses once a week in Dobbin's oats would make a colt of the aging horse, and greatly enhance his appearance. Grandfather experimented with the oats, and had gratifying results. Came winter and a hired man. One icy morning Grandfather decided to take

Dobbin over the hill into Windsor to have new shoes put on. It was the morning for the quart of molasses but the hired man had a different jug in the barn and put a quart of rum in Dobbin's breakfast. Grandfather knew nothing of it and happily hitched Dobbin in the shafts of the low home-made wooden sled. At the top of the hill Dobbin began to "feel his oats." Grandfather tried to check him too hurriedly and Dobbin lost footing. He sat down on the forepart of the sled as his hind feet failed to find hold on the ice, and trapped Grandfather by his huge coonskin coat. The astounded citizens of Windsor witnessed the descent, and to them it appeared that Dobbin was sitting on the forepart of the sled to enjoy the coasting and that Grandfather was clasping Dobbin in affectionate embrace. But when they were separated Grandfather waved his whip and shouted "No more molasses!"

But Grandmother insisted that it was a necessity, and that the hired man had caused the trouble. So he was let go. Came summer and haying. The new hired man was grateful for the buckets of cool well water that Grandmother placed under the shade of a bush. In the water she put a handful of oatmeal and a generous dash of molasses. "Put all you can spare," begged the hired man. "There is nothing so tasty as a big green grasshopper filled to the eyes with molasses."

Grandfather was near-sighted. He did not go near the bucket and he hated the talk about eating grasshoppers. When the final load of hay was on and near the finish the hired man returned from refreshing himself and said he had enjoyed a hopper that was at least three inches long and so full of molasses it couldn't hop. As he said so he gave a wild yell and almost thrust Grandfather from the load with a great forkful of hay. A grass snake had slid down the handle of the fork and inside the sleeve of the hired man's shirt. He raced wildly over the stubble, tearing his shirt from him in ribbons. But the snake had wriggled into the breeches, and by the time the hired man reached calmness he had nothing on but his shoes, while Grandfather, on the load, waved his fork and shouted: "No more molasses!"

Once more Grandmother insisted on her rights, and there was molasses. Came winter again, and the young folk had a candy pull at Grandmother's. Grandfather had retired, leaving his greenhides—moccasins made with the hairy side inward —by the fire to dry. One bright youth laid some strips of candy inside them. In the morning Grandfather failed to notice the candy. He wore the greenhides all day, and in the evening could not separate them from his home-knit woollen socks and hairy feet. So he slept with them on for three nights, when Grandmother surrendered and said: "No more molasses!

There is Falmouth next, and the beginning of the apple orchards. We saw sections that were mainly stumps. The apple trees had been removed to make room for a better variety of fruit. Now there were fruit stands beside the road, laden with berries and bottles of apple cider. Mount Denson provided fine views and there were excellent farms. Then we were crossing a bridge and around a turn into Hantsport. A fine memorial confronted us. We parked and realized that the honour paid to a gallant hero—William Hall, V.C.—must be threefold. Hall's was one of the very first awards made after the Victoria Cross was instituted in 1856. He was the first negro to win this most coveted of all decorations for valour. He was the first of any in Britain's dominions to win the Cross. Yet his name does not appear in any Canadian list of winners of the medal, this for the reason that he did not serve in any Canadian unit and won the Cross before there was any confederated Canada.

Hall was born in April, 1827, not far from Hantsport, where his parents were employed on the property of Sir Samuel Cunard. His father had been one in a cargo of "black ivory" on board a slave ship captured by the British Navy and brought to Halifax. His mother was a slave who managed to escape and get aboard a British ship during the burning of Washington, and was likewise landed at Halifax. Their son served as a Royal Marine through the Crimean War, then went on board the *Shannon* convoying troops to Hong Kong. From there he went in a force to relieve Lucknow, and his serving a gun when all others were killed or wounded won him especial recognition and the Victoria Cross. He retired in 1876 and returned to Nova Scotia where he did small farming to eke out his pension. In 1901 when the late King George V visited Halifax as Duke of York, he sent for Hall, and the veteran hero had a fine carriage to ride in and accept the homage of the people as he took a prominent part in the unveiling of the South African War Memorial on the grounds of Province House. Three years later Hall died, and now the memorial attracts the attention of passersby and receives more honours than the man received when he was living his last years in the county.

We drove on to Avonport, and there passed through one of the three remaining covered bridges in Nova Scotia. It was erected in 1869 of local timber and spans the Gaspereau River. The orchards closed in on us until at times there seemed but the width of the road between, and we were in historic land, land won from Fundy by the dykes of the Acadians, a land criss-crossed with ancient Indian trails and Acadian marsh footways and hunters' paths and New England Planters cart roads, haunted by the ghosts of three hundred years of warfare and invasion and defence. Far to our right we could see the great bluff that is Blomidon, holding back the fog and mist and raging tides from peaceful valleys that no words can adequately describe.

> Old Man Fundy had a laugh to wake the dead,
> It echoed from Annapolis,
> To Yarmouth and to Moncton,
> Rattled dishes in Saint John,
> And startled men in Digby;
> Some called it thunder as they listened safe in bed.

Alluring signs point to the right and "Evangeline Beach." We drove a distance and came to the entrance of Grand Pré Park. In the small canteen a charming silver-haired lady in charge proved to be Mrs. Gladys Porter, Mayor of Kentville, one of Nova Scotia's best-known and respected women. The Park is located in what was the centre of the Acadian village. The well is still there, and some of the ancient willows. On the site of the Acadian church is a chapel that partly serves as a treasure house of Acadian relics. Nearby is the statue of Evangeline, in bronze, gazing sadly over the fields, her gaze seeming to follow you wherever you walk. Here are the wide marshlands that made up the "great meadow," the land that attracted Pierre Melanson, his wife and five children, Pierre Terriau and his bride, away back in 1680. They left their holdings in Port Royal and journeyed by boat, wanting a place more quiet and safe from attack than the fortress village they had occupied, and possibly had been told of this sheltered and beautiful country by fur buyers who travelled up and down the waterways, dealing with the Indians. They built their cabins and prospered for fourteen years, being joined during that period by many other families. Then came the infamous Ben Church and his vengeful men from Massachusetts, too eager to attack the unarmed, and too cautious about doing battle with those armed. They cut the dykes and ruined the crops that had grown well in that week of early July. But when the raiders were gone more grain was sown and a harvest reaped, while a rude stronghold of logs was erected to defend the hamlet.

Gradually the Acadian village of Grand Pré spilled over its boundaries. The land was rich and there was never a poor crop. The cattle were fat, the poultry plenty. And so as more couples married they had to find new homes outside the village area, until there were more Acadians in the Grand Pré district than British at Port Royal. This was in 1720, when cleared farms at Grand Pré reached four leagues and produced endless bushels of good wheat and peas and flax and barley. There were fine orchards of apple and plum trees, and gardens filled with cabbages and pumpkins; herds of cattle and flocks of sheep fed on the slopes. Trading vessels came to the small wharves to purchase supplies for garrisons

at Louisbourg and Annapolis, paying in gold that the Grand
Pré folk buried in iron kettles.

Amid all the prosperity there reached roots of trouble to
come. The Acadians sold to the French garrisons, but had
little for the British. Some of the young men dressed like
the Micmacs and went on raids against British settlers. They
would pay no taxes to the British at Annapolis, but they
paid rent for land they held under British rule to the Lords of
Manors in Cape Breton, and their priests attended Louisbourg
councils. Many happenings there were that convinced the
British that Grand Pré might be used as a rallying point for
an attack on Acadia. Emissaries of French Quebec did
their best to stir up the Acadians against the English, and to
incite the Indians to acts of hostility.

Watching all that went on, the Governor of Massachusetts
felt that the time had come to take some precautionary
measures, so he sent Colonel Arthur Noble with 470 New
England soldiers to establish a blockhouse at Grand Pré. The
winter came early and their ship was frozen in the ice. The
blockhouse was not built, and so the men were quartered
in different houses through the village. They had no idea of
the number of inhabitants so did not know when some slipped
away and travelled overland to Fort Beauséjour to tell the
French soldiers there that a fine opportunity of surprise
existed. The French soon realized the advantage they held, and
made ready for the long tramp with sled and snowshoe.
Along the way they were joined by other Acadians who were
more than willing to strike a blow at the British.

A great snowstorm began on February 9th, and for thirty
hours the flakes fell thickly. Through it came the French,
silently and unseen, 346 of them, timing their arrival so that
it was about 3 a.m., when the British would be in their
soundest sleep. No locks need be forced. The attackers burst
in the unbarred doors and killed many of the sleepers before
they knew what had happened. Others rose in their night
clothes, groping madly to find weapons, and were shot down
as they groped. So fell Colonel Noble and his brother. But

all houses were not attacked at once, and when shots were heard the ones not attacked were suddenly ready for the foe. They gathered in a stone building and fought so determinedly that a truce was called in the morning, and the survivors were allowed to march back to Annapolis. Small wonder, then, that the Massachusetts governor, like the officials at Annapolis, knew that there never could be any security in the land while the Acadians remained. It was but a matter of time before arrangements were made for their deportation, a harsh move truly, yet made necessary by Quebec agents and some of their priests.

Sir Charles G. D. Roberts described Grand Pré graphically in *A Sister to Evangeline.*

There was the one long street, thick set with its wide-eaved gables, and there its narrow subsidiary lane descending from the slopes upon my left. Near the angle rose the spar of the church, glittering like gold in the clear flood of sunset. And everywhere the dear apple blossoms—for it was spring when I came home. Beyond the village and its one black wharf, my eyes ranged the green, wind-ruffled marshes, safe beyond the sodded circumvallations of their dykes. Past the dykes, on the other side of the Islands' wooded ramparts, stretched the glowing miles of the flats; for the tides of Minas were at ebb. How red in the sunset, molton copper threaded with fire, those naked reaches gleamed. . . .

On the 5th of September, 1755, Colonel Winslow, of New England, gathered the men of Grand Pré in the Church of St. Charles and told them his orders. They and their families were to be deported and their lands confiscated. The men were held and were told daily which ship they would sail on, and the day of embarkation. The women were told to dispose of their movables and to pack up their apparel and such items as they could carry with them, but they gave little heed to the instructions, feeling that the Government dare not send them away. Chests were filled with linen and treasures and hidden in the woods. Money was hidden in wells. Much of it was found years after, as were the rotting chests among old leafage. On the day of embarkation many of the men fled to the forest. Seventeen escaped one night from one vessel. Others were moved in to take their places. Then some relented and came from hiding, but could not get on their vessel again, but were placed on others. So it was that many families were not entire. On October 29th the fleet of twelve ships sailed away with 2,921 Acadians on board—one of the most tragic occurrences in Canadian history.

Longfellow was never in Nova Scotia. Seventy years after the Expulsion he heard the story of it from a man who heard it from a friend who had lived in the province. The fact that "Evangeline" was pure imagination on the poet's part did not hinder a mite in rousing the sentiment of millions of people. No publicity that Nova Scotia has devised has a fraction of the power of the story of the Acadian girl and her lover.

The Park guide points out to visitors the metal marker far out on the marsh that denotes the exact spot where the Acadians went on board the waiting vessels, and cameras grind throughout the sunny afternoons for the flowers are beautiful in Grand Pré Park and the view is superb in every direction. Among the throngs there are always those who drift apart and stand by the old willows, dreaming of that sad day two centuries ago, and painting in their mind's eye the village as it was before torch was applied to barn and dwelling.

Up in the present village, is the old Church of the Covenanters, built by first Loyalists who took over the district. The church has quaint box pews, a sounding board, and a pulpit halfway to the ceiling. When the Rt. Hon. Ramsay MacDonald was visiting Nova Scotia he explored Grand Pré and wrote as follows in his book *At Home and Abroad*:

On the right, at the top of the hill, overshadowed by the poplar trees, maple and ash, is the Covenanter Church built by Loyalists from the newly founded United States and Presbyterians from Ireland. Its plain walls tell of the severe and sturdy faith which used to be thundered from its heavy pulpit down upon its box pews. How heavily laden with the sins of their neighbours must the preachers have been whose feet wore those deep hollows in its pulpit steps.

It is but a short distance along the highway to Wolfville, but a kindly man indicated a branching road that would not take us out of our way and yet provide us with a magnificent view. So we drove up a long hill and at its crest parked the car and looked back. We were gazing directly over three thousand acres of marshland, with reddish, tide-ruled rivers catching the sunlight and all the view simmering in the morning's heat. It was a scene of tranquillity not soon forgotten.

Wolfville is tucked away among orchards and shade trees, one of the most attractive towns in eastern Canada. We had lunch at a place named Blomidon Lodge, a mansion-like house backed by added quarters, and were allowed to inspect the old front that had been, in its day, a most imposing private home, built by a retired sea captain. He had made a tidy fortune and intended to retire in state. During his last few years at sea he took on timber of rare value at various ports, mahogany and teak and walnut and oak. These logs he brought to Wolfville, had them milled and the lumber put away to dry. When he built his house he used the rich woods for panels in almost every room. He brought exquisite marble from Italy for his fireplaces, and, wanting the newest thing heard of, imported an entire Italian bath equipment which was installed on an upper floor, the huge tub occupying considerable space.

Acadia University has a campus second to none, and all through Wolfville the main street is lined with beautiful homes. A side street leads up hill to what is known as "The Stile," and there thousands of students have loitered to enjoy the moonlight and the remarkable influence it can have on young people. From the Stile one looks over the secluded little Gaspereau Valley with its checkerboard fields and orchards and gardens and quiet lanes. No painting holds more beauty than this scene, and each year countless artists and photographers try to capture the sheer loveliness presented. It is all beautiful country. "Where the five rivers flow down to meet the swinging of the Minas tides, and the great Cape of Blomidon bars out the storm and fog, lies half a country of rich meadow lands and long-arcaded orchards. It is a deep-bosomed land; a land of fat cattle; of well-filled barns; of ample cheeses and strong cider; and a well-conditioned folk inhabit it."

Such views Carman and Roberts knew and loved, and so we have such beauty in verse as:

> A grievous stream, that to and fro
> Athrough the fields of Acadie
> Goes wandering, as if to know
> Why one beloved face should be
> So long from home and Acadie.
> Was it a year or lives ago,
> We took the grasses in our hands,
> And caught the summer flying low
> Over the waving meadow lands,
> And held it there between our hands?

To the left of its main street, before the business section, a very old house is used as the Wolfville Historical Museum. The residents of the town have made it most attractive, and the stranger learns much history simply by moving from room to room and reading in the various items the story of the problems of the firstcomers, of their patience and ingenuity.

Between Wolfville and Kentville is the fast-growing community of New Minas, born as an escape from the higher taxes of the towns. A curb service restaurant there is the only one in the province. Kentville proved to be a bustling little town, with much of interest, some of the finest flower gardens in the east, a fine ball park, large fruit warehouses, a Government Experimental Station of over 400 acres, and a modern hotel. Nearby is Aldershot, where militia for both World Wars lived and trained and became overseas battalions. Along the town's main street is a unique relief map of Nova Scotia in miniature beside the local Tourist Information Bureau.

Once out of the town we saw a sign "Bird Sanctuary," and soon we had come to something novel—Palmeter's Country Home. A dozen or more cars bearing American license plates were parked at the rear of the huge farmhouse. To the right was an equally huge barn. To the left was a pond with a log cabin in miniature on the bank, and a row-boat nearby. We went up on the verandah and faced a wonderful display of handcraft, glass and china, more than the average store would carry. But it was nothing in comparison to what met our glances as we entered the house proper. The display kept visitors standing in open-mouthed awe. It is the finest and largest store of bone china in America, and, as Harper's Bazaar stated recently: "A store that bends over backwards to sell you the best bone china in the world."

If you are a visitor in Kentville, staying at the hotel, all you need do is phone and the Farm will send a car for you and return you afterwards—free, whether or not you made a purchase. And every afternoon delicious tea and sandwiches are served. If some of your party cannot decide quickly about their purchasing you need not be bored. There is a golf course large enough to occupy you for an hour or so, and bowling and archery. You can even row on the pond if you wish. The entire place is landscaped in a most pleasing manner, and as the Farm owns the land abutting the highway on both sides no one can come in and mar the scene. The story of Palmeter starting in business on a small amount of borrowed capital and rising to ownership of the present Farm is one for a Henty book.

We drove through pleasant villages—Coldbrook, Cambridge, Waterville to Aylesford, where we saw the waters of the upper Annapolis River winding through green meadows. The soil all around was exceedingly fertile, of a light sandy character, and there was scarcely a homestead without its surrounding apple orchard, while pears, plums, cherries and small fruits were abundant. Extensive cranberry bogs were seen, and at one place the development of a peat bog was underway.

Through this belt of country the New Englanders came, the Planters as they were called, in 1761-2. The general idea prevalent is that they came greedily to claim the lands left by the exiled Acadians, but that is far from the truth. They came to have religious liberty, which had become the one great need of their lives. New England was founded between 1620 and 1640 by about twenty thousand English who multiplied on their own soil in remarkable seclusion from other communities for nearly a century and a half. Connecticut was purely English, and Rhode Island was the only place having any religious liberty. Expansion then began to the back areas and a general movement to escape the strict discipline enforced was under way when the Proclamation called "The Charter of Nova Scotia" was made, promising religious liberty there to all Protestants, and representative government, with the laws of Virginia largely adopted. No other inducement was needed. Twenty-two shiploads came at one time to one place. Within two years they had settled all the Valley.

When the coaches began to run between Halifax and Annapolis it was found that there was not enough accommodation along the road, and the government offered a bounty of twenty-five pounds cash to any family who would open their home as an inn, offering food and shelter for man and beast. Near the Aylesford area there lived a clergyman whose wife had died and left him with four unmarried daughters. The good man heard of the bounty offered for those who established inns, and took himself and Angelina, his eldest daughter, to Halifax. There he stated his intention of opening his home to the travelling public, and was given the money offered. He took Angelina to a store in Halifax and fitted her out with all the finery of the day, from "pointed, high-heeled white shoes" to "lace-frilled collars," and told her she would be the waitress in the dining-room, while her sisters would serve in the kitchen. Then he took an auger and bored a hole through the smooth-board partition between dining-room and kitchen, thus enabling the sisters in the kitchen to hear the order given by the guest in the dining-room. When Angelina arrived in the kitchen the order would be ready for her hands and she would whip back quickly, thereby impressing the guest not only with her appearance but with her efficiency.

Soon there came a cattle buyer from Halifax going to Annapolis. He was served by Angelina and she impressed him to such an extent that he arranged to stop again on his return. He stayed overnight and, after breakfast in the morning, proposed to Angelina and was accepted. Father married them to keep the fee in the family. Then he took the finery from Angelina and gave it to the second daughter. One month later she had caught a sea captain by the same performance and father once more performed a marriage service. Then the third daughter was equally lucky, but after that father was in the kitchen and probably he fumbled many chances. At any rate the record shows that it was not until the following June that the fourth daughter secured a husband from those who travelled. Thereupon father closed the inn and moved to Halifax to make his home with Angelina.

Aylesford was the summer home of Bishop Inglis, he who defied Washington and his armed men by reading prayers for the King and Royal Family in Trinity Church, New York, when the General attended the service. For the reading he was banished, and he became the first Bishop of Nova Scotia. In 1797 the Duke of Kent had a chair made for him, and the chair now rests in an Aylesford home that was once an inn. Auburn, once Lower Aylesford, is just beyond, and there we stopped to look at a very old church and a man working near a small store came over. "Come along in," he said. "This is the St. Mary's Church you read about."

St. Mary's Church was built in 1790, and its walls are plastered with powdered mussel shells left at Morden on the shore where a group of Acadian refugees spent a winter. The wood frames and windows of the church were brought from Halifax on horses, and the handmade nails were carried by soldiers who were marched all the way from the capital, each man carrying a fifteen-pound packet of nails. There are three large gilt balls on the spire. One fell to the ground during a big storm forty-three years ago, and was found to contain a record of all details relating to the building of the church from the names of those employed to the pounds of nails used. The record was copied, then replaced in the ball and the ball placed back on the spire. The church is quaint inside, with the Ten Commandments inscribed on the wall, and the Creed. The little gallery has a very narrow stair up which the younger generation would climb to space now used as the Sunday School area.

There was an old house a few miles farther along the road, our guide told us, that was said to be haunted. No one lived in it for many years when an elderly couple returned from the States and bought the place very cheaply. Friends asked if they did not know there were ghosts. Oh yes, said the gentle oldsters, they come in once in a while, but we don't mind them. They're folks we used to know. But we couldn't bide if they were strangers.

Soon we were in Kingston, and a side road there leads to Greenwood, an air station during World War II where airmen from the United Kingdom were trained, and now a field where training still goes on. Dry sandy soil through the district has produced a large growth of pines. Wilmot was next, then the enterprising town of Middleton, where a fine school was being erected, and where visitors can scarce credit their ears when the hotel proprietor tells them they may go salmon fishing if they wish, without going out of town. All doubting Thomases are then given tackle and escorted across the main street and down a side lane to two good pools actually within the town limits. The town's champion angler, Gordon Marshall, works at a grocery store. He offered to go with us and bring a finny battler to the top of Cemetery Pool if we had the time to spare, which we did not. He said he never failed with a white buck-tail fly in May, and a squirrel-tail after that, adding that he tied his own lures. When a dull moment came during the spring Marshall would grab his tackle from the back shop and rush over to one of the pools. Netted result was seven fine salmon that averaged ten pounds in weight, small but mighty.

We had to have a look at the fine new school and, on the way back, dropped into a drugstore for a lime and lemon. A pleasant old chap was there and he immediately began talking of the good old days when the place was known as Gates Ferry. Later it was named Middleton because it is exactly halfway between Kentville and Annapolis Royal, two main towns of the Valley. There were New Englanders at first, then the Loyalists came, and in the lot were a family of three brothers from New York. All three were married and their wives were more or less awed by the mother of the three men, a frail person with bright red hair and eccentric ways, owning considerable property. She would not move to Nova Scotia under any conditions, she stated, but the first son who had a red-haired daughter in his family would inherit her fortune. The youngest son settled near Middleton, and in due time there was a daughter—with black hair. They named her "Hope," and kept hoping. The eldest brother's family commenced with a son. The brother in between had no luck at all. A year later Hope had a sister— with black hair. They named her "Faith," and her cousin of same age was a boy. Came another year and another daughter—with black hair. They named her "Patience," but grandmother was fast losing her's. The cousin matching Patience was another boy. Twelve months passed and there was a fourth daughter—with black hair, and they named her "Experience." The next spring grandma paid a visit to the province. She inspected four red-headed boys and snapped her fingers impatiently. Then she moved to the home of her youngest son and stayed until fall, when a fifth daughter was born—with red hair!

There was great rejoicing and the girl was named "Relief," a name popular in that part of the Valley for more than a decade afterward.

We drove to inspect another old church. It was at Pine Grove, Lower Middleton, Holy Trinity Church, erected in 1788, excellently preserved, with the original pulpit, straight-backed pews with doors and choir gallery. It was easy to stand there and visualize the parson turning the hour glass for his "thirdly" and the boys twisting uncomfortably against those hard backs, painfully aware of father's eye on them. The treasures of the church are the Bible and Prayer Book dating back to 1783.

3

The Oldest Settled Part

Paradise—Go Slow. The Apostles Inn. The Golden
Ball. Just call me "George." Fort Anne. The cherry
woman. Hedley House. The cook and the bag of bones.
The squaw man. Digby chicken.

THE sign at the entrance to Lawrencetown was intriguing:
"Lovely Elms. Dangerous Curves." We entered the town
slowly and saw that the elms were as lovely as elms can be.
It was drowsy and peaceful, and some small knots of people
were gathered by the few stores and garages. We slowed and
stopped, thinking that from the time we had entered the
province at Amherst we had not seen a dozen persons who
acted as if they were in a hurry. An amazing number of men
and women are seen about the towns. Some appear to be
going leisurely on unimportant errands, but the majority seem
genial citizens whom circumstances have placed beyond
worries of any sort. Through the country districts one sees
old folk in doorways or in chairs under shade trees. There
are mothers out with the children. Fathers standing together
and exchanging small talk. Strangers must feel that here is a
place where life is good, a grand country in which to retire.

We saw the usual apple-packing plants from where we
were parked and then were almost startled by a mellow voice
addressing us pleasantly from a few feet away. A gentle little
man with a genteel beard and no hat on his bald head was
standing by a tree as if he were its guardian, and he was asking
if we were looking for someone.

"No one in particular," we said. "We're just admiring.
This seems to be a solid restful neighbourhood."

"There isn't better," the man said with pride. "Every man's a good citizen. You can't find a trash-mire within miles of here."

"Trash-mire!" We savoured the word, and egged him further. "No, I don't know where it came from," he said, "and not likely anybody does. I've a son who went through Acadia College, and he knows more thirty-five-cent words than some of them at Ottawa, but I just know he couldn't explain 'trash-mire.' It's one of them words you inherit."

We agreed. "What does your son do?" It was a lovely spot in which to fritter away time.

"Not much of anything." The gentle voice held amazing candour. "Was a timekeeper on the road a while. He took law a time and switched to what he calls an arts degree, whatever that is."

"Do you mean his education has not been of much value?"

"I wouldn't altogether say that," came the mild rejoinder. "It's cured his mother bragging about him being a Hendler clear through. That's her people."

We nodded comprehension and wanted to change the subject but there was no need. An angular female with a hat bearing purple blossoms around the edges in the manner of the gay nineties walked from the nearest shop, gave the merest toss of her chin and had the gentle man scampering to join her. We watched him go, wishing he'd wave goodby, but he merely flicked a hand behind him in our direction. So we started on, forgetting the little man, then remembering him quickly as we saw the next road sign: "Paradise! Go slow!" He was headed toward Paradise, and we knew such gentleness as he possessed deserved high reward.

Paradise proved to be another quiet, serene community with neat homes and fine gardens, a dangerous intersection being the only item to catch the attention, but two boys riding bicycles wavered across the way and we braked sharply. A voice chided the youngsters, an old voice with plenty of heart and vinegar.

"I'm glad you're careful drivers," it said. "Not many are."

It was an old lady who greeted us, dainty as lace and apple-cheeked. She had a bowl of berries which she held carefully in both blue-veined hands.

"There weren't cars in my day," she went on, "and I'm just as glad there weren't. We'd no need of them. Times change mighty fast."

We thought there must be a motive in such manner of address, so we asked if she were going far. "Nearly a mile," came the pert answer, "and I don't mind riding in a car."

She got in carefully, holding her berries. "From my daughter who lives here. She always scolds about me getting rides with strangers, but I like it. I think I get about thirty or more like this every summer. Folks are kind."

She rattled on and on and we drove at ten miles per hour to listen. Berries were all right for a treat for a week or so, but apples were the only delight of mankind. Back in her day there were plenty of apples and nearly every farm home put out its quota of dried apples. They had a paring machine in every kitchen which they clamped to the table and turned with a crank. An apple was stuck on the three-pronged fork of the machine, and the turning of the crank rotated the apple against a knife which pared the skin from the fruit. The pared apples were then quartered by hand with a knife and the core removed.

"Mostly I did the stringing," she said. "We used twine and a big needle, and it was nothing to have a string seven or eight feet long before we tied the ends together for a necklace to hang behind the stove. Mother used to pare and my two sisters cut the apples into quarters. My, the bushels we handled in a fall. They shrunk like everything, and then we put them up in the attic until around the last of March, when all the barrels of fresh apples in the cellar would be used. Just put a kettle on the stove and put in a handful of the dried apples if you wanted a good sauce. Some kinds of apples never melted up good into sauce but stayed like prunes, and them kind was never served when we had company. My, though, the apples we've eaten. I've heard my pa say he'd bet the apples we'd strung would reach clear to the schoolhouse, and that was nearly a mile." She prodded urgently. "Here's where I get out, and I hope we meet again—in Paradise." She was chuckling over her joke as she scurried to a pathway, and how we wished we had a snapshot of her.

The clock over the post office announced five-thirty as we entered Bridgetown, so we looked for a place to eat and sleep, remembering a sign "Ye Old Homestead" we had seen on our way in. "Colonial House" sounded cozy, but the lady said she had every room filled and pointed to a restaurant "around the corner." We went around the corner and had something to eat. The *Bridgetown Monitor* office was not far away, but its editor, Frank Beattie, whom we had known from World War I, was not there. We returned to our car to find it neatly boxed by a truck loaded with lumber. Its driver had gone somewhere, as had the drivers of the cars fore and aft. There was nothing to do but wait, and so we strolled over to a store with "Rexall Drugs" on the sign and made inquiries. Then the lady used the phone, came back and shook her head. "No use, I guess. The town's full up tonight."

There is something perverse in all humans and it breaks out in a thousand different ways. With us the perversity rises to the top when someone tells us our case is hopeless. Just give up and go home. That's the time we'll sit in the boat all day in a rain and fish. When we'll eat our picnic lunch without anything to drink and stay on the spot the whole afternoon. So we eased away from the shop and walked off the main street into a different part of the town. Children were playing on the sidewalk quietly. There were people here and there in gardens, and we wondered if we could find the home of a couple of grand missionary ladies where we had stayed once when speaking at the dinner of a Men's Brotherhood. But we could not recall direction, and so we began talking to the kindest-looking folks. One woman asked if we had any luggage. We explained about our car, and she shrugged and went into her house. That made us more determined. Five houses later a tall woman with prim lips said she'd be glad to accommodate us—if we didn't smoke. We assured her we had no use for the weed, and she almost smiled.

Back at the car the situation had not changed, but a youngster noticed us and went somewhere shouting shrilly some name we could not catch. A short fat fellow in a red shirt came out from somewhere and climbed into the cab of the truck. "I had to talk to my girl," he shouted at us. "There's a dance on tonight and she wants to be dated." He backed away and let us out. "Sorry if I held you up," he called. "She's a talker."

We shouted back that we didn't mind in the least and we hoped he would have a good time at the dance. He grinned and waved as we drove away.

The prim woman was standing on her front porch as we returned, and she told us to drive the car into her yard. She had fine beds of flowers in orderly array, and not a weed to be seen. We doubted if one would dare try to grow there. A coal-black cat came from under a currant bush and rubbed against her as she accepted our compliments about her gardening. "Anything I do," she remarked, "I like to do right."

The room she gave us was large, and the wallpaper was cheerful. A large engraving of the Twelve Apostles gazed at us from the space beside the closet door. An angel in blue outlines with a rather heavy-looking harp watched us from the far side, and a calendar of a little girl patting a dog was over the head of the bed.

We made up our notes for the day and descended the stair, thinking to go out for a stroll and an ice cream somewhere. The prim lady appeared at her parlour door and invited us to join her. "I took you in for company, much as anything," she said. "It isn't easy for me to talk with some of the people around here, but I always get on well with strangers."

It wasn't an impressive beginning, but we entered and sat on big chairs that were very comfortable. The black cat came in and curled up on a horsehair sofa. The prim woman sat beside it and folded her hands limply, then began to talk. She asked what we were doing. We said we wanted material to use in a book on Nova Scotia, and would be grateful for anything interesting she would tell us. For what seemed a full five minutes she sat still, apparently considering, and then she began, speaking slowly and carefully, as if it were something she had learned by heart.

First off, she said, the place had been settled by the French away back in 1654. Then the New Englanders came over 100 years later, and one of the first houses was a big one of stone and wood that had mud to fill in the cracks, so they called it the mud house. When travel commenced it was used for an inn. After that it was the school house. They had a ferry over the river those days, and it was a long time before they could build a bridge. When it was finished they had a big dinner and named the settlement Bridgetown. We're proud of how it was done.

She paused and set herself more primly as someone blew a car horn insistently. I wish I were mayor of the town, I'd stop that noise. Then she talked on and on, and the black cat purred and the parlour darkened and night came down outside. She talked of Quakers who had populated Bridge-town in the early days, wearing their broad-rimmed hats and pearl-gray clothing, saying "Thee" and "Thou" and "Friend." There had been a hotel then, famed for three different things, its nickname of "The Apostles," its supper dish called "saupon," and the way the girls who worked there got married.

The proprietor and his wife were from Connecticut, and they had a passion for hooking rugs. So they made twelve circular ones for the lobby and dining-room, and dyed the wool with home-made preparations. Somehow they had far more red than they intended, and there was confusion. The husband was set on having an apostle's head represented on each rug, and his wife was determined not to waste any material. So it happened that eight of the twelve apostles in the rugs wore large and flowing red beards to say nothing of red hair. A favourite dish of the time was made by boiling Indian cornmeal in milk all the afternoon at an even heat. At the supper hour it was thickened and served with sugar. The trick of having it just right was to have a steady heat all the afternoon, and as maids were paid as much as eight shillings per month they could not sit idle while tending the saupon. So the innkeeper's wife equipped the girl with knitting needles and yarn and asked for socks. The girls were good knitters and took turns day about to sit by the fire. Soon there were plenty of socks, so long stockings were next in order. Then came scarves and caps. After that a venture was made toward underwear, and long before the winter had ended durable rigging had been provided that would last the proprietor and his wife three or four seasons more. Then the girls were permitted to knit for themselves if they paid for the yarn, and soon any maid employed at the hotel any length of time could be depended upon to have all the stockings and scarves and underwear needed for the first five years, to say nothing of a few pair of socks for her husband. Then saupon passed out of favour and the knitting needles were put away.

There was another silence. And the prim woman seemed to notice the darkness. She rose and switched on a lamp that placed her sharp features in silhouette against the wall. She talked about families. The Pineos who had built the big house with walls four feet thick. The Hicks who had come with the first, so that the infant settlement had been called Hicks Ferry. She said they had stayed in the town, generation after generation. That the present generation had one of the biggest lumber businesses in the province, and a son in the Legislative Assembly at Halifax. "Won his election easy as could be," she said, tilting her chin ever so little. "We're real proud of Henry Hicks here in Bridgetown."

Then she talked of another hotel, the "Golden Ball." It

had served liquor in various potent mixtures, and one had the disgusting name "Liver Hooper," whatever that might mean. At that time there was a beautiful girl in the town, the belle of the countryside. She had two suitors and could not make up her mind. Finally mother became annoyed and decreed that the decision must be made by October 31st. The girl tried to choose but it was of no use, so the men drew lots for the different evenings, and it came about that blond Nathan was the lucky man for the final evening. When it came, the loser, black-haired Philip, was so despondent that he visited the "Golden Ball" and there imbibed a "Liver Hooper" to revive his courage. Soon he went for a stroll, and observed that it was Hallowe'en, a fact he had quite overlooked. The "Liver Hooper" then began its evil work, suggesting that as mother was going out for the evening, and father was away, there would be no harm in smoking out blond Nathan before he became too convincing. A salt sack and a short piece of planking were obtained in short order. Then Philip mounted to the porch roof by means of the rain barrel at the corner. He went up the rather steep house roof by the help of a short run from the porch top, and was at the broad chimney. The salt sack covered the vent completely and the plank held it in place. Then Philip turned to descend, and slipped. The four-foot handmade shingles were slippery and he gained such speed that he could not quite get stopped on the porch roof but dropped over the eaves, spread-eagled. It was pure disaster. Mother was just emerging and she was wearing her new hat which was large in circumference and wonderfully laden with flowers and plumage. Philip's out-stretched hand caught the brim, the hat pins held firm and mother came to earth much against her will. She was wildly angry and legend has it that she, and not her daughter, made the decision that night regarding her future son-in-law.

"I have had one of mother's hats for forty years," said the prim woman, the shadow of her chin working fantastically on the wall, "and I still love to put it on sometimes and look in the mirror. You really knew you had a hat on in her day."

It wasn't her mother who fell, was it, we asked quickly. "Dear no," came the acid rejoinder. "Do I look that old?"

We hastily declared she did not, but felt we were quite pardoned and out of danger, when a remark about old courtships being romantic caused her to stiffen. She said she did not care to discuss such things. Then she went to a shelf and came back with a copy of a magazine. It was open at an article entitled "Last Stop Before Paradise." "That came out this June," she said, "and it's real good. We're real proud of it here in Bridgetown, because it's about us."

She rose then and made us some coffee and served very tasty cakes. In the morning she had a fine breakfast, and she served it without losing a particle of her primness. We asked her price for the accommodation, and she said "One fifty each, and you can print any word I said. I know my history."

We told her her charges were too modest but she refused to change them. Then, just as we were leaving, we noticed she had her wedding ring on the wrong hand. She caught our glance, and did not blush. "I married the wrong man," she said quietly. "So I wear it there. Good morning, and thank you."

There was scarcely any traffic on the road as we left Bridgetown, and it was a grand morning, but it was hard to get on with the job for we felt sure that not again in our travels would we meet a similar woman. Soon we were beside a cairn marking a historic site at Bloody Creek. Nearby was a garage, and the manager was polite but completely matter-of-fact. He had no time to talk history, he said, and he handed us a publication that had an account of eighty men proceeding up the river from Annapolis Royal on the morning of June 10, 1711. They were in a whale boat and two flat boats, going for firewood. They lost a tide and the whale boat got a mile ahead. It was ambushed by Indians hidden in the thick foliage on either side of the stream. The others coming in the flat boats heard shooting and paddled desperately to get near enough to lend a hand, but were caught in the same trap. Thirty of the eighty men were killed, and the rest made prisoners. Forty-six years later another force was ambushed near the same spot and twenty-four men lost. It was a grim tale, but cars and flowers and bright sunshine defeated any attempt to visualize the happenings.

Tupperville and Round Hill were next, and we knew we were quite near the Annapolis area. Apple trees in some orchards looked quite ancient, and we remembered reading the Journal of John Knox, who had spent some weary months with his troops around Nova Scotia. On November 3, 1757, he wrote:

About 50 men to orchards east about three miles from the fort. The covering party were arranged so as to prevent any surprise while the rest filled bags, haversacks, baskets and even their pockets with fruit; a most grateful break to our poor soldiers so long accustomed to salt diet without any vegetables. Indeed better flavoured apples and a greater variety cannot in any other country be produced. There is also plenty of cherry and plum trees. On December 1st we got more apples. Found a round storehouse partly underground with rows of shelves of choice apples and a few pairs of wooden shoes. We burned the place. I never saw such a plenty of hares and partridges.

Captain Pote's Journal tells of his tramping over Round Hill, and the path followed. The Indians, the Acadians, the New England Planters, the Loyalists, all had their different trails up and down the Valley, and then the highways were built by engineers who ignored all previous paths and cart roads. Yet the contour of the country assures us that travel in general from Annapolis came along much the same route that is followed today. The Rev. Jacob Bailey kept a diary of his travels in the province, and he wrote in detail about a journey from Cornwallis to Annapolis in July, 1782. He set out with his family and "a cart with two yoke of oxen containing all my wordly goods, guided by a couple of sprightly young fellows and a vehicle for the reception of Mrs. Bailey and her children, drawn by two horses." They were accompanied by "near thirty people of both sexes on horseback" who rode with them for fourteen miles. It took them four hours to reach Marshall's Tavern, where they "with much difficulty served an early dinner for our company." At one o'clock the Baileys moved on. Mrs. Bailey's wagon was covered with canvas, while Mr. Bailey rode a horse. They did not see "a single human habitation for eleven miles, the road extremely rough, encumbered with rocks and deformed with deep sloughs." They were caught in a shower and drenched.

Finally they reached a tavern of Mr. Potter where the eight of them crowded with the Potter family in a room sixteen feet square. The roof leaked so that the Rev. Bailey was soaked to the skin as he sat at the table, and a bearskin had to be spread over their feather bed to protect it from drippings. They could not sleep on account of excessive heat from a large fire, the mosquitoes and sand flies. So they started on at 5 a.m. in muggy weather and a heavy fog, having thunder storms all along the route and reaching Annapolis in late afternoon.

We drove the same distance in about an hour, and at a sharp turn read a sign: "Annapolis Royal welcomes you to a town of First Things." It was an attractive board, and the street was lined with beautiful shade trees. We drove to the Hillsdale House and had lunch. An article in the *Annapolis Spectator*, by Miss Charlotte Perkins, the town's historian, gave us the story of this noted inn.

Away back in the 19th century three Foster sisters ran a store in the town, and one of the three, Miss Susan, wished to branch out into further adventure. She bought the "exercising ground" for soldiers of the fort garrison, eleven acres in all, and built a fine house of twenty-five rooms beside store rooms, and a large carriage house, set well back from the road on the spacious grounds, which are in the heart of the town. She named it the Hillsdale, and built a fine barn, the basement of it being a hennery with a glassed-in sun room for the winter months. Next to it was an elaborate piggery, with a workshop above it. There was also an ice house on the slope, and a fancy picket fence surrounded all.

When all was complete Miss Susan was married in the double parlours to an Edwin Ryerson, who took upon himself the task of finding proper furniture for such a place. He attended all auctions and secured many fine antiques. Fruit trees were planted on the grounds, pears, quinces, plums, cherries, large grape vines, currants and a large apple orchard. A wedding-cake flower bed was established in front of the house, and shrubbery and flowers were arranged about. From the fruits Mrs. Ryerson made quantities of jams and jellies and wines, and they were quite ready to cater to first-class tourists.

The oldest register, dating back to 1870, contains many distinguished names. The late King George V, then Prince of Wales, and his suite, were there in June, 1884, on an extended fishing trip in the Annapolis area. A veteran guide was hired for the outing, and he had trouble in selecting fitting words with which to address the Prince.

"Just call me 'George'," said the Prince graciously. "It's easiest."

"Damn it, sonny, I think you're right," said the guide.

Mrs. Ryerson said she had thirteen kinds of wine in her cellar, which she invited the Prince to sample. He marvelled that one woman could accomplish so much, and when he got back to England sent her photographs of himself and his party. Later that year the Marquis of Lansdowne, Governor-General of Canada, and his suite, were guests of the Hillsdale. The same year Lord and Lady Alexander Russell, stationed in Halifax, came to spend a holiday at the inn, arriving in a grand barouche and pair, coachman and footman.

Mrs. Ryerson and the Perkins family, who ran the old Queen Hotel, were firm friends, and when Mrs. Ryerson died the property was sold to the Perkins, they moving in during October, 1897, and running it in the same style as before. They had many distinguished guests, admirals and generals and judges and governors. Three bungalows were built on the grounds and rooms added to the house, private baths

installed. Lord Tweedsmuir and Prime Minister Mackenzie
King spent time at the Hillsdale in 1937, and liked it much.

It is hard to imagine a finer presentation of antique items
than greets the guest at the Hillsdale. We can only mention
a few such as a Tambour desk with serpentine doors, an
Italian writing desk, a Napoleonic sofa, a circular rug, room
size, valued at one thousand dollars, a melodeon, a Sheraton
with reeded legs, tables, chairs and other furniture that is
simply priceless.

Annapolis Royal is crowded with historic treasures. We
walked a short distance and entered a very old building known
as the Banks House. Two charming ladies met us and
graciously let us explore. The house is said to be 250 years
old. The low ceiling, the wideboards in the floor, the old-time
H and L hinges, reported as "Holy Lord" letters that
restrained the power of witches from entering, the fine old
fireplaces, the thickness of the walls, all told of ancient days
and builders. There was the door of the dining-room that
opened outward, and there, legend has it, the Duke of Kent
kissed a very pretty serving girl when he was in Annapolis on
visit. The first owners had slaves, and the mistress was not
too kind to them. An iron rod fastened on an upper floor
is said to have been used as a sort of whipping post, and the
tale is told that one slave girl in a hurry missed a piece
of pie and it went out to the pigs. The mistress had seen,
however, and she made the poor girl go into the sty and
there eat the pastry. The usual ghost is there at the Banks
House, but the inmates are not in the least alarmed for
the phantom is a quiet, well-mannered old lady who never
bothers anyone. Away back when the house was built there
was some idea of insulation, and so a second roof was placed
a few inches higher than the first one, and serves well to keep
the place warm in winter and cool in summer.

From the Banks House we went further into the town,
turning in to old Fort Anne. We drove inside the earthworks
and out on the parade ground in front of what was the officers'
barracks. It had thirty rooms, each with a fireplace, and the

building almost sound proof. Now it is a fine museum under the management of Colonel E. K. Eaton, with a Port Royal Room, an Acadian Room, a Garrison Room, a Queen Anne Room and a Haliburton Hallway. The Acadian Room is intensely interesting as it was transferred bodily from an ancient Acadian home with the walls and ceiling beams intact, and all the furnishings of such a room are there. A tour through the various rooms takes one across the years of Nova Scotia's history. Then there are the earthworks outside, the powder magazine, the site of the blockhouse, and the grand view of Annapolis Basin that must have been balm many a summer afternoon or moonlight night for the sentry lad on duty and dreaming of home. One could write pages about this old stronghold that was captured and re-captured seven times before the flag of Britain went aloft to stay, but nothing written could be half as impressive as to spend a day there, as thousands do each summer, drinking in the historic atmosphere of over three centuries.

One needs little imagination to see again the place as it was in the middle of the 17th century, the new fort then, established by D'Aulnay, who had carted the Acadians away from La Have to build this new community seven miles from the site of the original Port Royal. It was given the same name, and forty homes were erected. The fort was mostly earthworks, and when it was finished to his satisfaction D'Aulnay went out across the Bay of Fundy to seize the holdings of Charles la Tour, claiming that the fellow was trespassing on his territory. He was repulsed, but tried again. La Tour hired Boston vessels and Boston men, and with the force chased D'Aulnay away and back to Annapolis, capturing a ship and a cargo of furs. The strife kept on, but each time D'Aulnay was defeated in his purpose until the day he found his rival absent and only Madame la Tour in charge. Treachery gained him access to the fort, and then he broke his word to the lady and hanged every man of the garrison. Gallant Madame la Tour died soon after, heart-broken, and D'Aulnay seemed successful in every sense of the word. But fate overtook him. An Indian guide he had abused upset him from a canoe in the Annapolis River, and he was drowned.

No tears were shed by the Acadians, for he had used them like slaves. His boys grew up along the Basin banks, went to France and died as soldiers on the field of battle. Charles la Tour came from hiding, wooed the widow of D'Aulnay and married her, a grand finale to the fighting of a decade, and a wedding of much arrangement and convenience. The entire agreement that was drawn up between them and signed in the presence of many witnesses at Port Royal, February 25, 1653, can be read in the Archives, or in any copy of Murdoch's History of Nova Scotia. Now came another scoundrel on the scene, one Emmanuel le Borgne, who claimed the possession of Port Royal, saying D'Aulnay had owed him much money. He came to drive la Tour out, and had little trouble as that gentleman was over at his old fort on the Saint John river. He intended to take that place as well, but a British force was there ahead of him, so le Borgne hastened back to Port Royal.

Soon the British arrived, and demanded its surrender. Le Borgne replied haughtily in defiance, so the British officer landed 300 men to attack. The visitor of today can stand on the grassy rampart and look over the scene of action, scarcely changed in contour since those days so long ago. A sergeant of the garrison led a party out to repel the invaders. He was killed and his men fled back to the fort with the British in pursuit. The sun glints on the river and bright sod, and you need little fancy to see those men in armour running clumsily up the embankment while officers in the fort shout orders. Le Borgne was not a soldier. He had 160 men, but they were poor fighters. So he surrendered, and all his stores and provisions were seized, the British not keeping a promise they had made at the capitulation, saying mockingly that they were not obliged to keep their word "with people who had exhibited so little courage."

The Treaty of Breda in 1667 gave back Acadia to the

French and another old document gives a word picture of Port Royal in 1679 when conveyances of land were signed by Acadian farmers who had lands along the Annapolis River, and who agreed to deliver one capon and one bushel of wheat the first day of each January as quit rent. The place had prospered, and six small craft were fitted out as fishing vessels, adding their gains to the welfare of the community.

Later there were letters telling of French warships putting in at Port Royal in 1688 with six ketches and a brigantine, British, captured along the coast. The booty was divided among the crews, and the captured ones sent to Boston in one ketch. Such procedure raised plenty of alarm in Massachusetts, and talk of capturing Port Royal once more was soon heard across New England. Early in 1690 a squadron commanded by Sir William Phips arrived there. De Menneval, governor of Acadia, was in command, with a garrison of eighty-six French soldiers. He had eighteen cannon, but they were not placed in battery. A soldier and two inhabitants were on guard at the "Gut" and fired a small mortar to warn the fort.

Phips sailed in close and sent a messenger with a demand for surrender, the messenger being a trumpeter. Menneval detained the man and sent a priest to the British camp to ask for good terms. These were that the garrison should be sent to Quebec or France and the inhabitants to be left in peaceable possession of their farms. Phips agreed, but was enraged when he saw the feeble condition of the defences. So he looked for an excuse to break the agreement, and had not far to look. While the bargaining was going on some of the garrison had got drunk and started removing property from the storehouse. It was enough for Phips. Port Royal was pillaged, and the officers were searched for money. The inhabitants were gathered and made to take an oath of fidelity to the British crown. Then Phips sailed back to Boston with his prisoners and plunder.

There was no security for the inhabitants left behind. Two pirate ships put in. They burned all the houses near the fort, killed cattle, hanged two of the inhabitants in sport then burned a house in which a woman and children had taken refuge. Records state that twenty-eight homes went up in smoke before the pirates were satisfied. The survivors built shelters for themselves and stayed on. In November came a French ship with soldiers, and Port Royal was taken over again as French property.

For ten years there was more or less peace and prosperity in the place, with many ships coming and going. When Brouillan, the Governor of Acadia, visited Port Royal in 1701 he tried to get the inhabitants to cut a road to Minas, but found them not agreeable to the proposal. He wrote a lengthy description of the strength of the fort and its fine site, and suggested that a wall of masonry be erected. He built a lime kiln and made a brick yard, finding the clay perfect, then requested France to send out thirteen masons and six stone cutters. He built a house for a hospital and had two surgeons on his six companies of soldiers. The time of his stay in Port Royal is aptly described in *Quietly My Captain Waits*, by Evelyn Eaton, a fine novel published a decade ago by Harper's. There was all manner of intrigue going on among rival officers, and some ladies of the place were not all they should be. Even the records of those days, written tersely to save ink and labour, make exciting reading.

In the spring of 1707 a New England expedition made a surprise attack on Port Royal. It was almost successful, but Subercase, the French commander, was a man of courage and determination. Furthermore, all the male inhabitants flocked to the fort to help as best they could. The New Englanders landed 700 men on one side of the fort and 300 on the other side, then advanced. The French went out to meet them and, although they were driven back, caused heavy losses, killing and wounding many soldiers. Finally the French were driven into the fort, and for two days there was a lull. On the third day the New Englanders advanced on the fort itself. Subercase fired all the buildings near the fort. The British began digging a trench that would serve as cover to get near the defences. The French sallied out in raids that were highly successful, so successful that after a few days of hard fighting the siege was abandoned.

The New England governor was disgusted at the lack of success and ordered another attack. On Sunday, August 20th, another force arrived, but disembarked so leisurely that Subercase had time to call in the inhabitants, many of whom were miles away. Monday noon the British formed up and began a roundabout march. Subercase sent his Indians and inhabitants to lie in ambush along the way. These killed and captured an advance party. The British colonel wrote: "Yesterday the French began to fire on our river guards and so continued until about three in the afternoon. There appeared about 100 Indians and French upon the same ground, who kept continually firing at us until dark. Several were shot through their cloaths and one Indian through the thigh. About four in the afternoon I suffered 50 men to go down to the bank of the river to cut thatch to cover their tents. All returned well except nine, who were led away by one Mansfield, a mad fellow, to the next plantation to get cabbages in a garden, without the leave and against the will of his officer. They were no sooner at their plunder than they were surrounded by 100 French and Indians who in a few minutes killed every one of them, their bodies being mangled in a frightful manner. Our people buried them and fired twice upon the enemy, on which they were seen to run towards our out-guards next the woods, which we immediately strengthened." The letter goes on to give a dismal account of sickness and despondency among the soldiers, and his bad cold. "In fine, some of the forces are in a distressed state, some in body and some in mind; and the longer they are kept here on the cold ground (it was in August) the longer it will grow upon them; and I fear the further we proceed, the worse the event. God help us."

Small wonder that the force withdrew the next day when the French flung some bombs at them. They took a new post opposite the fort, and Subercase attacked them there. They moved again, half a league back, and the French stole near enough to kill three sentries, causing them to move once more, out of reach of the fort cannon. Then the force embarked, stayed on their ships all night and at sunrise landed on the fort side, under protection of the ships guns. The point of land that looks today a small slope was then covered with bush, and 150 French were hidden in it. These remained passive until the British soldiers were within pistol range, when three volleys were poured into them. The British began to retreat and three parties of French took after them. Soon there were hand-to-hand combats. Two French officers were wounded and their men began to give ground. The British rallied and routed them, but another French force from the fort changed the situation and soon the British were hastily getting in their boats. They put out to sea and the attack was ended. The next year Subercase worked hard to put the fort in better repair, building a bomb-proof powder magazine, and a structure 80 feet long and 33 feet wide to serve as a chapel and quarters for the surgeon. A fine barracks was completed. A letter to France stated that three of the officers at Port Royal were insane and 75 per cent. of the soldiers were boys from Paris, whose parents had sent them out for misbehaviour.

In 1709 the French had a temporary plenty at Port Royal. A number of frigates made it their headquarters and went out to attack Boston shipping. In all they captured 35 vessels, sending back to Boston as prisoners 470 fishermen and traders. This was too much for New England blood to stand, and the next year an expedition was made ready to again attack the stronghold. Francis Nicholson, who had been governor-in-chief of Virginia, was in command, and on September 24th he reached Port Royal. One transport ran ashore and 26 men were drowned.

The British made no hurried moves but quietly sized up the situation, and the waiting was in their favour, for the nerves of some of the garrison gave way, and they deserted. On October 3rd, Nicholson sent a demand for surrender to Subercase, and was ignored. On the 6th the British began

landing and were unopposed. The next day they marched in
the direction of the mill on a brook near, and there planted
their batteries. Then the firing began, and at night 58 of the
garrison fled in the darkness. On October 12th the British
had worked three batteries to within 100 yards of the fort,
and the garrison was in mortal fear. Subercase had to
capitulate. His men and some of the inhabitants, 481 in all,
were shipped to France. The British flag was sent aloft to
stay, and the name "Port Royal," changed to "Annapolis
Royal."

Time and again the French attacked the fort, and many
times it was in a deplorable condition, but Major Paul
Mascarene was in command, was there for forty years, and his
was such a personality that soldiers did the impossible for
him. He withstood every onslaught and never again did the
French flag float over the old ramparts. No other spot in
America saw as much fighting, as many sieges, as many
changes in possession, as many different garrisons. For 150
years it knew nothing but warfare and pirate raids and bloodshed and privateers and warships and Indians and murdered
sentries and intrigue. No one book could ever contain in
terse account all the adventure that occurred around the
trenches and ramparts and outposts of this most storied fort
in America.

A long bridge over the River is in plain view from the
town, and Granville Ferry is a village clustered at the far end
of the bridge. Some very old houses are there, and with the
aid of a glass one can plainly see the ancient Entertainment
House that for well over two centuries has been a pleasant
meeting place and house of refreshment. The original sign
is still there, now inside instead of swinging on an iron post
beside the great oak that fronts the place, and the sign is a
stone well carved and framed with wood. One enters the
room to the right where once an officer rode his horse in the
broad doorway and asked for a drink, the imprint of the iron
shoes remaining still to prove the tale. Those who are
interested in history will linger a long time, and lucky indeed

are those who spend the night in the ancient bedrooms, perhaps sleeping on the great "sleigh bed" that remains in one. The kitchen is as it used to be, with the bake oven to the left of the huge fireplace that looks still ready for daily use with all the hooks and cranes and kettles and pots about. A great bread box is there, used as a seat when the cover is closed. Then there is the cradle of old days, a churn, a long toasting fork, an ancient settee on rockers, with pegs set high at one end so that a baby might be laid there to rest as mother gently rocked both herself and infant. A carpet bag of the old days, a Nelson corkscrew, the kneeling chair used by the devout, and other items too numerous to describe are there, and small wonder that there is seldom a vacant room at the Entertainment House. A small distance beyond is the oldest house in Nova Scotia, the home of Mr. and Mrs. John L. Amberman. Mr. Amberman is eighty-three years of age, one of the sixth generations of Ambermans to live in the house, which has great open beams and old-fashioned latches and all the features one expects to see in a house so very old.

Coming back into the street from Fort Anne, we went around a corner and located the home of Miss Perkins. Miss Charlotte Isabella Perkins is, first of all, a cultured lady, a gentlewoman of the old class, courteous, kind, keenly intelligent, and simply steeped in Annapolis history. She is an accomplished writer, and her articles are both interesting and informative. She can tell you of the fourteen times Fort Anne was besieged by the enemy, and of its being the capital of Nova Scotia for many, many years before Halifax was founded. She told us of the old houses in the town until we knew that nowhere else in the Dominion can be found a locality of similar historic interest. There is the old Commercial House, built as headquarters for ship-builders, then used as the Acadia Hotel; the old Bailey House, built cornerwise to keep a neighbour from looking up the street, and still solid as a rock, long an aristocratic boarding house for officers and professional men who came to the town. The Duke of Kent danced at a ball in this house in 1794. "Marm"

Bailey, who ran the house, was a large handsome woman, extremely capable, famous for her moose muffle soup which was so good that some of it was exported to England. According to Miss Perkins, after the preparation of the muffle were added knuckle of veal, onions, thyme, marjoram, clove, cayenne, salt, force-meat balls fried in butter, tomato catsup, yolks of twelve hard-boiled eggs, and, lastly, one bottle of old port wine.

No one knows when the Annapolis Royal Hotel was built, but carpenters making some alterations in recent years uncovered a coin dated 1749. A century ago it was famous for the turkey suppers given there and was known as Frederick Sinclair's Inn. The first Masonic Lodge in Canada was held in this old hotel in 1738 in what Col. Sinclair used to call his "large room below stairs." In 1791 County Court was held there. Only part of the Williams house, birthplace of Sir Fenwick Williams, remains. Its walls were set with clay and rushes of one foot thickness, and there was an enormous centre chimney for the large fireplaces. The interior finish was of pine, dark brown boards that shone like glass, the narrow crooked stairway being panelled, the walls sheathed with it, and the floor laid in planks of it eighteen inches wide. In the front rooms were hand-carved moldings and deep seats on either sides of the windows.

This Williams house was haunted. A young man sleeping in one of the rooms was startled to see a soldier come toward his bed holding up the stump of a bleeding arm. Forty years after this was still happening in the spare bedroom, and observant ones had noted that the uniform identified the ghost as belonging to the Royal Engineers. Some treated the tale as a joke, but it was generally believed. Great excitement stirred the town when the house was moved to make way for the Royal Bank building now there and a skeleton, with the right arm cut off above the wrist, was uncovered in the ancient drain. The house of Peter Bonnett is near the bridge on main street, and Mrs. Bonnett was a granddaughter of the Rev. Jacob Bailey who wrote of his travel to Annapolis.

This old house is built on the foundation of a French cellar going back to 1670. Another fine old place that catches the attention of visitors is the Runciman house in its setting of old trees and lawns. Its interior is unchanged, with an enclosed and winding stairway.

There is no one more qualified to talk of the quaint and beautiful than Miss Perkins, for she is an artist of talent and, though she had not mentioned it to me, her sister had shown me some of her work. So it was most pleasant to sit and listen to the tales of old gardens and fine flowers and gracious homes and hospitality dispensed in grand style during the days when Annapolis Royal was the centre of social activities and nearly every home had its possessions of pure linen and solid silver and cut glass and the finest furniture. But there was more than beauty and grace in her story of the Queen Hotel, that is just across the road from the Hillsdale.

A Mr. Ritchie married the sister of Mrs. Ryerson of the Hillsdale, and as he was expecting to inherit a fortune from relatives in England he decided to outdo his sister-in-law, and he purchased spacious grounds across the road and built a mansion of twenty-two rooms. A water tank was placed in the cellar and a force pump provided water for the kitchen. On the third floor was another tank with water to supply the bathroom and bedrooms, the small marble basins being set in wooden box-like compartments. The house was the first in town to have running water, the floors were of walnut and ash, the ceilings were lofty, there was a grand staircase and an iron grill ran around the roof. A special door bell made to order in Philadelphia impressed everyone. The place became a private boarding house, and Mr. Ritchie drove the coach to Caledonia. The chief ornament of the grounds was a large moose he had had mounted and which stood on guard in the centre of the lawn. The house was a school for a time. Then came romance. A girl of the town, daughter of the scrub woman, became a champion swimmer and won many honours, and considerable money, in the United States. She returned in style and purchased the big Ritchie house, put a ten dollar bill on the collection plate on Sunday, and installed a telephone in the rectory—a luxury in those days. She named the place "The Old Orchard House," installed the best of furnishings and these included a very fine and expensive music box. Came the opening, and she gave a large reception, greeting her guests in style. The music rolled forth and refreshments were served, and all tongues told of the wonders she had installed. But she had only begun, although the tourist season was a slim one that year. She had a fine hot water heating plant put in, and had a grand bathroom finished in oak. Then she got on a train and departed for parts unknown, escaping all her creditors. Legend has it that she married a sculptor and died in California. Not too long after the house became the Queen Hotel, well-known to every Nova Scotian.

Miss Perkins said it was too bad that people who would read this would never realize that these old places exist today in Annapolis Royal, and any visitor can see them. Every summer, she said, there are hundreds roaming around and making notes and taking photographs, shaking their heads, some of them, as if everything is unbelievable. I've heard them say a dozen times that if this town were in the United States it would be taken over by the government intact and kept as a national museum. And I've not mentioned the old cemetery, where one epitaph records the death of a girl two months before she was born, or the town hall which has mounted heads of nearly every wild animal in Canada or America even. Or talked of some inscriptions on old window panes that you can read. There's one in the old hotel: "Here I am after a hard day's ride. An empty stomach and a sore backside. Take my advice your stomach fill. Plaster your . . . and pay your bill."

Four boys from the old town of Annapolis gained high places in the naval and military world. One of these became General Sir William Fenwick Williams. He entered the military life at the age of fifteen, became an officer and served at Ceylon, Gibraltar and other places, then, in 1841, was loaned to the Turkish Government as a military expert. A few years later he acted as British Commissioner in the settlement of the Turko-Persian boundary dispute, and was decorated for his service—Companion of the Bath. During the Crimean War he was again with the Turkish forces and held the city of Kars from June 7, 1855, until November 28th of that year against repeated attacks of vastly superior Russian forces. After such a feat he was knighted and given many honours by Britain and France and Turkey, became Commander-in-Chief of the British forces in Canada, Lieutenant Governor of Nova Scotia, Governor of Gibraltar, and, finally, Constable of the Tower of London.

One of the boys he played with at Annapolis became Sir William Winniett, an officer in the Royal Navy and Governor-General of the Cape Coast District. The two other boys, Phillips Cosby and William Wolseley, became admirals of the British Navy.

We thanked her and left the town, wondering if ever a full history of it would be written. We drove across a bridge on the marsh and were on our way to Clementsport. To our right as we drove was the River and Basin, and far across the water we saw a dark oblong that was Port Royal Habitation, the oldest permanent settlement of white people in America north of the Gulf of Mexico. It stands on the site Samuel de Champlain selected in 1605, and the well he had dug is in the centre of the ancient courtyard. The group of buildings is arranged around the yard in the manner of 16th century farms in northern France, and is fortified by a stockade and by two cannon platforms at the southerly corners.

The entrance gateway is framed with hewn oak and is roofed with oak shingles as used in Picardy in the 16th century. The studded oak doors are handmade and hung and fitted with wrought ironware of period design. The peep-hole in the outer door was known as a "Judas." The coat of arms painted over the doorway is derived from that shown on Lescarbot's map of Port Royal. The arms are those of France (left) and Navarre (right), of which countries Henry IV was

King. The small building next the gateway is described in
a picture plan as "a small building in which was kept the
rigging for our pinnaces. This the Sieur de Poutrincourt
had later rebuilt, and there the Sieur de Boulay lodged when
the Sieur de Pont returned to France." The interior wall
boarding is spruce, the fireplace is of stone, the windows are
of leaded glass, and the candle sconces are as would be made
by the smiths of that time. The roof is covered with hand-
split pine shingles.

Next there is the blacksmith shop, where ironworkers
made tools, utensils and arrow heads, the forge being built
of hand-made bricks and stone. The windows are filled with
oiled parchment. The kitchen has its huge bake-oven in the
part known as the bake-shop, the whole being in two spaces
wherein was prepared enough food to feed eighty-four persons.
The community room was also the dining-room, and the great
table is there. Champlain and his fifteen gentlemen sat
around it three and a half centuries ago to form the first social
club in America, and our guide proudly reminded us when
we were there that the Order of the Good Time still exists
and members are scattered through every province of Canada
and every State of the Union. Other buildings are the
artisans' quarters, the chapel, the priests' dwellings, the
governor's house, the dwellings of the gentlemen, the storehouse, the trading-room, and the guardroom. To enter the
great gate is to step back to the beginning of the 17th century,
and there is nothing on this continent comparable to the Port
Royal Habitation.

In 1948 Andrew D. Merkel, who lives at Port Royal, now
retired from a lifetime as head of the Canadian Press at
Halifax, and author of *Schooner Bluenose,* headed a com-
mittee that erected a Memorial Arbour commemorating the
birth of Canadian drama there. In 1607 Lescarbot arranged
the first drama and wrote lyrics for the occasion, depicting
Father Neptune as greeting those arriving at the port. It was
as much pageant as drama, an elaborate ceremonial with
Lescarbot the manager, but definite parts were acted, and

so was born this type of entertainment in the new world. Lescarbot was something of a poet, and he composed verses for the occasion, the first poetry written in Canada. It must have been a joyous day, that 14th of November, 1607, for much wine was served to all the company and the arms of France were placed over the gate of the fort, environed with laurel crowns that Lescarbot had created with native growth. Lescarbot wrote a faithful story of each week, making a fine account of the colony that has been preserved and read by countless thousands of students of history. So there is nothing very far-fetched in claiming that at Port Royal Canadian drama and verse and prose were first created.

The Rev. Bailey wrote about journeying to Clementsport, fourteen miles from Annapolis:

In the second mile we crossed Allain River, a rapid rocky stream where we were bespattered. Our progress lay along horrid broken roads, so encumbered with rocks, holes, gullies, roots of trees and windfalls and sloughs that passage was dangerous. We were frequently obliged to dismount and lead our horses, wallowing knee deep through the mire. The last six miles conducted us over hanging precipices, wooded promontories and stony beaches. We crossed Moose River and a little before sunset arrived at the big house with two small apartments where I united in marriage Shupy Sprie and Alicia Van Voorhies. The bride was very pretty. Received half a dollar.

There was a unique arbour near the road. A steam roller had ceased to be active and someone had planted vines beside it, trained them over the uglier parts, and banked flowers fore and aft. The cab was now a cozy lovers seat, and the whole a most attractive feature. The road curved around the side of a hill, then dipped down to cross water at the head of the port. Across the wide ravine the road climbed the other side and vanished around the hill. We stopped and did some climbing ourselves to reach the old Loyalist Church of St. Edward, consecrated in 1788 and housing many relics. The architecture of the church is Norman, with pews of the old square type and doors with hand-made hinges and nails.

The lime for the plaster was obtained by burning clam shells and is now so hard that an ordinary nail cannot pierce it. This village had its beginning when the British Government granted land in the area to some of their German mercenaries who settled on what is locally known as the Weldeck and Hessian lines. The "Waldeck" line runs from Clementsport to the mouth of Bear River, while the "Hessian" line parallels it four miles distant, where some descendants of the original settlers still reside. Dutch, Hessian and other German Loyalists built this old church, and it was originally Lutheran. When it was finally transferred to the Church of England, a condition was made that a hymn in the Dutch language should be sung every Sunday morning before the beginning of the regular service. This was done until only two old men were left to chant, with aged voices, the hymn of their Fatherland. The old bass viol which furnished the instrumental music is still there, as are also some of the old Dutch psalm-books. When we went outside again we stood and gazed far over Annapolis Basin and could see plainly Digby Gap, the opening to the Bay of Fundy. It was easy to realize that the far-sighted first settlers had placed their church high on the side of South Mountain so that it would also serve them as a landmark when they were on their schooners coming in through the Gap.

Around the hill and a corner and soon we could see a city of buildings in orderly arrangement. It was "Cornwallis," the great naval establishment at Deep Brook, filled again with navy personnel and active. Next was Smith's Cove, and all along were signs pointing to holiday resorts. Small wonder, too, for it was beautiful along the Basin shore, with a wide panorama of sea and hill and sky. Here was old land, too, won in the hard way, making one think of verses of *Pioneer Home* by Mabel Staats:

> These stones, long quarried from the stubborn rock,
> Were set with aching toil in wild new land;
> These heavy beams were hewn by him who planned
> A home for sturdy sons of his brave stock.

His tools, too few and crude, made labor slow;
The matted turf was hindrance for his plow;
But yet he settled here and braved somehow
The savage raids of his marauding foe.

It was hard to realize that we were away from the lush
fertile lands of the eighty-mile Annapolis Valley, its sandy
plains and pine groves, endless orchards and pleasant towns.
Here we were edging along on land hard-won from rock and
timber, and we paused to chat with an old woman who came
to sell us a box of cherries from a fruit stand made simply by
nailing a board across a hefty stump. She had been a big
strong girl once, and there was evidence in her lined face
and stooped shoulders that in her hard-work lifetime had been
precious, not to be spent on unnecessary things.

"Cherries seem a good crop this year," we remarked.

"I've sold eighteen dollars' worth," she said quietly, "and
I can remember when we wouldn't take in much more money
than that all summer." She sat on a chair from where she
watched her cherry counter and talked about the family farm
that had been owned by her husband's people since 1800. At
that time the great grandfather had bought 250 acres for a
pair of oxen, and had built himself a log cabin. He had
raised five children in that homespun age, keeping sheep
because wool found a ready market, fattening steers for the
Digby market, working in the woods in the winter, growing
enough wheat to make all the bread needed. The farm had
been self-sufficient then, with everything from candles for
lighting to greenhides for footwear, produced on the place.
Then things had changed with the next generation. The
cobbler was no longer indispensable, for one thing. By 1840
the folks were wearing "store boots," and there was regular
coach service along the highway. It was hard to know how
the changes came after that, the woman said. She had been
born in 1869, and they were already calling it the machine
age.

"I remember the first mowin' machine come into the

settlement," she said, "and folks went around sayin' 'what next?'."

We remembered the hour. "Where can we get a good place for overnight?" we asked.

She hesitated. "Go to any of them that has the signs out and you can't go wrong," she said. "I reckon there ain't another part of Nova Scotia has so many good places in so few miles. That Out-of-the-Way Inn has been goin' since 1894, and they have eighty-five acres puttin' down to the shore. The Harbour View has even more space, and near thirty cottages. Then there's Mountain Gap Inn where they feed you good as at The Pines in Digby. But if I was you I'd just keep goin' till you see a sign for Hedley House, and I'd stop there."

"Good place?" we queried.

"First-class, and so mighty interestin'. That is, them girls that run it is. They were through the last war, one from England and one the U.S.A., then just happened to come over to Nova Scotia from Saint John to spend a few days on vacation. The U.S.A. one had an uncle in Saint John, and they come across for the boat ride. Well, they drove out of Digby and rambled along until they seen a big old house with a verandah across the front, and a grand view over the water. There was a sign up about overnight, and they went in. An old couple was runnin' the place, and tired out with doin' it, but they were so nice the girls just stayed there a few days and then the old couple asked them to buy it. Fact is, that offered it so cheap, the girls up and said they'd take it, and mind you neither of them had ever put foot in this country before. Neither had they any experience runnin' a place. But they set in and put a verandah all around and built some cabins and painted and fixed up till you woudn't know it, then hung out a sign. The uncle they'd visited over in Saint John was called Hedley, so they named their place after him, they were so glad it had happened the way it did. Well, that's four-five years ago, and they're now doin' a grand business. They're so handy. You should see the lamp in a lobster trap, the cute things they've rigged, and hear Penny Gott, she's the one tends the front, talk about over in Europe. She talks near any language on account she was an interpreter in the war."

The old woman was so in earnest that we decided to take her advice, and it was not long before we saw the sign she had mentioned. The view was there, too, and a fine parking space, so we went in and were lucky enough to find a vacant cabin. We sat to a wonderful meal served on the closed-in verandah. The little waitress moved about sure-footed as a cat and smiling cheerfully, and there was Penny herself pushing a cart simply laden with relishes and pickles and sauces and hot rolls, coming again and again, simply heaping plates with good things, and everyone eating with more sheer satisfaction than we had seen in years.

When we had finished we went to our cabin, then strolled down to the shore. A dozen or so younger folk were there, with some in bathing suits. Two men well along in years were seated on a plank placed on rocks and calmly surveying the water. They eyed us carefully, then invited us to sit, and the elder began to fill a large black pipe.

"I'm not a tourist," he said, reaching low to strike a match on a rock. "I just live back a way on the road, but this other is my brother from Watertown in New York State, and it's his first trip home in about thirty years. So I took the day off and we come here where we used to play a considerable few years ago."

We were alert at once, and told him we wanted to hear anything he knew about Smith's Cove. He put his pipestem back in his mouth and drew in a long and slow pull of hot smoke.

"I can recall my grandfather like yes'day," he said, "but he never told me any real history of along this way. But you'll find lots to write about if you git off this main road. You take over to Kedgemakooge, an hour's drive. There's them Injun rocks covered with Injun writin'. Pictures of birds and animals and canoes and ships and sunrise, nearly anything.

Some is deep cut and some you need glasses to see. I remember bein' in there when I was a boy and it was a dry hot spell so that many of the rocks was bare that hadn't been. We spent half a day lookin' at something different every stone we went to, and we found some they said was done by the first French, and some by the first English. It's always beat me that some-body hasn't gone in there and made copies before they're all worn off. Mr. Kelsal, the superintendent of the Gov'ment Experimental Station at Kentville, goes in there every summer with his wife and they copy a lot of the drawin's."

"It's all right if you like that sort of thing." The man who'd spent half a lifetime in New York State talked exactly like his brother. "If you don't, just go four miles in to Bear River. That's where cherries really grow. I've seen women in there with sunshades and sheets and tin pans, tryin' to keep the robins off long enough to git the fruit picked. But you should see the village. Built up on shelves over the river, every family lookin' down into the next man's yard, a kind of Switzerland, they call it. And in there Eber Peck grew up. He was world champion log roller for eight years straight, and he still lives in there. Now they've got Viola Paul, too, and she's the world champion female log roller. I'd give real money to see her on a log."

"Hell, Sam," snorted the elder, "are you forgettin' Blue Mary, that Injun girl that rolled logs from under a dozen men back when we were kids? I remember us goin' in there dozens of times to watch a rollin'. Mostly on Saturday afternoons, and sometimes on Sundays, when the preacher was out at Deep Brook. That Bear River is near old as Port Royal, too. The Frenchies were in there over three hundred years ago, and things has been found there."

"Things?" we echoed.

"One thing they found, them that settled these parts first, was a smooth stone floor about thirty by twenty. Not a sign of wall near it, but there was a well, showin' it had been a house, and a good one at that. Then there were old apple trees around there, and one summer when somebody was makin' a cellar they uncovered a three-gallon jug of rum. Bear River was drunk about a week after."

"Tell him about the mill cook that Christmas," urged the man from Watertown.

"Years ago there used to be a story on the rounds about two skeletons found over in a place by the brook they called The Flat. Some said there was more'n two. That five or six were there together, and when the first feller found them they all clattered down in a heap and ghosts run alongside him clean out to a house. He went near crazy and left on the next ship to follow the sea. They never got him back on land around here. Well, they set up a sawmill at The Flat and around one Christmas two men that had been on a bust come through the woods and begged the mill cook to feed 'em and put 'em up over night. The cook give them supper but was rather feared they might have fleas, so he bedded them on some straw and spare blankets in a store shed back of his kitchen. The cook was one of the old-timers that knew the skeleton story good, and he told it to them two visitors he had. At last they turned in but he didn't risk a light with them. Them days beef might be short a day or so, and the boss had the cook save bones for soup. The bones was put in a sack hung in that store shed, and just over the foot of the bed the cook had made up. They went to sleep all right, but it got cold in the shed and one of them begun to stir around, trying to find something more to pull over them. The other chap was havin' a dream, and a bad one. He woke up and yelled that the skeletons was right there beside them. The shiverin' one told him to be quiet, and hunched around more. But in the doin' he bumped against that bone sack and the peg holdin' it broke, for the sack was near full, and down rattled dry bones, fallin' all over both men. There never was such yellin'. They got out of there so fast they forgot their caps and near froze their ears off afore they got into the village. The cook said after it was lucky they had been cold enough to leave their larrigans on, else they'd run in their sock feet."

"It's a good story," the brother admitted, "but the

Caledonia one is better. That's down a bit toward the South Shore, and you ought to see it. Years back the first white men in there lived in one cabin while they cleared ground. An Injun woman did their cookin' and was good at it. Come Christmas they shot a bunch of partridge and give 'em to her to fix up for a Christmas feed. She baked 'em in the coals, feathers'n all, and did such a good job they all said she was the best cook in the country. Then they tapped a jug of rum and by dark they were well jagged and all got the same idee. They each wanted to marry the Injun woman, and they each asked her. She was purty confused and didn't know what to say so they agreed to draw for her. They did it with long twigs, and the next mornin' the winner took her and started out for Annapolis Royal to find a parson and git proper married. The squaw made no fuss, but when they were on the trail a mile or so they heard a wild yellin' behind them. Then they heard it again, nearer, and it was a real Injun whoop. The squaw begin to look scared. Next the man knew, up come a Injun in sight, wavin' a knife and yellin' like mad. 'He my husband,' said the squaw, stoppin' stock still. Well, that poor white man set to it and run for all he had in him. Somehow he kept ahead of the Injun and he reached town without bein' caught. A ship was in port and the poor chap went aboard, hired on as a deck hand, and sailed before night. He never come back to these parts until years after, and then nobody had the heart to tell him it was all a trick. The others in the cabin had hired the Injun to chase him, and had give the squaw a shilling to say it was her husband."

We came up from the beach satisfied with our day, and had cookies and milk served by our hostess, then retired to dream of old men and a quiet sea.

In the morning we were in Digby in no time. We turned sharp left as we entered the town and saw a fine Information Bureau in a park-like space by a bandstand. It was a new building and the interior was just as attractive as the exterior.

A display of handcraft occupied the back portion of the building and wide windows looked out over the Basin. We stood and watched the *Princess Helene* come in to the dock, arriving from Saint John, New Brunswick. She could carry forty cars a trip, we were informed by Miss Louise Daley, who was in charge of the Bureau, and seldom have we met a person more informative than she. First off, she told us of the view to be had up by the new school building at the top of the hill, and when we parked there we had no trouble seeing what she meant. The panorama was superb, a glorious expanse of water, yachts a-wing, far roads and fields and forest, all seemingly down at our feet.

Then we were told of the town's beginning in 1783, when 1500 Loyalists were brought there in autumn of the year. Winter set in early, and many of the people had no shelter, so they lived on ships that were anchored close to shore. There was not too much food in supply, but herring were plentiful and were eaten every day. When Christmas came there was no hope of chicken or turkey. Just the herring they had been eating at almost every meal. Some of the stout-hearted ones called the fish "Digby chicken," and the name caught on. Herring are called by the name in all that Fundy shore area to this day. The Hon. Robert Digby had been in command of the British fleet off New York, and it was he who superintended the removal of many Loyalists to Nova Scotia. He had especial interest in Digby, then called Conway, and so the town was named for him. He donated £100 sterling to the wooden church that was built in 1790, and gave the bell, which was brought from London, England, and now hangs in a more modern tower. The thankful citizens then reserved a pew for the Admiral, and had its door adorned with his coat of arms. He had a well dug that supplied many of the residents, and it was re-located a few years ago, near the wharf. The little site is fenced off and one of the many historic items of the town.

One of those first settlers was John Edison, from New

Jersey. He had been loyal to the Crown, and at one time was sentenced to be hanged for giving aid to British troops, but his sentence was commuted to banishment from the United States. He liked Digby, and there his son and his grandson were born. Then the Edisons moved to Ontario, the youth of the family being Samuel Edison, Jr. This was in 1811. He was married, and two of his children were born in Ontario when the ill-fated Papineau Rebellion forced Samuel to flee to the States, just as his grandfather had been forced to go to Nova Scotia. He settled in Ohio, and there his third child, Thomas Alva Edison, the great inventor, was born.

Digby is the home port of the largest scallop fleet in the world, and nine-tenths of the total scallop catch of Canada is made in Digby waters. Boats for hire, guides for fishing, fresh or saltwater, add to the natural recreational facilities of this famous summer resort. At the town limits is the beautiful Pines Hotel, and nearby a delightful golf course overlooking the Basin. From almost every vantage point in the town the visitor can look over the water to The Gap, or Gut, which opens into the Bay of Fundy.

Weary Old Fundy once rebelled against his fate,
 Rebelled against monotony
 And lack of recreation,
 Cursed his dim and luckless star,
 Stamped about and bellowed,
The Old Man's soul was in a most chaotic state.

Old Fundy snorted, heaved a rock against the sky,
 Then to vent his wrath some more
 Kicked the cliff in anger,
 Cut his great toe on Point Prim
 Making red the hillside;
Old Fundy's blood stained the earth and sea like dye.

Old Man Fundy grabbed his toe and hopped about,
 Gave another mighty kick,
 Nearly lost his balance,
 Kicked a hole right through the hills
 Wide as many a river,
Old Fundy looked aghast then raised a mighty shout.

In rushed the water beyond Digby and Deep Brook,
   Past the roofs of Clementsport,
   On to Granville Ferry,
   Filling up the valley land
   To make Annapolis Basin!
"Digby Gut!" Old Fundy cried, with wonder in his look!

                                        MARIE L. WELDON.

Anyone wanting excellent handcraft could find it in Nova
Scotia, said Miss Daley. She talked of beautiful rugs that
were made along that Fundy shore, of a lady who painted
exquisite scenes on fungus from trees, of a wood carver from
Annapolis who carved dogs in perfect detail and painted
them in true colour. She talked of the abundant wild life
around the Digby district for the camera hunter and lover
of nature. Often she would go to a little nook she knew
by a beaver pond and sit there in the moonlight with apples
in her hands. The beaver had become so accustomed to her
that they would knock off work every now and then and
come over to get an apple from her. Strangely, only the
younger ones were timid. The oldsters showed not the slightest
fear.

4

Through the Acadian Land

The wooden railway. The man who wouldn't talk.
Ox cart delivery. Green Tree Inn. 297 Yarmouth vessels.
International Tuna Cup Matches. The ship of death.
The quilt house. The Pubnicos.

IT is a lovely scenic drive through the Valley, but the highway
from Annapolis to Digby is simply thrilling, with height of
land overlooking the water, the Basin showing to best advantage, quick corners, tiny villages, ascents and descents, brooks,
hedges, fine homes. Now we were in wooded areas again and
finally climbed a long grade and dipped into Weymouth.
Here was a town where the Loyalists did not make good.
They settled it on quite a scale in 1783, and until recent
years traces of the old streets could still be found. They
called the place Sissiboo, an Indian word, but folks from
Weymouth, Massachusetts, finally settled the place and named
it to suit themselves. Colonel Moodie, a fabulous fighter in
the war of 1776, from North Carolina, settled in Weymouth,
and became an outstanding citizen. Weymouth developed
into a lumbering centre, and railroad history was made there
by the Stehlin family. The Stehlins were from the Alsace-
Lorraine district, and were famous engineers, working with
iron and steel. A Stehlin operated the first steam engine
in France.

In 1895 Paul Stehlin came to Nova Scotia, and settled
at Weymouth on the advice of a friend of the old days who
lived on Church Point. There was a large family, nine boys,
and lumbering seemed the key to a fortune. Ten thousand
acres of timberland were purchased seventeen miles inland

from Weymouth in almost virgin territory, and there the
Stehlins established a New France. They built great sawmills
and hired workers until fifty people were living in the
clearing. The name "New France" was adopted. A store
was built to supply the people, and a small school. Then
the idea of a railway grew, and soon the Stehlins were putting
down wooden rails the entire seventeen miles. A locomotive
was built in Amherst, and the road was in operation, hauling
many lumber cars, and one passenger car at the rear.

A large dam enabled the mill to operate with water power
but the Stehlins imported the first electric light used in any
Nova Scotia village. General Electric installed the motor and
all equipment for a total cost of eighteen hundred and fifty
dollars, and there was light in the mill, in every home and
the store. For a decade operations ran at full swing, then the
slackening began. The nearest lumber had been cut. The
wooden rails were giving out. Gradually operations ceased.
Today there can be found traces of the old wooden railroad,
and at the old mill clearing the site is outlined. Most of the
buildings have long since decayed, but some ruins remain,
and a public highway goes in as far as Riverdale. So it is
often that curious persons, knowing the history of the old-time
empire, go in for a day to see the spot where such activity
reigned half a century ago.

Weymouth seemed a bustling village in a bowl, with hills
all around.

"You'll soon see something different," said a fat man from
whom we bought some fruit. "It's the longest main street in
America. Around thirty miles, I reckon. Houses and stores
and churches and garages and houses and stores and schools
and churches and houses and garages, and people walking
on the street and signs in both English and French and the
biggest churches in Nova Scotia. Yes, sir, Acadian villages.
You know how they come there? No? Well, when the
Acadians were sent away they never lost their hankering for
this country, and in 1768 about three hundred families started
and walked back from Massachusetts. Yes, sir, they walked

the whole way, up around them rocky places in Maine, through the New Brunswick woods, and down into Nova Scotia. A lot of the old ones and some babies died by the way. Some families stopped off in New Brunswick when they found some of their kin, but most of the crowd kept coming, and when they were back to Minas here were New Englanders on their land, every acre taken. So the Nova Scotia government told them to keep on down shore and they would be granted land. In late fall they reached Annapolis, and there they stayed the winter, living in anything that had a roof, including some barns and the church. In the spring they were given near the whole of St. Mary's Bay Shore, and there they are to this day—their children, I mean. Yes, sir, the longest main street in America."

That night, at Hebron, we talked of that main street, and I am sure there is nothing quite like it elsewhere on this continent. It stretches through the District of Clare on the shores of St. Mary's Bay, from Weymouth to the boundary of Yarmouth County, peopled almost entirely by descendants of the exiled Acadians. They retain the characteristics of their forefathers, speak the French of Molière, go to church faithfully and keep on dividing their long narrow farms among their increasing grandchildren. Their homes are strung along both sides of the highway, neatly kept, with flower gardens, occasional hedges, until it is really difficult to tell where one village ends and another begins. Practically all the people are Roman Catholics, and they worship in a number of fine churches.

There was a huge stone church at St. Bernard's, and we were told that it took twenty years to build it. It stands on an imposing site and is a landmark for miles around. There were stores in each community, and we stopped to ask questions in each. Some of the people could not understand just what we wanted, but invariably they were polite. We were told that the first settlement was at Belliveau's Cove, and were shown a road leading to the first cemetery, a burying ground set apart in 1769. Grosses Coques is named after the big clams found there, said to be so plentiful that the first settlers lived on them through one winter. A simple stone memorial marks the site of the first log chapel.

At Church Point we saw the largest wooden church in Canada, St. Mary's, with a 200-foot spire, seating 1,800 people. At St. Ann's College there is a degree-conferring institution founded in 1891 by Eudist priests from France. At Comeau- ville we were shown a building that had been an inn for 124 years, and the owner has a document, dated 1772, conveying an extensive grant of land to the family. One hundred and thirty years ago a terrible forest fire swept the country in September. There had been no rain for weeks and everything was tinder dry. Bucket brigades could do little to stop the flames which leaped yards at a time, and eighteen homes were devoured by the raging inferno, the fire racing so fiercely that one family was trapped in the house and burned to death. Nothing was saved, and twenty-three full barns vanished. The Government of Nova Scotia sent money and clothing, food supplies and building materials, but there was great suffering through the winter, as the people lived with their neighbours and shared food as best they could.

Meteghan was a busy place. There were many men work- ing in the shipyard, and we were told that through World War II the yards there had set a record in production of a certain type of boat needed. An oldster who had been listen- ing to our questions, edged himself nearer and asked if we had ever heard of Jerome. No? Well, there was a tale to tell, to beat anything we could read in the mystery books he had seen for sale in Yarmouth. In 1854 a strange sailing vessel was observed in the evening not far off from Sandy Cove, "over on the Neck," the old man pointed. Digby Neck, a long spit of land broken by two ferry crossings, runs parallel to the "main street." In the morning someone observed the ship leaving, while down on the shore was a strange figure. The people went to investigate. They found a young man dressed in clean linen and well-cut clothing, seated, helpless, on the sand, a container of water and some biscuit within his reach. He was very pale and would not talk with anyone. He was also weak. Both his legs had been amputated.

Only one word did he say. His name "Jerome." After that complete silence. He was taken to a home and attended. Many came to question him, but no one could induce him to talk, priest or doctor or the lady teacher. Then he was taken to Meteghan, and there a family boarded him, receiving money regularly from the Provincial Government. Day in and day out, week in and week out, month in and month out, year by year, Jerome maintained his silence, taking no interest in anything, eating well, sleeping well, always looking toward the sea. There, on that St. Mary's Bay Shore he spent his life, living to a ripe old age and taking his secret to the grave. Polite enough, he made friends with none, seemed happier with children than any other, gave no heed to papers or books, simply sat and waited for time to pass. "One great, very great mystery," commented the old man. "He could have been a prince, a robber, who knows? One guess is as good as another. Only thing was, his health was always good. But then, so is everybody's along this shore."

He spoke true words. We made inquiries and were amazed at the number of old people residing along the "street." Further delving into statistics revealed that those who live in Nova Scotia are the best bets for a ripe old age. According to Dominion census figures there is one person 95 or more in every 3,321. The statistics given show that Nova Scotians have six times as much chance of passing that age as those who live in sunny Alberta, where only one person in 18,511 of population can boast of ninety-five birthdays. Next best province for long life is Prince Edward Island, where the ratio is one person out of 3,800. In New Brunswick it's one out of every 6,175. The other provinces are much higher, and the moral is, if there is one, that you should live in Nova Scotia if you want to add years to your life.

Captain John LeBlanc is a driving, energetic builder of boats. He looks weather-wise, and when you talk with him at his shipyard it is easy to think that he is a native who has not been out of the village except for some coasting trips along the Bay. But the Clare folks are like that. Captain LeBlanc knows New York City better than the average New Englander. He can talk of the hotels and shows and restaurants like an old-timer, for he has built boats for some of the real sportsmen of New York, and they have treated him well when he visited their city. He has operated tuna boats, too, and knows every angle of fishing.

We were talking of fishing as we left, and a dark-faced Acadian named Belliveau followed us to the car. He said Professor Willie J. Belliveau "from the college," would be along shortly and could tell us the history of St. Mary's Bay Shore, the history of the Acadians, the history of all Nova Scotia if we wanted it. Not many "had learning along the Shore," he said, because they quit school too soon to tend the weirs. We saw the weirs all along the way, brush tips like combs upside down, sticking up from the inshore chop of the Bay. We saw them with the tide out, mostly crude brush in a long fence, slightly curved, and were puzzled that they should be of any value in catching fish. We said so now.

"Ah, you do not know a herring," declared Mr. Belliveau. "They come against the weir but they won't turn back. No, not them, never. So they try and try and can't get through and the tide goes down, but still they try. Well, at the bottom of the weir there are pot holes made in the sand and mud, and soon the herring are in there like in a barrel, and we come and take them out. That is all there is to it. If herring were not so stupid we could not catch them that way."

We asked him what it was like in winter along the shore. "Not bad," he said simply, with Acadian cheerfulness. "One naturally likes indoors, and there is much visiting. I have heard my father talk of the winter roads. They were cut through the bush, avoiding the bigger trees, of course, and when the snow came and the first sleds had gone through, and the swamp bottom and swale were frozen, they had smooth roads. Oxen were hitched to a big sled filled with straw and everyone piled in and would go four-five miles to visit. Great times they had, and so much fun for nothing. Now you pay for anything there is to do."

Some men and boys and women, too, were working around the yard of a church, and we asked if some amusement were being provided.

"Oh, that is different," he said loyally. "No one minds paying there. That is for the church fair. We have them every summer all along the shore, every place, and raise much money. Any cars going by stop and help with the fun. The women make rugs and fine things to sell, and there are always buyers. Many tourists will watch for a Fair, for they knew how cheap they can buy from our people. Most always, too, they have fine weather, for they pick their times."

"You know the weather along this Shore?" we queried.

"Mostly we do," he nodded. "Sometimes there is a winter when it is hard to know. I have an uncle who can smell a rain coming. I have heard him talk of one fall when days on end there was dullness. Some mornings they had to pry the sun up with a crow bar, and when they got it up it was mostly a weather breeder." He grinned and shrugged. "It is much better now, and here is Professor J. Willie."

Prof. J. Willie Belliveau proved to be as gracious and learned a gentleman as one could wish to meet. We soon knew he was a member of the Historic Sites Advisory Council of Nova Scotia, and that he had selected for that body a suitable place to mark the first home of the Acadians in the district. He told of his search for the grave of a Mrs. Belliveau at Church Point, said to be the first woman in the area. He studied the records that were available and stepped off the land and arrived at the most probable spot. Time and again he went there in vain before he happened to glimpse a glint of stone under the sod. Quick digging revealed crude carving on the fallen slab, and he had located the grave. His grandfather had told him that as a boy he had seen the original log cabin of the first members of the family, and had described its location. There was not a trace of it. Instead, there was quite a hummock or small hill where the cabin should have been. One day it was decided to use some stones that were in the hummock, and when the workers began carrying them away they discovered that the hill was really composed of stone and rubbish that had been piled there as the fields were cleared. This made Prof. Willie eager. He cleared away everything—and there was the stone fireplace that had served his forefathers many a year. Someone had started piling rubbish and stone on the old cabin site, and in years the pile had sodded over, making the small hill.

A "Charley ox" was coming toward us slowly, dragging a cart that ran amazingly quietly. When it was near we saw it had old car wheels and rubber tires. What a change from the last century. In the cart were boxes of groceries.

"He will be delivering those to his neighbours," informed the Meteghan Belliveau. "He never comes to the store without doing errands for those in his road which runs back toward the woods. Look at him. He is eighty-one and thinks nothing of working in the field."

"Only in Nova Scotia," we said, "will you see groceries being delivered by ox cart."

"Groceries," exclaimed Prof. Willie. "Why Louis Gaudet of Concessions carried the mail to Church Point for over twenty years by ox cart. He never quit until 1947, when he was seventy-four. Day in and out he met the train with his ox and everyone of the train crew knew him and the name of the ox."

The next post office sign was Salmon River. Then we saw Beaver River. Here we had lost sight of the sea, and the forest was closing in on old clearings. A scarecrow in a grain field was wearing a large bonnet with tabs that flapped with every stirring of the breeze, yet crows were sitting on a fence close by as if no one ever wanted to drive them away. An old man who walked slowly was going up a slope that was a sheep pasture. There were sixteen sheep and lambs and they all followed him in file. The pasture fence was on his right, of ancient posts and palings and tilted to the right as if sagged in that direction. At the top of the slope a gnarled old tree leaned the other way, obviously the victim of prevailing winds.

We saw the old man enter a tiny gully that was no deeper than his knees. He lowered himself with the stiffness of age, tugged at something and stood again, bringing up a struggling lamb that bleated loudly. The next moment it was running with the others and all the sheep set to feeding. The old man came back down the slope and we waited for him, for there was something in the scene that gripped the emotions.

"I knew something were wrong," the old man said, resting arms on the fence that were as hard and weathered-looking as the rails. "I can always tell with sheep. I've tended them since I were a boy, and they're foolish like. That lamb were just back of a boulder, squeezed in like, and could have backed out, but hadn't that much sense. Just the same, you get to like 'em."

"I judge it has been some time since you were a boy?"

He glanced up at the question, then stroked his grizzled chin. "Past eighty years," he said quietly, "and never on a train. Biggest thing I ever knew were a circus at Digby a good many years back. But I've not a complaint. I've had good health and good hearing, and sight. I step out in the morning and see the barn I built. I see horses I've raised, carts I've made. I put up that fence years ago, and look at it. I drove the posts that way a-purpose. Wind's never hurt it, and sheep never try goin' through a fence leaning away from them." He looked up at the sky. "Be a shower tonight," he prophesied.

"Just things I notice," he said when we wanted to know how he could tell. "You see hens stand around arguing instead of scratching for grub, and there's going to be a change of weather. You see crows hanging near a wood, and there's bound to be a shower. There ain't much better'n a crow to tell weather by. In the winter I watch 'em, and if I see a lone one perch for an afternoon on a meadow tree I know a thaw's on the way."

The old man liked to talk. He asked us no questions. There was nothing he wanted to know about us. He had his

own life and was content—a man to be envied. Roman
literature lost no opportunity to glorify rural life. One of its
poets immortalized the Old Man of Verona, who spent all
his days in the fields, and who at the close of life could be seen
creeping with a cane around the very same land that was
his one and only home. He never lent his ear to voices
speaking of greener pastures, but was content with the freedom
of his own ground and the open sky. He worked in close
harmony with Nature, and grew old with the land, the
common mother of us all, which he grew to love more and
more, and which he made many another know and revere
as the greatest boon to mankind bestowed by a bountiful
Creator. Claudius said: "This man clearly had more of life,
even granted that another may have had more of the open
road."

His last comments before we left him there by the fence
were about the change in the highways he had seen. He had
known mere cart roads, almost impassable in the spring and
fall, often brushed over in the miry places, and now there
was the wonderful pavement and bus service and big trucks.
It all meant a changed world, so vastly different in so few
generations. He said he had an old paper in his home that
praised the county council for demanding that all carts be
provided with tires six inches wide, and then every man
from sixteen to sixty had to work on the roads a certain
number of days. Still, times change for the best, he said, and
then finished with a story that showed he had humour, too. A
sharp-tongued woman in a shore village gave her husband a
hard time while he lived, but when he died she purchased
an elaborate headstone and engaged the man to cut some
lines on it. He knew her reputation, and knew she could
not read. So everyone sees the name and details, and underneath is "Rest in Peace Until I Come."

A deer crossed the road in front of us and we stopped,
hoping to glimpse the animal again. As we were halted a
fellow came along in a panel truck, slowed as he saw us,
glanced around and halted, asking if anything were wrong.

We appreciated his willingness to be of help, and showed him the deer which had re-appeared and was gazing at us.

"We often see 'em down here," he said. "There is one that has come into our pasture reg'lar to play with a two-year-old colt. They play hide-and-seek around the bushes, and often there are many watching. But the deer never minds. Every fall my father gets a deer to eat, but I know he will not shoot the one that plays with the colt."

We murmured that we did not know hunters were particular about which animal was shot. "Oh, yes, my father is that way. There was a moose with gray on its back that often came out in our fields, and he would not shoot it because he said it was an old one. He knows many good stories, too, about Louis, our best hunter on this shore. Louis had set a bear trap, and found it gone although he had a block fastened to the chain. He started to follow the tracks, and when he caught up with the old bear it was a mother that had got in the trap and she was pulling it along while her two cubs were carrying the block. He is a moose caller, and proud of it. One fall he stayed by a lake half the night listening to a cow moose. 'She's a good one, all right,' he said. 'I listen all that time, and she only made two bad calls'."

The young man was interesting, but it was getting late. He told us he was going up the Shore to practice for a little show they were putting on in the hall. We expressed surprise and he told us with considerable pride that at one village, Saulnierville, more than 1,500 persons had witnessed a play "Evangeline" in the Parish Hall. It was the first time such a play had been produced, he said, and as it was about the Acadians at the time of the Expulsion the people could play it better than any others, for they had their emotions to keep them going. The actors had been graduates of St. Ann's College at Church Point, he said, and "Evangeline" was played by a married woman from Meteghan River. "We had many American tourists come to see the play," he finished, "and they all said it was good. There is nothing we cannot do on this Clare Shore."

There was more woods and then Port Maitland, a community that looked prosperous. Soon we were slipping into Hebron, and talking about the name. A sign said "Green Tree Inn," and we stopped. It was a lucky move. The proprietor is Jack Porter, a cultured gentleman, artist, poet, expert in handcraft, expert with flowers, expert with an inn. Our biggest surprise was his dining-room. He had transformed a barn into the most attractive quarters we have seen. We stood inside the doorway and feasted our eyes on the old beams, so cleverly used, the beautiful tapestry, the old brass, the quaint cow creamers, the oil lamps that heat the place on chilling mornings as well as furnish light. One has to see the place to appreciate it. There are ancient swords and pistols, here and there, placed just right, that would make any collector wild with envy. Insets above the fireplace and back of the stairway are exquisitely done. They hold flowers and are cunningly lighted. Red and blue and mauve glass set on the window ledges make striking colours and silhouettes. Mrs. Porter collects cow creamers and they led across the beam at the front and occupied four shelves above, all different and of striking designs. There are beautiful bell jars. One of the Moorish pistols is 500 years old. There is tapestry from Formosa that is of the same age.

The deacon who once owned the farm had a champion stallion he kept in the barn. The original doors to the stall are still there, but the stall is now a weaving-room, for the Porters excel in weaving. In the haymow part are bedrooms, each having a different colour scheme of rugs and curtains and bedspreads. Against the stairway is tapta cloth, made by Borneo natives who beat bark and use the shredded texture. The stair rail is natural wood, peeled, a strangely-twisted spruce that blew down on the property. The harness room is now the butler's pantry. The milk room is the kitchen. The original house dining-room is used spring and fall when the nights are chilly, and it is a delight to go through the house. Mr. Porter has done decorative painting on blueprint paper that is novel and charming. The "deer and pine" pattern of glass is on shelves, collected as a hobby. Every drape and dresser and cushion and table cover in the place has been made by Mrs. Porter, and Mr. Porter has made the parchment lamp shades. Five ships carved from blocks with sails and rigging accurate and in detail are masterpieces seldom equalled anywhere. Then, when we had seen everything, we found the food simply wonderful. Breakfast was in keeping. Fifteen persons who had heard of the Green Tree Inn had driven from overnight accommodation in Yarmouth to have the chance to eat in the unique dining-room. As we left Mr. Porter graciously autographed a copy of his *Furrow in the Dunes* for us, and as we read some of the poems in it we knew we had discovered a poet who should be more widely known.

Yarmouth seemed full of traffic as we entered the town, and soon we knew that the Boston boat had arrived. Down through the years boats from Boston and New York have meant excitement and prosperity for Yarmouth. They have been coming with passengers for seventy years. There was a period when rival companies struggled for supremacy and "bluenoses" were going over to Boston on the night boat for a day's shopping, then returning the next night, for a total of not more than ten dollars. This had to end, of course, with one company surviving. Rates went up to a saner basis, and travel was heavy until World War II came along. Then the boat to New York ceased to operate and, after a time, the one to Boston. The service is gradually being restored, and indications are that there will soon be greater boat travel than ever from American ports to Yarmouth.

Yarmouth was solidly Massachusetts in flavour at the beginning, and at the present half the people of the town have relatives in the New England States. In June, 1761, eighty colonists from Sandwich, Massachusetts, arrived and struggled to clear land and erect homes. There was some fertile ground that had been Acadian farms but mostly it was virgin forest.

The settlers had hard times that first winter, nearly starving. In the spring the first Yarmouth English child was born in a small cabin built around an Acadian apple tree. Some of the first homes were so crudely erected that they would not stand a gale, so this man had used an apple tree as sure support. Thirty years later the town's population was enlarged by the arrival of many Loyalists, and after they were established shipbuilding began on a moderate scale.

The building increased, and shipping expanded until before there was a Dominion of Canada the port of Yarmouth was known as the richest shipping port (per capita) on the North American continent, averaging in 1864 more than $500 for every man, woman and child living in the town. Despite the real or imagined effects of Confederation the shipping tonnage increased for more than another decade until at the height of Yarmouth's glory, in 1879, no less than 297 vessels were owned by Yarmouth citizens. Brigs and barks and schooners were built in the town or county, or bought elsewhere, and money poured into Yarmouth pockets until it seemed it would never end, all this despite the fact that back in 1832 a steam-propelled craft, the "Saxe Gotha," had entered the port, a cranky old side-wheeler that was hard to keep on an even keel.

Faith in sailing ships died hard in Yarmouth, and was ultimately embodied in the *County of Yarmouth*, a vessel of 2,154 tons register, the largest ever built in the County and launched in 1884. This big ship played out her dramatic rôle by losing her masts, bowsprit, anchors and chains in a gale off the coast of England in 1895. She was towed into Grimsby, re-rigged, sold and taken to Buenos Aires, where she became a naval training school ship.

Yarmouth had become a rich town, and the gradual loss of sail was not felt as keenly as in some other coastal towns of Nova Scotia. Every other lad in the place, it seemed, had become a sea captain and, until recent years, these fine old men could be found by the wharves on sunny afternoons, relating tales of the day of the windships. Their lives gave a flavour to the town. Tourists loved it at the beginning of the century, for there has always been plenty of accommodation in Yarmouth, and it is one place where relief from hay fever is sure. Today it is more or less a tuna town. We talked with W. Roy Cann, at the Government Information Bureau on the big wharf where the Boston boat arrives, and he spoke of the numbers of sportsmen who come from everywhere to go deep sea sport fishing out of Wedgeport, a little town just a few minutes' ride from Yarmouth.

The International Tuna Cup Matches are held there each September, and the competing teams come from Cuba and United States and Great Britain, with occasional anglers from Belgium and France and even South Africa. Franklin Roosevelt tried his hand at the game while on holidays. Through July and August and September a favourite outing for Yarmouth families is to jump in the car and ride out to the Wedgeport wharf to watch the big fish being hauled up to the scales. This is an important rite, for every catch is made with official tackle, and every world record for blue fin tuna, except two, has been made in Nova Scotia waters. Some of those records are surprising, too. In 1948, after the champions had been competing in the Tuna Cup Match, Mrs. Anne Crowninshield of Palm Beach, Florida, went out in a boat to try her luck. She caught a giant weighing 822 pounds, the largest fish of any species ever taken by a woman angler, and the largest tuna ever taken on a 39-thread line by either man or woman. One of the oldsters, congratulating her a little ruefully, remarked that the only field that seems exclusively left to the mere male is that of shaving in the morning.

Roy Cann knows his Yarmouth. He advised us to go to the spot at Yarmouth North where the first grist mill was founded, and there we would see the old mill stone. He was right enough, and had probably told many others the same, for there were three other parties, with cameras, taking pictures of the ancient stone. Then we drove over to Land's End, Cape

Fourchu, where the Yarmouth lighthouse stands and moans its foghorn warnings to mariners along the Fundy. Generally the wind blows in from the sea, so that it seems a lonely place, hemmed about with jagged rocks, polished by the waters, jutting out into the streaming sea, the white spray breaking over them, the wind wailing softly and gulls screaming overhead as they watch for the fishing boats to return.

We drove back through the town to the other side, cutting through a side road to visit Town Point Cemetery at Chebogue before starting out again on the paved highway that encircles the entire south-western peninsula. Cann had told us to see it, and we were grateful to him, for we saw something different, so unusual that we lingered long. A distance inside the cemetery gate a carved life-sized figure of a woman was lying on a pile of sheaves, her sickle in her hand, seemingly asleep. If one is not prepared they will receive a distinct shock, so life-like is the figure, so natural the repose. A Yarmouth man was walking over the fields one late afternoon and came upon just such a figure. He stood and gazed a long time, his heart filling with love, for never had he seen a more beautiful woman. Then he was startled as she awoke, but introduced himself and was accepted as a friend. In due time they were married, yet had few years of happiness, for the wife died young. The bereaved husband took pains to secure a real artist to make a marble effigy of his love, and there she lies in the Chebogue cemetery.

It is only a few minutes' drive from the main road to see Chebogue, and worth the time, for there is a remarkable panoramic view over the ocean and the Tusket Islands, and along the road are great clusters of lupine, growing wild. They were planted years ago and have continued to flourish so that the way is now called the "Lupine Trail."

Any mention of Chebogue brings to mind lurid history, Yarmouth natives will tell you. In 1736 a vessel, the *Baltimore,* which sailed from Dublin, October 7th, bound for Maryland, put into Chebogue Harbour in December. Meagre reports reached some of the Acadian settlers, saying that a woman had been taken to the wigwams of the Indians. Some of them went to investigate and found the story true. They also found some of the Micmacs dressed in fine blue jackets, the squaws arrayed in considerable finery. The white woman who was their captive was taken to a French home, and she stayed there until spring. She said she was the captain's wife, that a storm had driven them off their course and sickness had taken the captain and several of the crew. The remainder had gone ashore for fresh water and had been killed by the Indians. The Acadians looked at the ship and saw all the rope and canvas had been taken by the redmen. So they sent word to the authorities at Annapolis Royal.

In the spring some soldiers and an officer came to take the woman to the town. Eight bodies had been found near the Tusket Islands, undoubtedly seamen from the *Baltimore*. New rigging was placed on the ship and it was sailed to Annapolis. Meanwhile Mrs. Buckler, the white woman who said she was the captain's wife, went on to Boston where, she said, she had relatives. In late June the Annapolis authorities received word from England, giving them the truth. Captain Buckler intended founding a small colony in Maryland and loaded his vessel with supplies but could not find willing settlers, so was given a group of sixty convicts from Dublin jails. The convicts murdered the captain and crew at sea, then fought among themselves until only the female convict and eight men survived. They drifted into Chebogue, and there the men mixed salt water with rum and drank it, became frightfully ill, and were set upon by the Indians and killed. Examination showed dark stains on the decks, made by blood, and no one would purchase the *Baltimore*. It lay at anchor for seven years, then was taken out to sea and burned. The Annapolis authorities could not find "Mrs. Buckler" again, but they did learn that most of the supplies that had been on the ship had been taken off by a French fishing vessel that had taken the loot to Louisbourg. None of it, however, was recovered.

From May to August visitors to Chebogue see those large showy shore birds, the "Willets," localy known as "white-wings," and it is said that Yarmouth is the only place in the east where these rare birds may be seen.

Tusket was the next village, but we turned back a bit to go to Bluebird Inn at Arcadia, a beautiful little place of a few houses and lovely gardens and hedges. A sign pointed through a farmyard. We drove in and went down a lane through a spruce grove, emerged on the sand at the ocean, saw a number of small bathing houses and solid-looking stumps with wringers on them for drying bathing suits. Some cottages were there, and a wooden building called the "Bluebird." It is famous in all the county for its lobster dinners, and never had we tasted anything quite so good as that noon meal of lobster, followed by home-made straw-berry pie. At the next table an American lady exclaimed over every mouthful, then stood and said she must see the chef. She came back somewhat crestfallen. "It is a secret recipe they have," she reported. "He would not sell it to me at any price, let alone give it. What do you know! He says it brings him all his business."

Our sympathy was with the proprietor. He had found a way of making a lobster taste just a wee bit more delicious than you could find it elsewhere, and why should he not capitalize on his invention or discovery? We tested the water and it was quite warm, but we had just had a meal, and one should not go in the water until at least an hour after, the proprietor warned us, so, reluctantly, we drove on.

Driving through Tusket we saw a large figure—life-sized—on the end of a shop or barn. It was a figurehead from a ship, and well carved. The people living nearby had some relics of the sea and, as usual in Nova Scotia, a ship's model made by some retired salt who knew every jib and boom and mast and stay of a sailing vessel. The price, too, was reasonable. On the wall was a framed verse done by some expert penman:

> I sing of ships with virgin masts and sails,
> Manned by those men of iron nerve
> The seven seas have sailed;
> Of courage and the work of stolid men
> When ships along the waterfront
> Were builded side by side. . . .
> The stately trees came down from verdant hills
> To find new rootings in the hulls
> Of full-rigged sailing ships.
> The merry song of busy men rang out
> From quiet cove, from inland bay.
> White sails are spread, full-blown,
> Across the sea to every land whose shores
> Would welcome ships, with stomachs filled
> With home commodities.
> And from these wooded shores these wooden ships
> Plunged onward in their noble quest
> For rare and splendid things.
> And so for years the glory of the sea was hers,
> Staunch ships and stauncher men sailed far
> Beneath the sun and stars. . . .
> The glory that was theirs is still and gone,
> The iron men have passed, the ships
> Are rotted and decayed.
> All that remains of this bold arrogance
> Are pictures in their dull gold frames,
> Or models on a shelf.

We asked the name of the poet, and were told it was our friend at the Green Tree Inn, at Hebron, Jack Porter.

Highway 3 runs from Yarmouth to Halifax via the South Shore and the first fifty miles are by the sea, filled with wonderful views, rugged scenery, tiny havens. The salt of the earth are the "salts" of the sea, and the little coves are their homes in Nova Scotia. We drove through Eel Brook, as Acadian as the Clare district had been, and then had wild wooded country on our left and the broad Atlantic on our right, studded with islands. Soon we saw "Argyle" on a schoolhouse and knew we were in a distinctly English district, or rather Scottish one, settled in 1762. There was a small store, and we bought some ice cream in order to ask questions about the district. The woman who waited on us was plump and good-natured. "I'd get all mixed up if I tried to tell anything," she said. "I'll call grandpa."

Grandpa came from a field where he had been repairing a fence. He was wiry and salt-bitten to such a degree that we could not even guess his age, but he was willing to tell us without our asking. "I'm eighty-odd. Wife says eighty-four, but I figger I'm eighty-five. We've never 'greed on it yet, and it ain't likely we ever will. Anyway, I'm too old to go fencin' like I do. Wish we had a stone fence like over there."

He pointed in a general direction, and emitted a real South Shore mouthful. "Them blistered nags is back again." We gazed and could see two rather hairy horses of pensioned age walking in file, but not until the old man got us to cross the road and climb a vantage point did we see that the horses were walking on a stone wall. "Six feet wide, five feet high and a mile long," he declared with pride. "Put up by an old Scot who come here with the first. Where'd you find the like goin' up today? But this land around here ain't hurt none. Do y'know that from Central Argyle to the county line there's a strip twenty miles wide that's jest as much wildness as when the first white man come. Pure barren and bogs and brooks and lakes and swamp and rock and woodland. Only fit for moose and fox and rabbits. In my day I've tramped over near half of it. Come and look in my barn and you'll see a real moose head. One I shot thirty-odd years ago. My wife wouldn't let me put it up in the house."

We obliged him, and in the stable saw a ghastly skull with broad pan and antlers above the oat bin. We had thought to see a head mounted, but it was evident that grandpa had let time and nature remove all meat and skin until the hard gray bone was all that remained, with the duller and blacker teeth, and huge sockets where the eyes had been. We sided with grandma as we gazed, but did not say so. "Up the road a mile or so, there's somethin' worth a stop," said grandpa.

"Likely you'll see hooked rugs for sale at Aunt Mary's. Go in and see her quilts. They beat anything this end of the country."

It semed there was no more to be seen so we drove on and saw two perfect pictures for an artist or photographer. The first was the stone arch of an old bridge that had been used many years ago when the road ran at a different angle. Now it was about fifty yards from the paved highway, looking unnaturally high above the shallow brook. Under the arch, keeping cool during the hot afternoon, were a pair of black and white oxen, standing quietly together as if they were yoked, peering out at the world as if they were apart from it and content to be. The second picture was placed in colour by some busy farmer-fisherman. He had a hedge of spruce that had not received enough attention and was growing thick and uneven, but a gateway or passage through it led to the stable, and in a moment of turning back to get something he had placed an oxyoke so that it fitted perfectly in the top of the gap, the neckrings pushing back the brush. Framed in those rings was a glimpse of blue water beyond and in the water a small dory with a tiny sail rigged. No photographer could ever have arranged anything so neatly.

We began to look for such pictures, and soon saw haystacks built on pole platforms to keep their bottoms from dampness. A four-foot space was beneath, and under one of them a number of crows were having a family gathering, ranting vigorously in crow language. Farther on we saw lobster traps piled three deep on a hillside, glistening darkly against greenery, while below them, piled on the grass, were red and white marker buoys. Then we saw the quilts. They were hanging on a line, four of them, blue and white, red and white, green and white, yellow and white, all a block and circle pattern. On the fence beside them a small board bore the legend "Hooked rugs for sale here."

Aunt Mary was a tall woman with a dreamy look in her eyes. Her rugs were only average, but we must say in fairness that she only asked an average price. But her quilts were a delight. When she saw that we admired them she took us up a broad stairway to a room under·the sloping roof and opened a huge chest. It was filled with quilts, and as she displayed them she had a little story for each. One was "quilted" while the teacher was sick with the mumps. Another was done when her daughter's first baby was near arrival "and I had to have something to put my mind on."

There was one quilt with a "clam shell" pattern, looking extremely difficult to do. Another was the Mariner's Compass. Others were Job's Tears, King David's Crown, the Hand of Friendship, the Rose of Sharon, the Snail's Trail and the Spider's Web. One had been made from wedding gowns. But there was a pattern I could not understand as it seemed to have no set design. Aunt Mary saw that it was a puzzler, and she explained.

"I call that one 'Tracks in the Sand.' One day I wanted something new for a quilt and I was walking down on the sand beach when I saw a doe and her fawn come out of the bush and walk a piece. The fawn kept going back and forth around its mother, and when I saw the track I just copied it on paper and had a new pattern for my quilt. You should go look at the sand. It's white and clean and shows every track. That's a cranberry bog just over there, and there's the path to the sand. You go down and I'll have some tea made when you come back."

We did not want to go particularly, but we had bothered her, and it seemed but right that we should humour her whim. The path was easy to take and soon we were in sand that filled our shoes. So we took them off and left them by the upland.

In no time we saw deer tracks. There was spruce and white birch and alder along the shore, and no doubt deer fed there. Soon we found a tangled maze of footprints. Some were big and broad, the mark of a buck. There were smaller ones, fawns a few months old. Some tracks showed where the deer had leaped straight ahead, leaving angular cuts to the rear of the prints. Some jumped sideways in the moist sand, no doubt in play. Where they had trotted the hind feet had often been placed squarely in the prints of the front feet. We saw the track of a fox, the two claws and toes to the front, then a muskrat's trail, the groove made by its tail swinging back and forth between imprints of its webbed feet. There were marks left by crows and gulls, even a rabbit's track, and we were amazed to find an hour had gone before we turned to go back. Aunt Mary just smiled, and nodded wisely.

"If everybody could take time out to walk by the sea in quiet places there'd be a lot of hot and foolish heads cooled," she remarked. "People don't get enough time with outdoors, and that's more'n half what's wrong with the world. Now don't ask me about old times around here. There isn't a thing to tell. But go along to the Pubnicos and you'll have a bookfull."

She was right enough. We were bewildered by the number of them—Pubnico Head, West Pubnico, Middle West Pubnico, Lower West Pubnico, Middle East Pubnico, Centre East Pubnico, Lower East Pubnico and Pubnico.

"Go over on the west side," advised the first person we spoke to about the numbers. "They've wrote it up in a magazine, and what they said about it you can fit to all these others. They're all fishermen and farmers. Any of them as can goes after Irish moss. Nearly all have some oxen. There's nine villages in a ten-mile stretch."

Lower West Pubnico was chosen, we thought after a survey, because it is the real home of the d'Entremonts, descendants of those who first owned all the district. At Centre East Pubnico there used to be a little tower of concrete one of the d'Entremonts erected as a sort of Memorial Tower, but the old gentleman is dead and none of his relatives seem as interested in the family history. They'll talk easier about lobster fishing or oxen. The lobster season lasts from December through May, and in good years brings considerable money to Pubnico homes. Some of the oxen weigh 1,500 pounds each. They work a life-time of from ten to fourteen years, then are made into a winter's supply of beef, and you can't do that with a horse. That is why there are about thirty oxen to every horse in the village of Pubnico, most of them red-and-white animals, placid as their owners. Seventy-five families get their mail from the Lower West Pubnico post office, and over eight hundred of them have the same name—d'Entremont. A hundred or more have the same names—Mary d'Entremont or Paul d'Entremont, and how the patient postmaster knows to which Mary or Paul a letter is addressed is far too complicated a matter for outsiders.

Marie d'Entremont looked startled when we asked her, jokingly, if there were no traffic officer for Pubnico itself, which links the "West" Pubnicos with those on the "East" side of the harbour. Then she stated primly that they had no officers of any kind, as there was no need of them, police or truant or traffic, because they had no crime in the Pubnicos. Half the folks never locked their doors. There was no jail, no unemployment, no poor relief and there never had been a divorce. On the west side, she estimated, there were over 1,400 Acadians, sharing only five names—d'Entremonts, d'Eons, Amiraults, Surettes and LeBlancs.

H. Leander d'Entremont, the man who erected the Memorial Tower, compiled a book on the history of the whole shore. According to his story there were some clearings made by a few early Acadians but in the main nothing much was done until 1652, when a French nobleman, Sir Philipe d'Entremont, was granted half a county's acreage and made Baron of Pubnico, the word "Pubnico" being derived from the Micmac word "Pogomkook," meaning "land cleared for cultivation." Sir Philipe told his friends that he had a territory of vast size, forested with pine and spruce, fertile if cleared, fronting bays and harbours filled with fish of every sort, the marshes and meadows the home of thousands of waterfowl. Some settlers came. They found the fish plentiful, the Indians friendly, the weather kind. Then, as now, the Pubnico area was blessed with long summers of comparatively cool days and bracing nights, with mild winters, almost without snow. So word went back with the ships that the wild Acadia offered much, and the settlements thrived for ninety years, living quite apart from the rest of Nova Scotia.

They took no side in the many struggles for possession that went on in the rest of Nova Scotia, for the simple reason that they were so isolated on that South Shore that half the time they did not know there was any fighting. When the Expulsion took place in 1755 the Pubnicos were left alone, as they expected to be. But three years after relentless officials sent soldiers to the settlements. The redcoats burned the villages and carried the people away to exile. Eight years later the first families drifted back and stayed. Soon others returned, and in this respect the Pubnicos were different from any other French sections of the province. In all the Cumberland and Minas and Port Royal areas no Acadians regained their lands, but were established along the District of Clare. The exiled ones returned to the Pubnicos, however, and took up the old homesteads, so that they now form the oldest Acadian villages in the world.

It is hard to find a more orderly or contented people. Every home is owned by the people who live in it, and there is no class distinction, no keeping up with the LeBlancs. Thrift and careful living are respected by all, and schools and churches are their community centres. Everyone is educated. At Pubnico the storekeeper said we would not find a man, woman or child in the nine villages who could not read and write, nor an adult who could not speak both French and English. They have radios and keep abreast of what is going on in the world. In the summer they entertain relatives who come to visit from the New England States. The only person who might complain about lack of business is the doctor, a LeBlanc, who said that the Pubnico people were so calm and easy-going that they had no ailments, and many of them lived far beyond the usual three score years and ten. Marie Surette was the last living member of the Acadians who were deported, and she lived to be one hundred and ten. Today at Pubnico there are those who were born before she died, making a real link with the past.

Mostly the men work independently, but there are two small industries, employing about forty men in each, a fish-packing plant operated entirely by d'Entremonts, and a seaweed-processing establishment.

"You must have a problem when there is a wedding," we said to Marie. "Do you invite certain ones, or can all come?"

"We try to do it a fair way," she smiled, "and no one gets cross because, you see, if you do not get to one you may be sure there will be another soon. Why there are so many birthday parties and wedding anniversaries that no one wants to go to them all. I think you can say we are more like the Evangeline people than any others, and do you know that when the government wanted an 'Evangeline' to take to New York and Boston for a big booth at the Sportsmen's Shows, they came to Pubnico for one of our girls. So she had a grand time at Grand Central Palace, answering in French any who wanted to ask her questions, or speaking as well in English. She wore the dress of 1755, and there was a crowd packed along the booth front every day she was there."

We stopped at the Acadian Handcrafts Shop and inspected fine work done by the Pubnico women during the winter months. They make cunning things with needle and thread, and there were carved pieces made by the men and boys that American visitors purchased readily to take back as unique souvenirs of Nova Scotia. The woman who explained each item to us, and told of the way the work is carried on, was most courteous, and did not urge us to buy in any way. We knew at once it was such politeness and graciousness that sold for them their complete stock every season. She followed us to the car and talked about Lobster Bay on our right, so named because in the old days the men could go out at low tide and take in lobsters with long-handled rakes. Far off were islands—Seal Island, named by Champlain in 1604 because it was covered with seals; the Mud Island group, and John's Island.

"The petrified woman," she said, "is buried in a secret grave over on that Mud Island you see. There was a shipwreck many years ago and seven bodies were found and buried. Thirty years after some men were going to build something and, digging for the foundation, they uncovered the body of one of the drowned women. It had not changed in the least, and was hard as stone. They hastily re-buried the corpse, but told of their discovery. Soon others rowed to the island and dug up the body to view it. This was done several times until those then living there made a secret burial at night, so cleverly that the grave had not been located since."

We thanked her and drove on the fine paved highway, our heads ringing with "Pubnico" and "d'Entremont" until we were almost shouting the words, and so it was that we were in Wood Harbour, gazing at one of its lobster packing plants, before we realized we were really away from the Acadian villages. Here we saw a few gardens with beautiful roses, their fragrance meeting solidly the damp breath of the sea. A man was going down the road pushing a wheelbarrow, and in the barrow was a sack of feed. We stopped and, to make talk, asked how far we were from Shag Harbour.

"Four mile," he said briefly, making it singular, but he rested the barrow. "You a fish eater?"

We took it that he meant a Nova Scotian, and nodded assent. "A body never can tell," he explained. "Yes'day there was some come in a car with license plate like yours, and before I was through talkin' with them I found they were from Vermont, and had borried a cousin's car. Then a crowd was down last week with a span-new Ford with a Maine license plate, and they was just along at Shelburne, had borried the car from relatives visitin' 'em. You never can tell."

He said he had been "raised" at Wood Harbour, so we queried him about local legends or history. He sat on the sack in his barrow and fingered it thoughtfully. "Seems a sin to spend cash for hen mash," he said, "but my wife can't stand any fish taste in eggs, and I never argy ag'in her. Well, there's two stories out of here that I've heard since I were big enough to split cod. Back around forty years ago there was a vessel broke up in a storm a-tween here and Shag Harbour. Next morning everybody's on the watch for any salvage, and some picked up chairs and tables. Seems there must have been a cargo of furniture. Well, one boat had two old fellows in it whose wives told them they wanted a table. They couldn't see one anywhere, but in close they spotted somethin' draggin' along. It was a piano, and they got ropes on it and were fetchin' it straight to the wharf when one of the men yelled 'There's a keg of rum.' There weren't any debate. They jest slipped ropes off that piano and let her go. Then they took after the keg and got it aboard. I hear tell the cussin' was so loud them on shore heard it. The keg was filled with vinegar!"

Our friend shook with silent laughter until he wiped his eyes. "If you could have knowed them two you'd laugh your head off," he observed. "The other story is true, but it ain't funny any way you look at it. Away back when this settlement was first made there was a demobilized soldier and his wife come here. He was a proud one on account of the regiment he'd been in, and he'd been a sergeant. Well, they weren't here a great while before he took sick and died, and the widow—their name was Andrews—noticed there weren't any graveyard here. The more she thought of it the more she decided her sergeant should be buried in Halifax, where he'd been on garrison duty a spell, and some others he served with were buried. Mind you it's a good two hundred miles to Halifax and there weren't any roads worth the name. Mostly there were jest blazed trails, with a tree or two felled to make a bridge over the brooks. Rivers mostly had to be forded. Jest the same she sewed her man up in a piece of old sail and started luggin' him. She was a big able woman and she never give in. Folks along the way fed her and did their best to get her to bury Andrews in handy graveyards but she jest wouldn't. Some of them took her in their boats and give her a day's lift up along the coast. So, one way and another, she reached Halifax with the body. Well, nobody knew her and the ones lookin' after the graveyard she had in mind wouldn't let her bury her man. So she left him back of a fence somewhere and went lookin' for Bishop Inglis, who was head of Church things in them days. Finally she found him and he tried to put her off, but it weren't any use. She had her way, and her husband was buried proper. After that she lived around Halifax and made a pest of herself, naggin' the church people to tend the graves better, 'specially her husband's. She'd walk into most any house and ask a meal, and generally they give it to her. They also left a place in the graveyard for her alongside her husband, but she never was put there. Her folks lived in Scotland and she wangled passage on a ship to visit them, and died on the way over. You go to Halifax and look in the graveyard for the name Andrews, and you'll see the very spot." He stood to go. "She must have thought a pile of her man. I doubt my woman would carry me outdoors for buryin'. Good day, folks."

Shag Harbour was a smaller place, and more picturesque. A pair of oxen plodded along the paved way, swaying with their pace, guided by a thin man in overalls nearly faded white with sun and many washings. We tried to make conversation with him, but he showed an aversion to strangers and we went into a store to ask questions. The clerk nodded comprehension, and pointed to a lady near the door. "Anything you want to know, ask Mrs. Richardson. She's the one who wrote *We Keep A Light,* and her island is just a short boat ride from here."

Luck was with us. We have never met a more charming person or one more at home with tides and islands and coastal geography, weather signs and violence of the sea. She wanted us to go to the island—Bon Portage—as so many do after reading her book, but we were content to view it from the Harbour wharf, looking little more than a strip of rock. Mrs. Richardson told us it was three miles long but no higher than twenty feet above sea level at any place. She had been a school teacher and had sea facts at her finger tips. Nova Scotia might not be much more than 300 miles in length, but its shore-line is so cut and eaten away by bays and coves and harbours and inlets that the corresponding number of capes and points and headlands make up 4,625 miles of coast, which has to be guarded by no fewer than 356 lighthouses and fog alarms. Some of the lights are large and of importance to trans-atlantic shipping; some are small, as along the Northumberland Strait, while others are in the between category.

Mrs. Richardson's book is filled with such realistic description that the reader can smell the salt air and hear the crash of surf on the rocks. She said she was never lonely on the island for she could see the mainland all day, and at night there were the lights—Seal Island's to the west; Cape Sable's to the south-east; West Head's to the east; Emerald Isle's only two miles away, and Wood Harbour's to the north. Sometimes the big storms were a bit scary when they made the lighthouse rock and the big metal lantern vibrate, and there was the whistle-buoy at the reefs, The Groaner, to add to the wind's threat.

The Harbour got its name from the numbers of "shags" or cormorants that used to nest there, but it has its place in the history of three centuries ago when refugees from Port Royal in 1613 are said to have built a small log fort there. After that one of Acadia's best-known traders, Denys, visited it and no doubt it was a sort of trading post. One of the items of interest at Shag Harbour is the "wreck chair" made by Gilbert Nickerson, who afterward made "maple leaf" souvenirs to sell to visitors. Pieces of wood from twenty-three different wrecked ships were used in the making of the chair, and hundreds of persons have viewed and heard the story connected with each arm and leg and ornament of the curio.

The hour we spent at Shag Harbour was one to remember. In no time at all we had met many interesting people, and though Mrs. Richardson had to leave us to go on her three-mile boat ride to Bon Portage, we lingered with a trio of old salts who knew countless tales of the coast. One of them talked about the old taverns there had been between Shag Harbour and Yarmouth in coaching days. There had been the McDonald Inn at Clyde, serving mutton and eels three times a day when beef was high priced. Powell's Inn farther along the way, Kendrick's Inn at Barrington Head and Travellers' Home at the Passage. At Powell's Inn the proprietor was troubled a good deal by Indians who were camped along the Clyde River. They were forever at the back door begging for bread and scraps or old clothing, and inclined to be surly if not well treated. So a way was devised to be clear of the lot. The next who came were warned away by shouts from an upper window "Smallpox!" The tricksters knew well that the Indians would watch the place from the woods, and so the next morning a grave was dug beside the apple trees, and that afternoon clothes stuffed with straw to resemble a corpse were used in a burial. A slab of wood was then placed at the head of the "grave." The ruse worked. No more begging Indians were at the door. But in the spring a procession of them appeared, and a grave large enough to admit five bodies was made beside the bogus one. The proprietor went out to remonstrate but was waved aside with a shouted word "Smallpox." Before the summer was over six more burials had taken place, and the proprietor's wife, visualizing her garden filled with graves of smallpox victims, finally induced her husband to sell out and move to Yarmouth.

The talk turned to large families. Sixteen children in one home at East Pubnico had seemed a record, but a fisherman at Shag Harbour had been the father of eighteen. In the old days, however, a Dudley Porter of Chegoggin, in Yarmouth County, had got himself plenty of publicity by being the father of twenty-two children. But the champion of them all, claimed our informants, was James Doucette, of Tusket Forks. He had twenty-nine children. It was a hard struggle to feed them all, but when the twenty-ninth arrived blueberries were a rich crop as there was a ready market in Boston, and the berries were shipped from Yarmouth. Whole families went picking berries on the plains, and had their meals picnic style. The children mixed during the day and had their good times together, which troubled Papa Doucette.

He was never sure he was not feeding an extra child or so
not belonging to him, or that all his own were bringing their
bowls of berries for the family buckets. The second season
of the blueberry market a pedlar came through Tusket Forks
selling calico and other materials. Papa Doucette, thinking
of his fourteen daughters of berry-gathering age, purchased an
entire bolt of one pattern, and Mama Doucette made it into
fourteen pink and white dresses. But the pedlar had had
more than one bolt of the same material, and Papa Doucette
stared in anger and amazement. Then he gave strict orders.
Every daughter of his had to turn her dress inside out and
wear it that way. It was done, and down through the years
the name, the "inside-out Doucettes," stuck fast.

The older of the trio recalled a Granny Doucette along the
shore who was a weather prophet of more than average
ability. So correct were her predictions that couples planning
to be wed would consult her about fine days. She also knew
the best times for planting different seed, and knew all the
moons; the March moon when hens began laying; the April
moon when the fish arrived; the May moon, for sowing
different kinds of grain; the June moon for luck with a boat
launching; the July moon when berries were ripe; the August
moon meaning eels in the sand, and the September moon,
the time for moose hunting. She cured everything from boils
to kidney trouble with herbs she gathered from the woods
and fields.

5

The Salty South Shore

The "shaving mills." Fort St. Louis. The new Cause-
way. The Ross-Thomson House at Shelburne. The
Twenty-third Psalm. Lockeport. Bunyan Green and
Buffalo Bill. The Perkins House and Liverpool.

BARRINGTON PASSAGE was a larger place than we remembered,
and a new prosperity was there, for the Causeway, replacing
the former ferry to Cape Sable Island, had just been opened.
Car traffic was moving briskly, and the oldsters were thinking,
no doubt, of bygone days when a rowboat ferry was the only
service available.

We had been told of the Old Meeting House at Barrington,
so kept on driving and were at Barrington Head before we
knew it. The fifty-four miles we had driven from Yarmouth
to Barrington had been so interesting with marine scenery
that time fairly flew. It is rugged country, a shore line of
granite boulders and harsh contours, grim and unyielding,
yet picturesque to a degree unknown along the St. Mary's
Bay Shore. The sea had been to our right all the time, while
on our left had been broken country, wilderness, stony farm
land, forest, plains, barrens, brooks and occasional swamps.

We met Frank A. Doane, eighty-six but surprisingly active,
and there is no other man living who knows as much history
of the Barrington area, the oldest along the Shore. The first
settlers were mostly fisher folk from Cape Cod, and they found
how hard a new country may be during their first winter of
1781-1782, when the vessel that was bringing their fall food
supplies was wrecked. In no time their own vessels were frozen

in ice three feet thick, very unusual in Nova Scotia. The snow was deep. There were no roads and no neighbours. They had no firearms or ammunition with which to secure moose or caribou by hunting. So they went to the shore and chopped holes through the ice and lived largely on clams until they were told by some men on Cape Sable Island that the French at Pubnico speared eels through holes cut in the ice. These were French who had escaped the soldiers in 1758 and returned to their old settlement. The newcomers tried the eel spearing and were successful, so managed to get through the winter. Holes were cut the size of flour barrels and the round piece of ice thus loosened was thrust down under surrounding ice. The eels were got at the Barrington River mouth where soft silt was deposited, making an ideal eel bed into which thousands of eels squirmed to make their winter quarters.

Half a century later, in 1815, another supply ship was delayed and no food brought to Barrington, but the situation had changed. The Barrington men owned muskets and had learned woodcraft. The snow was deep and they made snowshoes, took dogs with them and went after moose. The dogs could run on the crust with ease, but the snow broke under the weight of the moose as soon as they left their "yards." Over three hundred moose were killed before spring came, seemingly a terrible slaughter, but game was plentiful then, and had not there been such a supply of moose meat the cattle in the barns would have had to be butchered. The moose hides were cured and sold to Boston markets. Even in comparatively mild winters the killing of moose was large, and the records tell of ninety-five moose hides being sent to Boston on one boat.

We had a copy of Frank A. Doane's *Old Times in Barrington*, we had dozens of newspaper clippings shown us, and we had dozens of stories told us by the people of Barrington who observed us walking about the cemetery back of the Old Meeting House. They told us the Old Meeting House was built in 1765 and was used by the settlers for public meetings

of all kinds, afterward as a place of worship, so that it is now
the oldest Nonconformist church building in Canada. The
graves are very old, one being that of Mrs. Edmund Doane,
who died in 1798, the maternal grandmother of John Howard
Payne, author of "Home, Sweet Home."

The story of Edmund Doane would make good reading for
those who have found it hard to realize what the pioneers of
Nova Scotia endured. He had a two-storey house in Massachusetts and was told that high winds in the "bluenose"
country might cause him some trouble, so he had the house
taken down and the posts cut shorter to make but one
storey. Then he hired a vessel to remove him to Barrington,
placed all his household possessions on board, with seed grain,
his cows, a pig, his mare and his farming implements. He set
sail for Nova Scotia but a gale caught the vessel and drove
it on the rocks. Doane's cargo was strewn along the beach.

He salvaged all he could, and hired another vessel. His
second attempt met with more trouble. Another storm caught
him and swept him far from his course. It was getting late
in the year, and so when he had a chance to put in at
Liverpool, he did so. They would be in Nova Scotia at least.
But ill-luck haunted him. As he was taking a boatload of his
effects ashore the old pig became excited and crashed about
until the boat was upset and its contents lost. However he
took most of what he had to land and he lived the winter
in an old storehouse that was scarcely a shelter. Wind tore in
at them through the many cracks, while the roof leaked
badly. The season was mild, though, and everyone was
healthy. Food was dear, and Doane had to sell the most of his
belongings to get through the winter. In the spring he moved
to Barrington, and about all he had was his old mare.

His credit was good, nevertheless. Records show that two
years later he was receiving a shipment of fifteen hogsheads of
salt, two barrels of pease, one barrel of rum, two barrels of
wine, two barrels of flour, one cask of sugar, one case of
men's shoes. He was running a store and doing fairly well.

Mrs. Doane, who had had two other husbands, proved a valiant worker in the new community. She was a practical nurse, and sought by every family that had sickness. In the spring there were many claims for her attention, but the travelling was bad. There were only paths, and trees cut down to serve as bridges. Many spring freshets made brook crossings seem hazardous, and Mrs. Doane would often sit in a large basket and be carried over a stream by husky neighbours. It was said that tansy tea was one of her favourite remedies for almost any ailment.

After the Meeting House was built it was difficult to find a parson who would stay a year for the princely stipend of fifty pounds, paid or promised. So after two or three had remained no more than six months a goodly man from Connecticut was given a grant of one thousand acres, and was so encouraged that he remained for seven years. The records show that one settler had the honour of "setting" the tunes, and that there were rigid regulations relating to general conduct. No person was allowed to dance or sing gay ballads. There was no cooking on Sundays, and no visiting was allowed on that day. Services were held and the preaching was long, often two hours. When the parson made his rounds the entire family would respond to the catechism.

The Barrington pioneers were worried about their supply of shell fish, and they passed a law forbidding any but property owners of the area to dig clams on the township flats. Community effort placed sheep on the various islands for pasturage, and a man was paid to gather them for shearing. Many stories were told of the "shaving mills" then in operation, a "shaving mill" being an open boat filled with men who were out to plunder either side during the American Revolution. These fellows were not overly brave, for there is an account of one lot being driven from Cape Island by a woman armed with a musket. One crew came to Barrington and was friendly with the people, so much so that they went to one of the houses and were being provided with a fine dinner when a British ship arrived and seized them.

There are many tales of the Barrington settlers aiding the other side during the Revolution. Granny Snow kept a place of entertainment that was a favourite place for American fishermen, and she had so much sympathy with their cause that she let them erect a Liberty pole. Six Britishers tore the pole down and burned it. It was said that many Barrington men had such flattering testimonials from American privateers they had assisted that they were permitted to sell fish and buy goods at Massachusetts ports during the War. In 1780 the Barrington schooner, *Betsy*, was seized by an American privateer and taken to Salem, but there the people protested so strongly over the seizure that the vessel was restored to its owners.

Barrington men used to go out to some of the islands on sealing trips, and during one such project two men were left stranded when their mates thought them lost in a fog. It was late in the autumn, and they had no food except cranberries until they found a wreck piled on a far part of the island, and two lame horses pasturing there. They killed the horses and ate them, and the meat lasted a long time as it was easily frozen. They found casks of biscuits in the wreck, quite undamaged, liquor and clothing. So they kept warm and lived in the cabin until spring, when they managed to hail a passing vessel and were taken to Boston with a load of soldiers' coats and silk stockings and dress material which they had salvaged and made ready to take along. They sold the goods in Boston, paid their rescuers for their passage, and still had plenty of cash to take back with them as they returned home on a Barrington ship.

Not all the Barrington men were received kindly all the time in Boston. The captain of one schooner took his wife along on a trip, and while visiting shops in the Massachusetts town kissed his wife in public. Such an offense could not be overlooked at that time, no matter who the culprit might be.

So the worthy captain was arrested and was sentenced by the magistrate to be publicly whipped. Later, the magistrate tried to be friendly, explaining the nature of the crime, and the captain apparently took the explanation in good part. He invited the magistrate on board as he was about to leave, but instead of standing him a drink, as was expected, had him seized and given thirty-nine lashes at the gangway "to lather some common sense in his head."

Twenty minutes from Highway 3, beyond Barrington, is a spot that grips the imagination of all who stand by the simple cairn of field stone and learn why it was erected there. Claude de la Tour, a Huguenot, and his son, Charles, came to Nova Scotia in 1609, and soon the young man was a boon companion of Biencourt, so that when the latter moved away he bequeathed his holding to Charles. It would seem that Charles distrusted the Port Royal area after the attack on it, and he settled at Port La Tour near Cape Sable. His father was on a trip to the homeland when the ship on which he was a passenger was captured by the British and he was carried a prisoner to England. There he made the best of it by winning the favour of the King through his descriptions of Nova Scotia, and soon he had married one of the Queen's maids of honour. This act caused him to be created a Baronet of Nova Scotia, and the King granted Sir Claude and his son Charles a grant of land extending along the south shore of the province from Yarmouth to Lunenburg.

This seemed a grand gift, and in return for it Sir Claude promised to strengthen the Scottish colony at Port Royal and to induce his son to join forces with the British. It was known that Charles had erected a fort at Port La Tour, and it seemed a smart move to have his father win him over. When the British ship arrived, however, Charles proved a real patriot. He prepared to defend his stronghold. His father went ashore and pleaded with all his eloquence, but his son would not admit him to the fort nor listen to his arguments. So the patience of the British captain wore thin and he turned his cannon on Fort St. Louis. Then he landed with a force of fighting men fitted in the armour of that time.

The battle was brief and somewhat bloody, with the invaders being routed by the bushmen Charles had gathered to his garrison. A second attempt was made, and also failed. Sir Claude was in disgrace. Here he was in this new land, with great things seemingly awaiting him, and Charles blasting all his hopes. Then Port Royal was lost to the French and Sir Claude was no longer wanted, while Charles was commissioned Lieutenant-General of Nova Scotia and sent men and stores and ammunition. Sir Claude had to find his way humbly to his son's fort and ask for shelter. He was not allowed into the stronghold, but Charles built a place for him nearby and provided it with a garden and small orchard. The inscription on the cairn reads:

In 1630 Claude de la Tour arrived here with an Anglo-Scottish expedition, and strove in vain to induce his son Charles to surrender this last foothold of France in Acadia. From the consequent displeasure of the Scots at Port Royal, Charles later offered him refuge near this fort.

We stopped at a small canteen to have ice cream, and to chat with the smiling lady in charge. She told us of the thrill she had had the night before when, coming home, a large moose had sauntered across the road, not hurrying in the least. "We often see them down this way," she said. "I guess we pretty near live in the woods. Did you see this paper?"

The newspaper proved to be an edition of the *Journal-Bulletin* of Providence, Rhode Island, and it was credited to one Marc Greene. He wrote:

Let's take a jaunt to Nova Scotia, the land of summer charm and the simple old-fashioned way of life. You leave Boston in the afternoon and you are in Nova Scotia, barring fog, at a reasonable hour the next morning. Trains and busses wait at the wharf, to bear you up the peninsula on either coast, along the Bay of Fundy or on the South Shore—that is, the Atlantic coast. This side is more like the old days. It is mostly a fishing village, and the manners and tempo of existence are those of half a century ago. People are friendly and hospitable. They will stop to ask the obvious stranger how he likes their town and what they can do for him. They will discuss the weather at length and detail, for it is even more a topic of conversation up here than in many weathered New England, where Mark Twain is alleged to have said that if you are not pleased with it, wait a few minutes.

Along some fifty miles from Yarmouth, right at the southeast corner of the peninsula, is the little village of Barrington Passage. The Passage separates it from big Cape Sable Island. Hereabouts the Atlantic beats on a rockbound pine-fringed coast, just as back yonder in Maine. Most of the men, ruddy-faced and hard-headed, pursue the succulent lobster. Sometimes they harpoon a swordfish, and tuna are not unknown. They live in small cottages a little way back from the sea, and in the evening they gather at the village store to talk of fishing and the weather.

I don't know just why I left the train at Barrington Passage. Anyway I took my bag and typewriter and wandered up the village from the station amid the spruces. "Yonder's the tavern," the agent directed. The proprietor of the little inn seemed to be a very amiable person and as it turned out was willing to feed me any hour of the day or night. "Dollar for the room," he said, "and sixty cents apiece for meals. Two dollars and forty cents by the day 'tis, and twelve dollars by the week. Come in and set." The house was clean and furnished with all the necessary conveniences. At lunch, called "dinner" in a Nova Scotia village, they had several kinds of meat. One was good roast beef such as I for one, hadn't seen in some time. At supper there was steak, and this menu was unchanged each day. "Raise most things on the farm here," explained the proprietor. "Got five hens and chickens, one hundred turkeys. One turkey took the prize last fair. Weighed twenty-eight pounds, he did. A pretty hefty bird."

And there was fresh farm-made butter, good rich milk, strawberries just picked. Hard by was a blacksmith shop. In it a big farmhorse was being shod. What a delightful sight, recalling many memories. I asked the owner if he used such horses for plowing. He said there were too many rocks in the fields for plowing by horses. "Plow by oxen," he said. "They go slow, come up ag'in a laydge, they storp. Take hosses, they don't storp. Plow gits stove up." The simple life in Nova Scotia. That is about the way it runs because this land hasn't been discovered yet.

We asked the woman if the article were true. "He wasn't too fussy about the truth in some of it," she said, "or maybe he was tryin' to be funny. But I guess we are a bit like it says."

Through that section we saw several stone walls. They seemed weather-furrowed granite links that held together little patchwork farms. Some curved around old sheep pastures where thin-soiled ridges evened down to brooks running toward the sea, the clear cool water crossed by humble pole bridges. Often they lined small side-hill mowings or made boundaries between swampland and small orchards. Often rutted lanes ran alongside, leading from barnyard to boulder-studded pasture. Over the gray stones lean birches and alders, pines and maples. The walls show their old-man mosses among high-bush blueberries and plumed goldenrod. Along their tops scamper chipmunks and squirrels, pausing each few yards to sit up and view the situation. Hornets and wasps build their gray nests among the gray rocks, and woodchucks dig tunnelled homes beneath them. Where they end, deer tracks can be seen in spring and summer. First settler accounts fairly groan with tales of stony ground along this South Shore, and it was but natural that stones and stumps should be used to make their first fences. Here and there are piles of stones, dragged there on field sleds or stone boats drawn by patient oxen.

There was stone in plenty for the building of the new Causeway to Cape Sable Island, opened in August with great ceremony when Premier Angus L. Macdonald cut a white ribbon to symbolize the beginning of a new era in travel to the Island. As he did, the ferry steamer, *Joseph Howe,* with flags flying and whistle blowing, made a final voyage across the Passage, and a dream of decades had come true. On the platform with the Premier sat ninety-one-year-old Bradford Crowell, who recalled when the passage to "Cape Island" was made in rowboats. The completed roadway is 410 feet across. One veteran at the opening ceremonies was Frank Hitchens, who rowed a boat across the Passage for many years. One of his patrons was a preacher whom he took back and forth

every Sunday for years, waiting for him to preach on the
Island—a two-hour service—and then taking him back to the
mainland, all for a fee of fifty cents. Steady motor traffic
now crosses to the Island, and many are visitors headed for
Clark's Harbour, an enterprising little town that has three
lobster canneries.

From Barrington, Highway 3 cuts across the Baccaro
Peninsula to Clyde River, running through six miles of land
best suited for blueberry barrens.

The Clyde River flows through the villages of Upper and
Middle Clyde, pooling here and there by an old mill site.
At one spot two young boys were fishing with the typical alder
pole, using a squirming mess of angleworms for bait. Nearby
an oldster sat on a stone and watched the lads. We stopped
and asked him if he had ever handled a rod. "Years ago," he
said. "Around fifty-odd, I reckon, but I sit here and look and
it ain't any trouble to skip back and be right there with them
in my bare feet. Only there wouldn't be any cars on the road,
and the road would be dust and ruts, with more sheep tracks
on it than wheel marks." He talked of the size trout were in
those days, and the few there were who bothered to catch
them. "All young fellows wanted to do then was go moose
huntin'," he said. "I had my turn at it, too. Likely I tramped
an average of two hundred miles or so for every moose I got.
We had old muzzle loaders till after the Boer War, when we
managed to git some rifles here. First I had was a Swiss
Mauser. Heavy to carry, but had power. My father was ag'in
moose huntin'. He said we wasted too much time. My brother
and him argued over it one fall, and there come a cold
morning that looked right for huntin', so my brother up and
dressed and had a bite while father was out to the milkin'. He
started out the back way and wasn't no more'n over the fence
than he sees a big bull moose standin' by the pasture bars.
He ups with the Mauser and lets go. The bullet hit the
bull's near antler, broke off a spike, and you never saw
anything git madder than that moose. It charged over the
fence like it was only a foot high. My brother was about sixty

yards off and he had a flyin' start. Father had just come out with two pails of milk. My brother yelled at him and he dropped the milk. The two of them just got through the little barn door ahead of that critter. They hadn't no time to shut it and the bull charged in. He was too big to go through and stuck there, found he couldn't back out and started surgin', so in no time he'd torn the big barn door right off its three hinges and was back out into the yard with it. By then my brother'd got back to the Mauser, and he run up close and fired the finish shot when the bull took into the barn ag'in after father. They had to chop the door off that bull, and father said. 'Don't ever ag'in bring moose into the yard. Go into the woods to do your huntin'.''

"Do you mind," we asked, "if we use that story in a paper?"

He stood up and grinned, looked interested. "Not a mite," he said, "but if you really want a moose story you go see the mail driver, Bonnycastle Dale, Junior. He knows more huntin' and fishin' stories than any two men, and if you look in rod and gun magazines you'll see some of them. If'n you don't have time to look him up I'll tell about the year an old bull got its horns caught in a loggin' chain and drug a pine log clean out to Healey's mill. . . ."

We thanked him, and said we were sorry but we would have to wait until another day. We wanted to get into Shelburne and find a place for the night. "Go to Bower's place," he said. "He's the County Clerk, and he knows more history than the man that wrote it. Good place to stop, too."

It was no trouble to find Charley Bower's place, and it would be hard to find nicer people. He took us out to have a look at the third finest harbour in the world, Sydney, Australia, being first, and Havana, Cuba, second. Shelburne is third according to the decision of the British Admiralty many years ago. He took us to see an ancient fire engine, nearly two hundred years old, and to see some of the old "town wells," dug in the street so that they were available to all, and then, during the evening, he drew for us word pictures of Shelburne's beginning that helped us see the stirring scene that Shelburne presented in 1783. There is nothing quite comparable to it in the history of North America. The aristocratic Loyalists in New York wanted to reach friendly soil in Canada and, most of all, they wanted to found a town of their own, to be run by themselves according to their ideas. So Port Roseway was mentioned and its fine harbour described. No further urging was needed, and on April 27, 1783, eighteen ships loaded with Loyalists and all their possessions, including a very large number of slaves, sailed for Nova Scotia.

They weren't the first whites to try a settlement at Port Roseway, called Port Razor by the French. The Acadians had been there first, but a pirate killed their cattle and New Englanders burned them out. Then a Portuguese took over the land they cleared on an island, and paddled about on a raft, even going as far as Barrington for meal and molasses. Alexander McNutt, an over-enthusiastic land agent, named the place New Jerusalem and used the title to attract a number of Scottish-Irish families, but they soon had enough of trying to clear the forest, and passed on. Then came the New York aristocrats, arriving on May 4, 1783.

The gentlemen landed, and surveyors ran out five parallel streets, and lots were marked out. The slaves helped the labourers with clearing trees and beginning cabins. The ladies stayed on the vessels until shelters were provided. The weather was fine and rations were provided from Halifax, and the world seemed a much more pleasant place than it had been during the last few years. Five thousand persons poured in, and there were a thousand slaves. Tents and all types of shelters were used during the summer, but vessels brought loads of framed timbers and boards and planks so that frame houses went up rapidly, and when the Lieutenant-Governor came on August 2nd he was entertained in one of the new homes, and from its verandah named the new town Shelburne, in honour of Lord Shelburne, Secretary of State for the Colonies.

Five thousand more Loyalists arrived in September, and more streets were laid out. There was much building, and prosperity seemed in the air. Large barracks were built on the west side of the harbour and a road made around by the troops so they could march in the three miles for church service on the Sabbath. The Loyalists had been publishing the *Royal American Gazette* in New York, and they started it in Shelburne. A rival, headlined as the *Port Roseway Gazetteer and Shelburne Advertiser,* announced its rates as twelve shillings per year, half to be paid in advance. It carried many advertisements, and groceries of the day were referred to as "wet goods." The Merchants Coffee House was opened for business, and was quite a social centre. More and more frame houses were built, and fine furniture was brought in, silver and crystal and linen. Ration tickets, good for flour and pork and molasses, became a sort of currency.

Many coloured people came as servants or slaves. One aristrocrat—Stephen Shakespeare—had twenty in his retinue. A goldsmith, Charles Oliver Bruff, had fifteen to do his errands. Four other families had nine slaves each. Soon many of these were freed, and they established a small town of their own under the direction of Colonel Burch. Soon the place was called "Burchtown," and today is known as "Birchtown." Colonel Stephen Black, a mulatto schoolmaster, became the leader of the coloured people, and did much to improve their circumstances. He was beloved by his people and highly respected by all the Loyalists. When Prince William Henry, later King of England, visited Shelburne two years after its beginning, he was entertained at Colonel Black's home.

Teas and parties and balls, every type of social event, was taking place in Shelburne during 1784 and 1785. Many stores were opened, and ships brought in goods continually. Very little land was cleared, as it was found to be poor and stony. There were fish in plenty in the sea, and in the lakes and rivers. Hairdressers and tailors did a great business. Tower headdress was in fashion, and columns of Shelburne's papers declared that the correct way to dress the hair was to measure the lady's head from chin to crown, then dress the hair one

inch higher than the measured height. Bombazine was in
demand for the ladies gowns. Men wore brown, blue and
green coats, with ruffles at the neck and wrists, and dressed
their queues with white hair powder. Snuff was used, and
everyone had brandy and rum in plenty, so much so that a
whipping post had to be erected on Stanhope's Hill for the
punishment of the troublesome drunks.

Gradually the free spending ceased. The cash that had
been brought from New York was nearing an end. The Nova
Scotia Government offered a bounty of ten shillings per ton
on all vessels over forty tons built in the province, and eight
vessels of eighty or ninety tons were built at Shelburne the
next year. The *Roseway,* 220 tons, was launched on December
22, 1786. The fishing improved, and thousands of quintals of
dried cod, over five thousand casks of pickled fish and smoked
salmon, and thousands of gallons of fish oil were shipped
from Shelburne. But the pinch continued.

The town was impressive at first glance. Wide shaded
streets had been marked out at proper intervals and at right-
angles to each other. Public wells had been provided. A
stupendous amount of work had been put into the construction of the town, and it was modelled after the city of
Philadelphia as it was at that time. Three newspapers were
then operating, and all the institutions that went with a real
town had been established. A brave start was made at the
whaling industry but, like the fishing industry, it did not
thrive. Gradually people began to leave, and then it was as
if a panic had been created. In a decade the population had
dwindled from ten thousand to three hundred. Houses
constructed so proudly were dismantled and taken to new
settlements. Others were torn down for fuel, and still more
were allowed to fall into ruin and decay. Grass grew in the
streets and boulevards. Cattle wandered in an out of homes
that had entertained so royally. Weeds grew where flowers
had flourished. In some settler cabins along the shore were
seen tall old clocks, carved chairs, secretaries and tables of fine
walnut, sold for trifling sums by those eager to get away.

Thomas Chandler Haliburton wrote about Shelburne. He visited it soon after the people began to leave, and described it thus: "The houses were still standing, though untenanted. It had all the stillness and quiet of a moonlight scene. It was difficult to imagine it was deserted. The idea of repose more readily suggested itself than decay." Of the houses that had been removed or burned for fuel, he wrote: "The chimneys stood erect, and marked the spot around which the social circle had assembled. Hundreds of cellars with their stone walls and granite partitions were everywhere to be seen like uncovered monuments of the dead."

Many legends arose about the exodus from the town. One concerned Granny Kirby. She was dearly loved by all who knew her, but rather feeble with advancing age. Her family had talked of going, and it was getting late in the fall when a ship arrived and Granny's grandson discovered that if he could have everything ready he could obtain passage for all. The ship was to leave on the evening tide. News of the passage to be had electrified the household. They began packing all belongings and taking them to the wharf as soon as they were ready. There were several members in the family, and there was no arrangement concerning Granny. She was told to put on her coat and shawl and make herself ready to go on board.

Granny wrapped herself warmly as bidden and was about to make her way to the ship when she remembered the crocks of strawberry preserves that were stored in the cellar. She hoisted the trap door and went down, hoping there would be one crock small enough to be carried. While she was groping about someone thought the trap door had been carelessly left open, and closed it. This left Granny trapped below in utter blackness. By the time she had found the stairway the family was gone. They hurried to the ship and worked fast and furious to carry everything they had on board. Then up came the anchor and away the ship sailed.

It was the custom of those who remained in the deserted town to explore the abandoned homes and see if anything of value had been left behind, a procedure easy to understand. So in the dusk a trio of women came to the house and poked into the cupboards and closets. They stopped and listened, then bolted. The place was haunted. They declared to their families that as they stood a voice singing the Twenty-third Psalm had come from the walls about them. Some of the bolder ones scoffed at the idea. They went with lanterns and peered in. The place was perfectly still, and they were about to leave when they, too, heard the voice, barely audible, coming from nowhere in particular.

For three days the survivors of Shelburne talked of little else than the mysterious voice. It had been heard several times, both in the daytime and in the evenings. Fearful ones declared that the house should be burned, and there was general agreement. On the fourth day a hunter came into the settlement. He heard the story and went to investigate. He sat on the stairs of the house for an hour or more and heard nothing. It was a warm day and he dozed. Then he woke suddenly, for the voice sounded clearly. His hunter's instinct was aroused. He listened intently and explored. Soon he lifted the trap door, and there sat Granny, still wrapped warmly but wanting a drink of water very much. He helped her up and she wanted to know where her family were. She said she could only remember the one Psalm and had sung it to keep herself company. Kind friends got her passage to Saint John where the family had gone, and she was soon with them again. She had eaten from one of the crocks of strawberries whenever she felt hungry, and it could be truly said, as it was many times, that she was remarkably well preserved when she emerged from the cellar.

Anyone who walks around Shelburne with Mr. Bower will have no difficulty in seeing, in fancy, the aristocrats parading around the streets, the military bands coming to play on Sunday afternoons, the proud ships at anchor. Then Mr. Bower will continue with the story of Shelburne's grand come-back. Ship-building was begun again, and soon it prospered. More and more people came to the abandoned lots and built new homes on old cellars. Soon the population had tripled, and some of the most famous yachts on the Atlantic coast were built in Shelburne's shipyards. Donald MacKay, America's most famous builder of racing vessels, was born at Jordan River, but learned his trade in Shelburne's yards. He later went to the United States, and there constructed the finest clipper ships that sailed from American ports. The town became known as "the birthplace of yachts." From its yards were launched the *Malay,* winner of the Bermuda Trophy; the *Haligonian,* winner of the Havana Trophy, and the *Mistress,* second in the Transatlantic Contest. Many fine boats are still built at Shelburne, and in World War II the harbour was a base for many types of warships. Six generations of the Cox family have worked in the same shipyard there.

Mr. Bower shows visitors the old Anglican Church, with wide aisles, wide deep pews and heavy timbers. Then he takes them to see "the old Thomson House," recently given to the Shelburne Historical Society by the Webster family, who purchased it some years ago to preserve it as a link with the first growth of the town. Two Scottish bachelors came to Shelburne with the first settlers. They built a rather pretentious house, one that must have stood out prominently on its street when constructed. It was large and long, built to serve as a home and as an office and warehouse for the brothers' shipping business. Each brother had rooms on different floors, though they ate in a common dining-room on the first floor. The kitchen was in the basement, and slaves prepared the meals. The brothers prospered, largely because their Scottish clerk, named Thomson, was a perfect jewel. They entrusted him with both buying and selling, and he went out with the different ships of the firm and did business in many ports. They regarded him with great affection, and when the brothers died the big house became Thomson's property.

The shipping boom was over, but Thomson taught school in the warehouse space, and made a fair living. His son

Granite Ledges at Peggy's Cove

Children in a Fishing Village

Mending Nets at Indian Harbour

OXEN ARE USED IN THE HAYFIELD

WOODEN SHIPS ARE STILL BEING BUILT

Shad Fishermen of Nova Scotia

One of the Three Remaining Covered Bridges in Nova Scotia

An Artist at Work

GOING DOWN ALONG FOR A VISIT

A VETERAN OF THE SEA IN A NOVA SCOTIA COVE

Paved Highways Skirt Ocean or Lake Shores

Haliburton Memorial Museum, at Windsor

THE HUGE CHURCH AT ST. BERNARD'S ON THE ST. MARY'S BAY SHORE

GRAND PRÉ MEMORIAL PARK

OLD FORT ANNE AND THE ANNAPOLIS BASIN

"CORNWALLIS" AT DEEP BROOK, NEAR DIGBY

LOBSTER TRAPS AT SANDFORD

OXEN ON THE LUNENBURG WHARVES

An Old Well at Shelburne

Mahone Bay, the Town of Spires

The Waterfront at Lunenburg

Liverpool's Tree-shaded Main Street

BRIDGEWATER'S MAIN STREET
AT WALLACE, NOVA SCOTIA

AIR VIEW OF HALIFAX WATERFRONT

GRAND PARADE AT HALIFAX

AIR VIEW OF THE CITADEL AT HALIFAX

THE OLD TOWN CLOCK OVERLOOKS HALIFAX

THE NOVA SCOTIAN HOTEL AND C.N.R. STATION, HALIFAX

THE NORTHWEST ARM AT HALIFAX

IN THE PUBLIC GARDENS, HALIFAX
THE JUNIOR BENGAL LANCERS OF HALIFAX

A View of the Cabot Trail

A Bit of the Cabot Trail
Sunrise Valley in Northern Cape Breton

The "Lone Shieling" near Pleasant Bay, Cape Breton

Massive Masonry in Louisbourg National Historic Park

An Afternoon at the Gaelic Mod

A Pipe Band at the Highland Games in Antigonish

VIEW FROM KELTIC LODGE AT INGONISH BEACH

SWORDFISHING FLEET AT GLACE BAY, CAPE BRETON

HEADQUARTERS OF CAPE BRETON NATIONAL PARK
BADDECK, ON THE BRAS D'OR LAKES

inherited the property and was for years Shelburne's post-master, keeping the office in the front part of the house. By that time the militia of the town was meeting in the big upper room where the goods were formerly stored, and there racks for the muskets were installed. The Thomson House is the only building in Shelburne reaching back to its first settlement. Time has laid heavy hands on some of its interior, but the old timbers are staunch and the old fireplace stands solid in the kitchen basement, and many relics of the shipping era are still there. The Historical Society hope to prepare the house as a sort of museum, making another in the fine list that contains such places as the Uniacke home, Haliburton's and many others.

At the foot of King Street in Shelburne a tablet on a boulder commemorates the founding of the town. Its inscription reads: "Shelburne, the Loyalist Town of Nova Scotia. Settled in the years following the close of the American Revolution, by men and women determined to remain under the flag and rule of great Britain rather than become citizens of the United States. The Harbour was first known as Port Roseway, the site chosen by the Port Roseway Associates of New York. First fleet of settlers arrived 4th May, 1783. The town was laid out in same year. It was officially named Shelburne, 22nd July, 1783, by John Parr, Lieutenant-Governor of Nova Scotia."

The concluding paragraph in "The Loyalist Town" reads: "When remembering the relics of the past one should not forget those mute and silent cellar holes gone wild with tansy, sweet may, farewell summer, and sweet wild roses, still to be found along old deserted streets that now are shaded alder paths that lead into the delightful land of trees and flowers and murmuring brooks that is the hinterland of Shelburne."

The coloured folk at Birchtown had their own hard times, and during the autumn of 1791 Lieutenant Clarkson met them in the meeting-house used by Moses, a coloured lay preacher, and read to them the terms and proposals of a company that offered them a new home in Africa. Each married man would have thirty acres of land, and each male child fifteen acres, in the new African settlement. They would have a free passage to Africa, and on their arrival would be furnished with provisions until they could clear a spot from which to secure their own food. After that the company was also to furnish them with any provisions needed, for which produce of the plantations would be received as pay. The majority of those present at the meeting accepted the terms and were willing to leave Nova Scotia. Their kindred to the westward soon heard of the land of promise and resolved they should have a share in it. For a time small parties from Barrington, Argyle and Yarmouth were arriving at Birchtown, and on the sailing date, December 3rd, there were enough to fill two ships. These joined with others at Halifax, and the little fleet sailed from there on January 15, 1792 and, in spite of storms, all reached Sierra Leone, Africa, safely.

The few that did not go were the ancestors of the coloured people who live in Birchtown today.

Highway 3 winds through Jordan Falls after leaving Shelburne, and from it we saw branching roads leading to Lower Jordan, Jordan Ferry and Jordan Bay. The latter place is famed as a tuna hot spot, and there the famous novelist, Zane Grey, caught one of his record blue fins. The depth of water is no more than thirty feet anywhere in the Bay, so the tuna cannot sound deeply. In 1937, Mrs. William Chisholm, of Cleveland, Ohio, was angling in Jordan Bay when she hooked a giant blue fin that tore around the water like a torpedo, but could not sound to any extent. The battle ended with the big tuna being boated by Mrs. Chisholm. It weighed 760½ pounds, a world record that stood for more than three years.

There is a Jordan River, too, and the natives have their own songs about it. Old records show that in June, 1785, the ship, *Prince William Henry*, took from the River the first entire cargo of Nova Scotia lumber to be shipped to England.

An American car was stopped beside the highway, and

two men were studying a map very carefully and talking with
a farmer who leaned over his fence in neighbourly fashion.
They were armed with several good cameras, and they wanted
to visit Tobeatic Sanctuary. The farmer was telling them of
the wild life they should see, and how easy it was to travel
by canoe as there were the headwaters of at least five rivers
in the area, in addition to a great number of lakes. "I reckon,"
we heard him say, "you'll get pictures of about everything
from a moose to an Injun devil. No-oo, you won't git near
anough to take one of them. Injun devils! You mean to say
you ain't ever heard of them. I don't rightly know what they
are, maybe like a cross atween a wolf and a wildcat, only
they're tied up with the devil, so the story goes. I've heard my
father tell of one that come out and yelled near the village
when he was a boy. The men grabbed their muskets and took
after it, for there was soft snow for tracking. They got into
the woods and then they quit. There was the critter's tracks,
plain as day, but when it come to a big tree there was half
the tracks one side of it, and half the tracks the other side.
They weren't followin' that sort of a thing, not them. But
you'll see scads of moose in there, and beaver so tame you
can feed them apples, and deer and bear and raccoon. One
feller come out with about a dozen pictures of a pair of bear
cubs. Said he spotted them on an island in a lake and jest
went over and got his camera to workin'. The cubs climbed
a spindly spruce and he sure got cute snaps of them. We
asked him where the old bear was, and he said he didn't see
no old bear, they was jest the cubs. Don't it beat all how
some can flirt with death and not even know they're doin'
it?"

As we drove on the farmer was launching into a salty
yarn about a moose that chased the game warden up a tree
and kept him there two days until a thunder storm scared
the big animal to deep cover. The visitors were enjoying
the talk hugely, and it was evident they were in no hurry
to get doing. Along the South Shore it is hard to find a man
in the smaller places who has not roamed the woods as well

as the sea, and who has not a fund of woods tales handed along from generation to generation. It is a characteristic of those who live along the Queens, Shelburne and Yarmouth county districts.

A short dip off the highway led into Lockeport, a small town possessing a crescent beach of more than a mile of hard sand which gives the locality distinctive charm. We had lunch at a cosy inn named "The Billows," and discovered that Miss Bill, the proprietor, was very learned in the history of the whole countryside. Lockeport is one of the older places along the sea, founded in 1755 by settlers from Plymouth, Massachusetts. Their leader in those days was Jonathan Locke, and the settlement was named after him. The fishing was very good and the tiny village prospered. During the beginning of the American Revolution many American privateers scouted along the Nova Scotia coast, and were given much aid by the people who had come from Plymouth. Great was their indignation, then, when whale boats from Rhode Island arrived and treated them as an enemy, raiding every house for food and other items, leaving them with little for the coming winter. They held a meeting and wrote a letter, dated September 25, 1778, reading: "These raids are very surprising after we in this harbour have done so much for America, helped three or four hundred prisoners up along to America, given part of our living to them, and have concealed privateers and prizes from British cruisers in this harbour." The letter was sent to the Massachusetts Council, but gained no satisfactory response, nor was any recompense made. This was too much for the hardy Lockeport folk to endure, and their sympathy with the American cause vanished overnight. The men had to go to other settlements to obtain food supplies for the winter, and while they were away on one such expedition another American privateer hove in sight. The women were as determined as the men about the situation. They brought out the muskets and began firing at the approaching vessel. Some wrapped themselves in red shawls and took places at different points, as if a company of soldiers were present. Only one or two muskets were available for each hasty post chosen, but other women were along, and they had broomsticks and fork handles which they aimed through bushes. The privateer's men thought they were to be opposed by a strong force. They put about at once and fled the scene under full sail.

Since that day in 1778 there have been no more loyal Canadians than the people of Lockeport, and a record number of its young men have volunteered their services in both world wars. It is a town that lives largely by fishing. There are cold storage plants, a fish meal plant, a fish oil refinery and a cannery taking the harvest from the sea, and every man and boy in the place can talk intelligently about fishing and trawlers and handling. We drove away with regret, and, at Port Joli, reached a new element altogether. Here were a shore people who spoke little about fish. Their main topic was the wild goose, and rightly so, for they told us their port is the only winter home of wild geese in Nova Scotia. Their feeding grounds are at Port Joli and Port L'Hebert Harbour, where eel grass abounds, and the areas have been established as a Sanctuary. The only shooting allowed is on the hills between the two harbours, as the big birds fly over.

We had talked with half a dozen veterans at Lockeport without securing a story containing anything of the unusual, and so were not too hopeful as we stopped where an elderly fellow was hoeing his garden. It was a hot afternoon, and he was wearing a woollen cap. He looked up and grinned when we asked him about it.

"These fellers that go around tryin' to sell insulation tell it keeps heat in through the winter, and heat out durin' the summer. That right?"

We agreed. "Then," he took off the cap and scratched a bald spot, "this here cap is my insulation. I wear it the year 'round, and I wouldn't want any better."

Our comment was that every man was privileged to select his own headgear, or go without, as many did during the summer.

The oldster nodded, and scratched his head again. "Our young folks is gettin' the habit. Copyin' off'n them American visitors they see down at White Point Beach. Makes me think of Bunyan Green. His father was one of the first settlers along here, and a bit strong on religion. He had two copies of *Pilgrim's Progress* in the house. One was kind of worn, and he read it on week days. T'other one was bound in real leather and he only read it on Sundays and Christmas and the like. So it was jest natural he named his first boy 'Bunyan,' on account he thought there never was born a better man than John Bunyan. When the boy had learned to read the old man give him a new copy of the book and ordered him to read it end to end."

The old man removed his cap once more and scratched his head. "It's a habit I've got when I'm thinkin'," he said, glancing toward his house. "My wife's always at me about it. She says how folks will think I've got company in this here cap." He laughed softly and replaced the helmet.

"Well, time this Bunyan's growed up he's jest as bad as his father over this book, *Pilgrim's Progress*. In fact you might say he's even worse, because he'd worn out the first book with readin' and he could recite a whole chapter, if anybody would listen. He was, maybe, around thirty when he got the notion he was Faithful, and he took a cane and a loaf of bread and said he was going to look for the Valley of Humiliation. Nobody give him much heed on account a smallpox scare was going around the country, and so he was clean away and crossin' through to 'Napolis in a day or so. It were purty thin settled through that way, and Bunyan called in at a house where three old maids lived. They kept house for their brother, but he was away. Bunyan was give a meal of potatoes and pork, good enough for any, and as he finished he discovered one of the old girls was named Charity and another one Prudence. It set him clean off his base. 'I knowed I'd meet up with you,' he shouted. 'This here other is Discretion, and don't try to tell me different. Now let's begin talkin' accordin' to the book.'

"You couldn't blame them females for figgerin' that Bunyan was gone potty. They didn't know how to respond, but jest nodded or said after him what he wanted. What they was thinkin' was that the next house was two mile or better away, and their brother wouldn't be home until Sunday. Furthermore, a crazy sailor had gone through that way once and killed a bunch of sheep and calves with a bone fastened to a stick. Called himself Samson, he did. They didn't want any stock killed, and they didn't want him loose around the place. So they jest set to and pushed him into the closet off their sittingroom. It was a smallish place, with a foot-square window, and a good door that locked. They turned the key and begin watchin' for somebody goin' by. Bunyan hammered plenty on the door and yelled his head off. But they jest got a plank from the wood shed and braced it ag'in the door to make sure it couldn't open.

"Well, it must have been a longish evening, for not a soul had passed, and the sisters had their supper with one sittin' on the plank to keep it in place, and one at the window, watchin' for a lantern. All night they took turns holdin' the plank. They thought of goin' to the next house for help, but each one wanted to go, and no two of them would stay. Come mornin', and still nobody went by. There ain't no point in draggin' over the story. Fact is, it were late the second day afore their brother come, and Bunyan was still in the closet. He'd busted the glass out of the window, and the sisters put a barrel up and from it they handed Bunyan in all the food he needed. He didn't make too much fuss, either, only askin' for a light. So they hung a lantern outside the window. When they let him out he was a changed man. Didn't so much as mention Discretion. You see the brother had been to Boston and had fetched back a bunch of them Buffalo Bill books. Dime novels, they was, the first out likely. The sisters hadn't dare burn 'em, but they'd tucked them in a corner of the closet, where Bunyan found them. He read every last one, and he begged a couple from the brother. Then he put back home and afore he finished he'd read the Buffalo Bills like he'd read *Pilgrim's Progress*. He sent away and got a big hat like Bill wore and trained his mustache to grow like Bill's. He weren't ever called anything but 'Bunyan Bill,' after that."

Port Mouton was next, a fishing village named by Champlain in 1604. He was with the De Monts expedition that founded Port Royal, and they put in at Port Mouton. They stopped a while and a sheep jumped overboard, earning the name of the port. In Champlain's Journal the account reads:

On the 13th May, 1604, we arrived at a very fine Port, seven leagues from Rossignol, which we called Port du Mouton, where there are two small rivers. The soil is very stoney and covered with underwood and heather. Here are great numbers of hares and plenty of water-fowl in consequence of the ponds there. As soon as we landed everybody began to construct camps, each after his fancy, upon a point at the entrance to the Port close to two ponds of fresh water.

There is no record of how long De Monts and his party stayed at Port Mouton, and it was long after before a real attempt at settlement was made there. In September, 1784, a large number of disbanded soldiers who had served under Sir Guy Carleton arrived there and began to establish a settlement. They built over three hundred cabins and received rations through the first winter. When spring came they found that no good earth for farming was readily available and regretted that they had not chosen a better site. Their problems were solved by a disastrous fire that burned all but two of the homes. No lives were lost and the people simply moved away to the eastern part of the peninsula where they settled what is today the town of Guysboro. The name had been given their temporary settlement, and they took it with them to the new site. Port Mouton was a favoured haunt of American privateers during the War of 1812. They would lie there in wait to capture vessels headed for Boston. Great beaches of white sand at Port Mouton make excellent playgrounds for summer visitors, and at Wobamkek Beach golf is played over the white dunes with a red ball. Summerville Beach is wide and long and the coast is bold. F. E. Wood, the proprietor of Summerville Beach Cabins, told us of an ancient wreck that the sea had cast up after a great storm. A terrific gale had lashed the coast, and waves roared in with such strength that the very bottom of the bay was in upheaval. Then when calm had come a blackened hulk was lying fairly near the shore. It had been resurrected in the same manner fifty years before, old-timers said, and their ancestors had talked about it appearing back in 1848. Investigation showed that accounts of 1762, when the first settlers were along the shore, told of the burned wreck of a sailing ship off what is now Summerville Beach.

Mr. Wood and others, chiefly from Liverpool, went out and explored the old hulk. The wood had been British oak, and was hard as metal. Everyone obtained a bit and mechanics were called to assist in making cribbage boards of the souvenirs, a most difficult task with such hard material. There was not a nail or spike in the wreck. Everything was tree-nailed. The interior of the keel was blackened, showing that a fire had gutted the vessel. It had been of fair size, probably a four-master, but no one knows its name, its home port, or how it came to grief at the edge of deep water at Summerville. We were proud indeed to be given a small block of the wood, and we hope to contrive something more clever than a cribbage board—when the right tools can be secured.

Souvenirs are found in almost every home along the coast, and many of them have come from ships. During both wars there was heavy salvage at some points, and at one home we were shown a bale of towels that fishermen had picked up while visiting their nets. Some brought in cases of canned goods, and clothing. It was best policy in war-time to be polite in the fishing villages and to ask no questions if you saw some youngsters playing with unusual items, such as a town child would never possess. And in the homes to make no remarks about anything that might have been salvage.

An arch over a gateway proclaims a road leading to White Point Beach Resort, where every facility for recreation and entertainment is supplied. The highway skirts the sea, and all along are rugged contours, stretches of white sand, surf, and countless cottages. Then we are at Liverpool, a salty storied town as interesting as a book. The Micmac Indians named the place Ogomkegea, meaning "a place of departure," and knew it well, for here is the mouth of the Mersey River, long known as one of Nova Scotia's finest salmon streams. The redmen speared and hooked the big fish summer long in the old days. Liverpool is a quiet town with a narrow main street almost roofed with chestnut, ash, locust and elm trees. There are many fine gardens and sedate old houses colonial in appearance, for this is a town possessing the dignity attained by a long and honourable history.

The first white man who paddled up the Mersey was an errant fur buyer named Rossignol whom De Monts and company discovered trading with the Indians. They seized the poor man's ship and cargo of furs, claiming he had no right to be there, then gave his name to Nova Scotia's largest lake, which is on the river. Captain Sylvanus Cobb was a daring New Englander who had seen much service at Louisbourg and Chignecto and Halifax with a company of Goreham's Rangers and as captain of a sloop *York*. After the capture of Louisbourg Cobb joined with a number of Cape Cod folk who founded Liverpool in 1759, the most of them being descendants of the Pilgrim Fathers. Cobb soon went off on other ventures and died in the West Indies, but his house was a landmark of Liverpool until a few years ago when it was destroyed by fire.

One of Liverpool's settlers, Simeon Perkins, came from Connecticut, and he was destined to be the human anchor of the little settlement throughout its early struggles, and to be its historian as well. He kept a diary that reposes in the Dominion Archives at Halifax and relates a faithful story of pioneer life in a salt water town. He built a sawmill at Milton, and built a fine home on the town's main street that is now a Museum of intense interest, representing the social life of Liverpool in the 18th century. The town's story is one

of Indians and salmon fishing, of lumbering and West Indies
trade, of ship building and pulp mills, of the paper mill and
baseball champions. The American Revolution wrenched the
hearts and troubled the minds of the settlers as it did in so
many other sea ports along Nova Scotia's Atlantic coast. Many
Liverpool vessels were built for the West Indies trade, and
there came a time when they were captured by privateers of
the King's enemies. This was too much to take, so Liverpool
money built ships and Liverpool men manned them. Letters
of marque were obtained, and they sailed forth to do a bit
of privateering in their own fashion, for this was a time when
Britain was at war with about half the world. The Liverpool
battlers tackled Dutchmen, Spaniards, Frenchmen and Ameri-
cans in the North and South Atlantic, snapping up some
ships within sight of Boston Roads, harrying the coast of
Cuba and cruising the Spanish Main as if they were its
masters. One of these Liverpool privateers was named *The
Liverpool Packet,* and some old records from American newspapers of 1813 tell the world what was going on. The New
Year issue of the *Boston Messenger* related, concerning the
Packet, as follows:

The depredations repeatedly committed on our coasting
trade by this privateer seem to be no longer regarded the
moment we hear she has left our Bay, for the purpose of
conveying her prizes safely into port, although the property
taken be enormous. That an insignificant fishing schooner
of five-and-thirty tons should be suffered to approach the
harbour of the metropolis of Massachusetts, capture, and carry
home in triumph, eight or nine sail of vessels, valued at from
$70,000 to $80,000, and owned almost exclusively by merchants
of Boston, in the short space of 20 days from the time she
left Liverpool, Nova Scotia, would seem incredible were the
facts not placed beyond any doubt. Let it be remembered,
too, that this is the fruit of but one cruise, that this same
marauder had, a few weeks before, captured within 10 miles
of Cape Cod, vessels whose cargoes were worth at least $50,000.
Why have four or five gunboats been quietly moored at anchor
in this harbour while a paltry privateer of the enemy has
captured more property in 40 days almost within sight of

Boston, than would cost the United States to support twice this number of gunboats a whole year?

Liverpool, of course, did not escape all the alarms and miseries of war. The press gangs had their turn around the town and its waters, carrying off several luckless fishermen, sole support of their families. And a French warship sailed in near enough to bombard the town and fling cannon ball along the streets. Few found real targets, but were unearthed many years after when the railway went through. Smallpox was a dread curse to many settlements, and it ravaged Liverpool until the people submitted to an ordeal called vaccination. Perkins wrote in his diary:

My Family are inoculated by Doctor John Kirk, all in the left hand between the thumb and forefinger, though not in the loose Skin but in the hand. By making a Small Incision and laying an Infected thread into it about three-eighths of an inch in Length. He then put a Small Square rag doubled, and over that a bandage to keep it in place. My wife stood the operation very well. Some of the children were faint.

It is a wonder they survived. The inoculation was preceded by a "Course of Physick," which included Rhubarb and Calomel, followed by copious doses of Cream of Tartar, Salts and Tincture of Jalop. The faithful Perkins wrote that as many died of the vaccination as by the ordinary route of smallpox, and his reports of the "pest houses" established at the outskirts of the town read somewhat like accounts of the great plague of London.

Visitors cannot grasp the import of Liverpool in the old days, but they can read the inscriptions on a stone cairn and on buildings. The plaque on the cairn bears the following:

In memory of the privateersmen of Liverpool Bay, who maintained and defended their trade with the West Indies, and waged successful war upon the enemies of Great Britain in ships fitted and armed at their own expense. Foremost among them were: Alexander Godfrey of the brig *Rover,* who routed a Spanish squadron off the Spanish Main and captured its flagship, September, 1800; and Joseph Barss, Jr., of the schooner *Liverpool Packet* who, in nine months of the War of 1812, captured more than 100 American vessels on the coast of New England. They upheld the best traditions of the British Navy.

A little lighthouse stands on the site of Fort Morris, and there are old buildings in the town that deserve inspection. The Rectory is very old and was first occupied by a relative of Daniel Webster. The Town Hall stands on the site of the old Goreham mansion, the ground donated by the Gorehams. This family also donated a Temperance Hall and a school. In the Town Hall can be seen great oil portraits of the donors, prim Mrs. Goreham with a poke bonnet on her head, her spectacles in one hand and a Prayer Book in the other. Grim James holds a scroll marked "Temperance," and one can easily imagine the fervour with which a temperance crusade would be carried on in the old town.

Nova Scotia reveres such names in the literary world as Haliburton and Howe and Roberts and Carman, but at Liverpool there is an adopted son who has become one of the most famous literary figures of Canada—Thomas H. Raddall. His field is historical fiction, and his love is for the out-of-doors, the woods, the rivers and the sea. He is a workman who has spent years in intensive research, a writer of outstanding ability, and his tales of Liverpool and Nova Scotia are being read the world over. His love of history has urged him in his labours to preserve things belonging to the past, and it is largely through his efforts that the Perkins House has become a shrine for history lovers. He was out of town when we called or we would surely have had some interesting episode to spice our picture of this great port of wooden ships and famous seamen. Liverpool is fortunate beyond words in having such a man as a citizen.

There are huge fish in Liverpool waters, the largest blue fin tuna ever taken by rod and line, weighing 956 pounds, being brought to gaff in Liverpool Harbour. And there sport angling for tuna had its beginning away back in 1871, when Thos. Pattillo, a schoolmaster, rigged home-made tackle and went out in a dory to try and catch a blue fin. He quickly hooked one, and his line held. Soon he was being towed back and forth across the harbour and at length ran foul of the fishing nets, making angry the watching fishermen who promptly cut his line.

Pattillo persevered until he boated a big tuna, then wrote about his adventure thirty years later in a British magazine. He was the pioneer tuna angler of America.

6

Along Canada's Ocean
Playground

**One-sided main street. The Bluenose. Mister and
Missus Santa Claus. The Inglis House. Horseshoe Cove.
Prince William Henry. The Maroons. The Halifax Ex-
plosion. When Adam walked in Eden.**

THE great Mersey Paper plant is at Brooklyn, once known
as Herring Cove. New houses line the hillside, for the village
has grown with the industry which supplies some of the
biggest newspapers of New York City. We did not linger but
drove on to Mill Village, situated on the Mersey River, a top-
liner among the salmon streams of the province. It is a pretty
village, and nearby roads run to Greenfield, headquarters
for anglers and near the best pools, and to Port Medway, a
quaint village by the sea. An oldster was working by the
roadside, cutting weeds and small bushes with a scythe. We
stopped and asked if he were working for the government.

"I am that," he stated, "and I've been on road work for
gov'ments fifty years, off and on. You new down this way?"

"In a way we are. We're looking for things to write about,
but we know the Medway is a good salmon river, and we
can't leave the main highway."

"Too bad you can't," came his dry response. "The best
things there is is always off the main road. You talk about
knowin' the Medway. Do you know seals bother the nets
of the fishermen jest outside, or that there's eels down in the
big pool by the bridge? Some years back there was some

167

women boarding at Mill Village, and they wanted to paddle
in the water, so they put on bathin' suits and went down to
the pool. They got out on the pad of eel grass there and it's
jest like a mattress, heavin' up and down with the current.
Well, they squealed with the fun and declared they'd come
there every day, keepin' trampin' about all the while.
Suddenly one let out an awful screech and fainted. The others
were feared she'd drown and she was hefty so they had a time
holdin' her up. Then another yowled like a cat with its tail
in the door. You see them eels had begun squirmin' up
through the eel grass to see what was goin' on, and they jest
crawled over the tootsies of them old girls. Somehow they
got ashore, but I never heard such yellin' and half the village
was down to the bridge afore it was over. I don't figger any
of them women has been near a river since."

He paused and rubbed the blade of his scythe with a
handful of grass, inspected it with a critical eye. "Too bad
you can't drive in to East Port Medway. It's only a few
minutes in a car, and mighty worth while. Used to be
called Cohoon Settlement, and where the first houses were
is now under water. Shows this old world is tippin' a bit
here and there. Well, one of them Cohoons owned a place
that was goin' to the sea, so he moved inland further and dug
a cellar. Then he took down his house on account he wanted
the stones from under to build his new cellar wall. The old
wall was well set, and he had to lever stones out with a
crow bar. He dug a place to git back of the wall—and struck
an iron kettle filled with gold coins. The old chap tried to
keep it quiet, but word spread around and folks told him
that the Gov'ment would collect a treasure trove tax. He
swore they wouldn't, and when he built his house on the new
cellar he laid them gold coins along the sills and put timbers
fair over them. Had enough to go along two sides, he did.
'Bout a month after he'd moved in some 'ficials come and
said they were to see his gold and collect from him. He said
he hadn't any to show them, and they searched the place
upstairs and down afore they give up. That fall the place

caught fire and burned to the ground, meltin' all that gold
to nothin' in the ashes. Folks thought the old boy would
be near crazy, but he jest went and joined the church. Said
it served him right, lyin' about it the way he did."

Our informant made a few lusty strokes with his scythe,
then returned to the car. "If'n you drive along the shore
'stead of on this main road you'll find any amount of things
to write about, like witch brooms and the like."

"Witches!" we echoed.

"Sure. Here and in Lunenburg county. Inland you'll find
right new houses with two chimneys. One to use, and one
for witches to go out by. I'll warrant you could find, if you
knew where to look, a dozen houses that still has witch
brooms hung up in the kitchen. They're made of so many
switches of hazel, and so many of birch, all tied certain ways,
and used to sell for three dollars. I knowed well an old man
that made them all his life, and earned a tidy bit by it. He
could cure cows of givin' bad milk, too. Used to draw a
picture of the witch on the barn door in a rooster's blood,
then shoot it with a silver bullet. You come with me any
day and I'll show you an old barn with the hole still there in
the door. This old man I knew was better'n average. There
was a new schoolma'am went in there to teach one year, and
she made all manner of fun over witch brooms and the like
'till she got the old fellow mad. So he says to her 'I'll show
you what's what. When you come out of school tomorrow
noon and go to cross the brook bridge you'll blat like a sheep
any time you try to say anything.' Course she laughed more'n
ever at that, but next mornin' she's purty nervous at teachin',
and when noon come half the school followed her to the
bridge. She turned to laugh at them and instead she 'baa-ed'
like an old ewe. The kids laughed but she was near crazy,
and the more she tried to say something the more she 'baa-ed.'
So she ran to where she boarded and there she went hysterical.
They sent for a doctor and she went from bad to worse 'till
the doctor hustled to fetch the old man and told him to take
the spell off or the girl would lose her mind. So the old boy

went in and put his hand on her head and said a long piece in words she couldn't understand—and like as not he couldn't either. She jest stared at him and listened, and then he give her a white pill to put on her tongue and told her to wait 'till it melted, when she could talk all right again. She did exactly like he said, and when the pill was gone she said. 'It's the truth. I can talk again. Please help me pack my trunk.' They did, and she left the place that very day and never went back. All the old man said after was he was glad he found that old peppermint in his pocket, else he wouldn't have known what to try."

Our friend sliced off a few weeds with a quick slash. "I reckon that's enough for this part of the county," he said, and we agreed, thanked him and drove on.

Highway 3 affords every type of scenery, the sea, shore, rocks, surf, pasture, beach, cliffs, woods, barrens, lakes, shore again, wharves, lighthouses, islands, boats, oxen, grain fields, swamps, rivers, rocks, hills, meadows, boulders, little towns. When a fine rain descended it only enhanced the delicate colours of woods and fields and far shore, making detail vague and the blending excellent. We finally drove up a long hill and entered the town of Bridgewater, passing a long wooden hospital and buildings used by the annual exhibition, and driving along beautiful residential streets with fine gardens and fine trees. Soon we descended and found a unique main street that had only one sidewalk and one side. The river, La Have, flows along parallel, and is crossed by a bridge in the centre of the street. If one didn't cross the bridge by turning right the main street continues until one is away out in the suburbs, still following the river. In fact there is no prettier drive than all the way up to New Germany, on a grand paved road.

The long bridge fascinated us, as did the river views, and we were told that when the Fair is on during the fall and coloured lights are strung the length of the bridge the effect is something to be remembered. A clerk in a shop where we purchased a paper told us to go to the Town Hall and look at the relics there, but we hadn't the time. There were, he said, old coins, Indian relics, sea curiosities and first settler possessions. Turn right, instead of going over the bridge, the clerk advised, and a few minutes drive will put you on the site of the first colony in this county. We would like to have gone, for his story of the place was most interesting. *

De Monts reached the mouth of the La Have River in 1604, and named it "La Heve." A cairn there bears a tablet reading:

La Heve. Following the Treaty of St. Germain-en-Laye in 1632, France determined to establish permanent settlements in Acadia. Isaac de Razilly was appointed Lieutenant-General. Here he built a fort and established the capital of the colony.

The Capuchins, a branch of the Franciscan Order, sent six members from Paris with de Razilly to establish a seminary, and their record states: "We are inhabiting two houses or hospices." This was the first school founded in Canada and it was afterward moved to Port Royal. By 1634 de Razilly had a settlement of forty families, and much land had been cleared, but he died and the entire community was moved to the site chosen by De Monts at Annapolis Basin. Others came to the site, and a wooden fort was built there, but it was attacked by a British force and several men were killed in the fierce fighting. Still the place survived and had a mild prosperity until in 1705 a Boston privateer raided the homes, burned every dwelling and destroyed the crops.

The bridge is the real core of Bridgewater. Young couples moon along it every evening. There is parking space along the river bank and there cars are lined up and people sit in them to watch traffic over the bridge. Practically every store has a view of the bridge, and all who live in the first half of the town can see it. So it was with keen interest that we scanned the story of the building of the original structure, reading as follows:

The first bridge at Bridgewater was built about 105 years ago. The stringers were round timbers, hewed on one side to receive the plank roadway. They were sixty feet long, and ten inches at the small end, and were cut in a hemlock forest on the hill at the rear of Mr. Solomon Hebb's house. Other timber for the bridge was rafted down the river. It was a strong and serviceable structure with neat side rails. There were but few of the many men at work who did not use intoxicating liquor freely, and it was found that too much time was lost in bringing it from the tavern, so a small room, purposely for rum, was partitioned off in a shed erected near the bridge for the safe deposit of tools. On the evening the bridge was finished a general celebration took place, and an old soldier, drinking, set the shed on fire, a blaze that consumed all the rum in store there as well as the tools that had been used in the work. The liquor used by the workmen was charged against their wages, and it was found that several had not earned enough to pay for what they drank. Fourteen puncheons of rum were purchased, and thirteen were used.

The bridge stood for 20 years, when the upper woodwork was found to be decayed and it was rebuilt from high-water mark. In 1869 the bridge was rebuilt from the piers, the height of it somewhat increased and it was otherwise improved. The present bridge was built in 1891. The length is 300 feet, with an 18-foot roadway and two footways of 6 feet each. The abutments are solid granite masonry, and the piers are formed of filled tubes, three to a pier.

We liked Bridgewater immensely. Its people are friendly and its situation is unique. The La Have is a fine salmon stream and many anglers stay in the town during the fishing season, for it is but a matter of minutes to excellent fishing pools.

From Bridgewater, we followed the shore road around to Lunenburg, a drive of delightful scenery, following the river and then glimpsing the sea. Many of the old-timers of this district have full-rigged models of sailing vessels in the parlour, and on one lawn we saw a model of a modern cruiser that was eight or ten feet in length.

Lunenburg! We gazed at the lovely roses climbing on trellis' beside almost every home. We glimpsed the harbour and many ships along the wharf. We remembered the history of this town, and we were thrilled. When Halifax was founded there was a large assisted immigration of foreign Protestant settlers. These came mostly from the Palatinate and the upper Rhine. Three hundred of them reached Halifax in September, 1750, and several had died on ship during the two months' voyage. In the spring of 1751 a thousand arrived, and a year later there was another thousand or more, so that a real problem had arisen in providing them with the land they wanted. It was decided to take them to some suitable harbour and there found a colony. First thought was of a site along Eastern Shore, but it was thought too near to Louisbourg, held by the French, and so Lunenburg was chosen. Early in 1753 fourteen vessel loads of the settlers arrived there, cleared land, put up a stockade and nine blockhouses. Lots were dealt out by use of a deck of playing cards, those drawing aces and faces getting first choice. All were given seed grain and tools and building supplies and weapons.

They had no easy time, those first settlers, for the Indians were enemies who killed from ambush and attacked lone persons, but more and more land was cleared and more homes built, and when a knowledge of the woods was gained, the redskins were no longer feared. These Hanoverians became excellent farmers, and also excellent ship-builders. Soon they had many fishing schooners, and they continued to prosper until they had the largest deep sea fishing fleet in the world. Their rival was the fleet out of Gloucester, Massachusetts, and back in 1920 so keen had their rivalry become that an annual international race for deep sea fishing schooners was arranged. The race was held off Halifax in October, and the American vessel took two straight wins from the Lunenburg representative. This was a sad blow for Nova Scotians, but they bided their time, and the next spring a new challenger bearing the proud name of *Bluenose* was launched from a Lunenburg yard. The *Bluenose* had a season of deep sea fishing, then entered and won eliminating races for Nova Scotia vessels. Following that came the race for the International Fishermen's Trophy, and the *Bluenose* won handily, went on from there to win again and again as long as there was competition, and in the end there were no schooners to make a challenge, and the *Bluenose,* after a long and victorious career, was sold to alien owners and lost in the south seas. But the name, *Bluenose,* is treated with real respect in Lunenburg, and always will be—an undefeated world's champion that deserved a far better fate. The *Bluenose* was built in the yards of Smith & Rhuland, that had launched 120 other schooners, and was owned by Nova Scotians. Her keel was laid with due ceremony by the Duke of Devonshire, then Governor-General of Canada.

This Queen of the sea was no toy built for pleasure, but an honest-to-goodness fisherman, following the usual hard life of a typical Lunenburg schooner at the Banks, a steady grind from March until October, carrying a crew of twenty-one, paying her way. The schooner rides at anchor and trawl lines, a mile and a half in length, are set out, the ends of the lines being attached to kegs or buoys which act as markers. Four times a day the caught fish are removed and the hooks re-baited, by dorymen rowing out, two men to a dory. The *Bluenose* holds the record for the largest single catch of fish ever brought into Lunenburg. Her overall length was 143 feet, and her displacement 285 tons. Stories and books and articles have been written about this grand champion of the Grand Banks, and we saw a dozen fine photographs of the schooner before we had been in half as many stores along Lunenburg's main street.

It was a hard and dangerous life, fishing, in the old days, and the Lunenburg churches held many memorial services for their various members lost at sea. In 1925, however, a public memorial service was held, conducted by the mayor, who was assisted by the various clergymen. The following year an August gale sent two Lunenburg schooners to the bottom with all hands—fifty-two men, and hundreds of people from surrounding districts came to the annual Memorial Service. Then came the tragic fall of 1927 when four schooners went down, and after that the Fishermen's Memorial Service was established as a deep tradition among the people of Nova

Scotia. Combined choirs assembled in Lunenburg's town square and sang hymns of the sea. The names of those lost that year were read at the conclusion of the service, and then the assembly moved to the wharf where wreaths were given to the deep.

Lunenburg, named after Luneburg in Germany, was first known as Malagash, and the year after its founding the British Government built a church for the people at a cost of £476 and supplied a missionary. This church is still in service, called St. John's Church, and worthy of a visit from any who visit the town. No changing or re-modelling was done until 1870, when a chancel was built and the ceiling opened. In 1889 more changes were made and wings added. This fine old church possesses a Royal Foundation, the communion vessels being presented by King George III. The choir is thus entitled to the scarlet cassocks that are worn. Another old church in Lunenburg is the Zion Evangelical Lutheran Church, built in 1776, and in its steeple hangs the Saint Antoine Marie bell taken from Louisbourg at its capture in 1758.

We were lucky that day in Lunenburg, for there was to be a launching, and we had not been to one before. *The Doris Susan,* a motorized fishing vessel, slid down the ways, and to see the faces of those watching the launching was to glimpse the hearts of those who live by the sea. It may be said that the average Nova Scotian lives by "the mighty waters" and the atmosphere of the sea never vacates the innermost recesses of his mind. Wherever chance may take him in life, this love expresses itself in frequent visits to the home port to hear again the pounding of surf on the shore and walk the wharf planking with men newly back from a deep sea cruise. The expressions we saw that day in Lunenburg on the faces of those attending the launching was a mute testimony to the symbolic nature of the ship being sent forth into the unknown future, and the hushed air of expectancy when the "tri-shore" was knocked out and the ship gathered speed down the ways was so tense that a girl sobbed suddenly. To us it was all tense, the launchers watching the tide gain the right depth, the crew with pin mauls getting to work at the wedges, the supporting poles being knocked out, the cry "knock down." Every inlander should attend a launching for the good of his soul.

One of Nova Scotia's unforgettable characters is Earl Bailly of Lunenburg, one of Canada's better artists and widely known. He was stricken with infantile paralysis when three years old, and his body, arms and legs were left useless. His mother had been a schoolteacher, and she gave him an education of mind and spirit that has carried him far. He began by holding a pencil with his teeth, making lines with it, and so learned to write. Then he began drawing, first with pencils and then with pen and ink, finally winning a drawing contest in a newspaper. At ten years of age he began to paint in watercolours, making Christmas cards. Long practice and natural talent won him recognition. He had special apparatus put on his wheel-chair and painted in oils, and soon his work was selling. He studied art at Eastport, Maine, under the noted George P. Ennis. He had an important picture exhibition in Montreal, had others in Toronto and Halifax, studied more in New York, and won acclaim.

When the champion schooner, *Bluenose,* went through the Great Lakes and up to Chicago, Earl Bailly went along with it and exhibited his paintings. He had two accepted by the Pennsylvania Academy of Fine Arts. He and his brother bought a trailer and travelled to Florida, where he held an exhibition at Palm Beach. They spent the winter there, and since that time Earl has travelled over half of America, holding exhibitions in most of the important cities. Two premiers of Canada bought his paintings, and many other men in high places. Thousands have visited his Lunenburg Studio, as we did. He is cheerful and talkative, has a fine baritone voice and once sang in recitals. He attended the World's Fair at Chicago as a guest of "Believe it or Not" Ripley. He obtained the Queen's autograph during the Royal visit. He has a programme autographed by Marian Anderson, his favourite singer. His latest venture was a visit to New York City, where he appeared on a television programme.

Earl Bailly is an inspiration to any person, however gifted he may be. His work stands on its own merit, and its continual sale to patrons who do not know of his handicaps is a wonderful tribute to his courage and talent.

"You want to see a real rock garden?" a lad asked us.

It was so pleasant there in Lunenburg that we nodded assent and followed him to the home of Captain Angus Tanner, expecting to see, perhaps, some unusual flowers. But it's not the flowers that make the garden; it's the rocks. They have come from as far north as Newfoundland; as far south as Columbia; as far west as Vera Cruz, and as far east as Puerto Rica. We counted fourteen name plates on small posts beside the most important of the rocks, and near one bearing the name of Mexico was an image that experts told Captain Tanner was two thousand years old. It is carved from Mexican granite and was given the good captain by the Free French in Mexico during World War II. The rock marked Cuba, we were told, was obtained from the site where the treaty was signed between the United States and Cuba to end the Spanish-American War. The most important rock, Captain Tanner thinks, is one obtained from the home of Christopher Columbus in Santa Domingo.

A real rock garden! It certainly is, and when you stand and view it you know you have come upon something far out of the ordinary.

Several towns in Nova Scotia have information bureaus for the convenience of visitors, and there are none better than that conducted by Ernest White, of Lunenburg. We spent an hour with him, listening to his tales of the county, and then, through his guidance, visited a blacksmith shop that is but a step off the main street, and saw an ox being shod. It was something to see. The big animal was driven into an arrangement something like a stall. Then great bands were placed about the body fore and aft and, as the shoeing commenced, a large windlass wound up the chains and the ox was raised, completely helpless to struggle, from the floor. They are suspended only inches from firm footing yet the feeling of helplessness seems to grip them so that they make no effort to free their legs.

"If Ernie White is busy with tourists," said a man in the bookstore," go and see Harry Zwicker at the clothing store. He knows everything about this town and county, and he'll even try to sell you the Ovens." The Ovens, we found, were great caverns in the cliffs easily reached by boat, where gold was once panned in considerable amount, so that a small town mushroomed overnight. Legend has it in Lunenburg that once an Indian paddled into the largest cavern so far that he became lost and kept paddling all night—to emerge on the Bay of Fundy. We found Mr. Zwicker to be as helpful as declared, and it was he who steered us across the street and to the home of Mr. and Mrs. Willie Anderson.

Do not make the mistake of thinking that the name is William. He was christened "Willie," and proud of it. He and his good wife were for years the "Mister and Missus Santa Claus" of the county, visiting schools in remote areas at the Christmas season and handing out toys and treats to every child. It was said that a decade ago a letter simply addressed "Mr. and Mrs. Santa Claus, Nova Scotia," could, and did, reach them. Then they made hundreds of scrap books for children in hospitals, and Mrs. Anderson said that for five years the glue pot was never off her stove. Their home is like many others in Lunenburg, having the parlour and bedrooms on one street level, the kitchen and living-room on the street below. The heavy bedroom furniture was built in the room and could not be removed. But it is the museum of the Andersons that intrigues every visitor. They have every type of relic of early settlement, tools, household implements, even the first "store" operated in Lunenburg, a trunk four feet nine inches long and two feet in depth, with heavy iron hinges and lock, in which a woman kept needles and thread and thimbles and combs and ribbon and all the smaller items needed in a household. There are relics of three wars, curios of every sort, completely filling a large front room. Mr. Anderson has talent of a nature that all envy. He travels like a moose in the woods, the townsfolk say, and none can follow him when he takes his rod and line and hikes back into the forest to "go fishin'." It often is the hottest part of the summer, which makes no difference to Willie. He will be gone the day and at night will return with a limit catch of the finest speckled trout an angler could wish. To meet these folk and talk with them is a treat in itself. Remembering them, and Harry Zwicker and Earl Bailly and Ernie White, we could scarcely drag ourselves back to the road and our journey.

The road dipped and rose and turned and circled delightfully around marine vistas that made one want to pause often, then followed the curves of the shore into the town of Mahone Bay. Many call it the "town of churches." If it is entered from the other side seven steeples cross the skyline like fence pickets, and make it a picture postcard town. We stopped at a filling station and asked what there was of interest. "Go around the corner to Percy Inglis' store," was the answer. "You'll find all you want."

No truer word could be spoken, and we pass it on to all who are interested. We entered a small store that was stocked from floor to ceiling with china of varied quality, and when we asked prices and examined it we knew that here was a shop of honest dealing. Mr. Inglis himself was a kindly man no longer young who spoke gently and asked us to step into his house which the store abutted. We did so, and stood amazed. The place was a museum of valuable and beautiful china and glass and hammered brass and furniture. Tables were arranged tastefully, bearing precious burdens. China was hung on every wall, platters and plates and cups and saucers. There were old swords and muskets and pistols. Brass from the Far East that was centuries old. And Mr. Inglis knew the story of every piece, and its probable value. Representatives of the New York Museum had heard of him and his collection, and had made him tempting offers for the contents of his rooms. But he is a loyal Nova Scotian, and would prefer that his place be taken over as a museum of furniture and glass and china of the 18th century.

Mr. Inglis is a remarkable man. He can sew and knit and hook rugs and make lace as cleverly as any woman expert. He took us upstairs to see some beautiful rugs he has made, and he had what he called his "hope chest" filled with needle-work. He has an astounding memory and knows the history of the town correctly without referring to a book or notes. Name a citizen of former days and he will tell you the day and the year that citizen died. He will give you any dates you wish to know. Before we left him he took us to his garden and showed us flowers as amazing as his collection. Small wonder it was to us that the people of Mahone Bay, when they want flowers for any special occasion go to Mr. Inglis and buy them, for they know they will get better than from any flower shop.

Mahone Bay, we learned, was known to the Indians as Mushamush, and was a favourite camping ground. Captain Ephraim Cook founded the town in 1754, bringing with him the timbers of a blockhouse, ready fitted to save time. The Indians were hostile for a long time, and there are many grim tales of those early years. The biggest story is about an American privateer, the *Young Teazer,* which entered the Bay during the war of 1812-1814, pursued by a British man-of-war. An English deserter was serving on the American vessel, and to his dismay saw that capture was inevitable. He began to think of what would happen when his identity was made known and, desperate with fear, ran below and hurled a torch into a barrel of gunpowder. The explosion resulting blew the vessel to fragments and all the crew was killed. Next year, on that date, June 27th, people of Mahone Bay were startled to see an apparition sailing into the same water where the *Young Teazer* had been destroyed. As it came nearer they recognized it as the privateer, and then it vanished in a huge puff of flame and smoke. The story spread through the country, and on the next anniversary many were on hand, watching for "the fire ship." Sure enough, it appeared again, and it is legend to this day that many persons now living have witnessed the appearance of the ghost ship, and have seen it disappear in flame.

A good story we were told before we left the town was about a Scottish settler who walked about the Bay and prodded the earth with a crowbar, decided there was no good land available and so took him off to a village known today as New Dublin. There he cleared land and built himself a small cabin. His first possessions were some pewter dishes, horn spoons, an axe, shovel and pair of oxen. He prospered, in his own way, for the river was full of fish and potatoes grew in abundance. He had brought from Scotland a heavy woollen cap fitted with heavy earlaps, and this cap he wore for twenty years, summer and winter. He bought a pair of three-year-old steers and worked them for fifteen years, when he sold them for beef. He never used a vehicle with wheels, but used sleds the year around, looking for wet weather in summer to do his hauling. All his firewood, and the cordwood he sold, was hauled over a "jumper road" which was a trail cut through the forest on which was placed peeled skids about three feet apart. Over the skids, wet and slippery, the sled ran easily, while the slow-moving steers could pick their way carefuly, never tripping over the poles. He wore moccasins summer and winter, made of skin taken from moose knees, pounded and washed until it was tough and pliant. This settler was best known for his reluctance to talk and his savage strength. There was not much law in the settlement then, and the men agreed that all disputes would be settled by a great oak tree, with lookers-on to make sure of fair combat. The Scot had trouble only once. The man he met was a big fellow, but the Scot seized him in a grip that could not be shaken, held him and bit the man's nose off, retaining the edge in his teeth. The onlookers rescued the victim before more damage could be done, and escorted him away. The Scot went home and placed the nose tip in vinegar, and for years after kept it on a shelf to be shown to any caller who had courage enough to mention the event.

Western Shore seemed a long village, and there were signs offering fresh lobsters for sale. We purchased some to have excuse to talk with the woman who waited on us. She had been born there, she said, and had been tired of the place and motor boats and fishing, so had gone to work in Boston when she was seventeen. "I stayed three years," she said, "and they were the longest three years I'll ever live, but I hated to give in that I was homesick. At last I met some folks from home, and it was more than I could stand. I walked right out of the place where I worked, packed up and went back to Halifax in that car. I never give notice I was leavin' or got my pay. At Halifax I got on the train and come home here, and when I got off I jest stood and looked 'till my eyes were tired. No, you can have all the Bostons and big places in the world, but I'll stay right here."

A man who had been listening offered to take us over to Oak Island. It didn't look far from shore. "Back a piece, by Martin River which you come by," he said, "you can walk over when the tide's out."

The island got its name from a heavy growth of oak trees that covered it when the first settlers came. In 1796 three young men went over to hunt, as moose often went over to the island, and bears were killed there. They walked around a small cove and were astonished to see an old ship's block hanging from the limb of a giant oak that had been sawn off five feet from the trunk to serve as a sort of derrick. Underneath there was a depression in the soil about thirty feet in circumference. The young men went back to the mainland and got shovels. They began digging and found it easy to remove the soil within the circle, while outside was a hard blue marl. At a depth of ten feet they encountered a flooring of oaken plank. These were removed and the digging went on, though it was slower, for a bucket was used to pull up the earth. At twenty feet a second oaken floor was found, covered inches deep with charcoal.

The trio were now convinced that something was buried below, but winter interfered, and the next year they formed company with a doctor from Truro and began work once more. The floorings were found at each ten feet, and some were covered with a strange matting of heavy seaweed. The last one was covered with putty, and was at a depth of ninety feet. The putty was taken up, and there was enough to serve for the windows in a dozen or more houses. The depth of ninety-six feet was reached on a Saturday night, and work ceased until Monday morning. Then the workers returned to find the pit flooded to within ten feet of the top. Pumping failed to keep the water out, and borings were made which revealed that at a depth of 150 feet there were several chests and hogsheads of treasure. The auger passed through inches of oak, then into metal, and some links of gold chain were brought to the surface. Tunnels were driven in from other shafts as company after company was organized to combat the water menace, but no one could reach the treasure.

Then someone discovered that the water was salt, and an exploring of the shore uncovered a channel leading to a small tunnel, covered with the thick seaweed and a layer of sand. The water channel was blocked and then holes were made to the tunnel and explosives dropped below but still the water flooded in. This work went on for over a century until there are so many old shafts and pits and tunnels that one can scarcely tell where the original one was made. Interest is still keen in this most famous of all treasure pits. A new owner of the island is working on a scheme for uncovering the entire treasure area by modern machinery. The most intriguing feature, however, is the mystery of who dug a shaft 150 feet deep and constructed a water tunnel three by four feet to the sea, then cleverly concealed its entrance by seaweed and sand. It was an engineering feat that seems incredible, and the entire shore population long for the day when the mystery of what is below will be solved.

We crossed a bridge over Gold River, then went down a long grade, through an underpass, and into Chester, known as "the American's town," as many families from Pennsylvania have owned homes there for nearly half a century, and American yachts sail up and down the bay summer long. New England families settled the place in 1759, named it "Shoreham," and erected a blockhouse in which twenty cannon were mounted. Such a defence kept the Indians away from the settlement, but they hung about the outskirts and murdered several families. The little village prospered, was named Chester, and most of its inhabitants lived by fishing. But its location, overlooking a beautiful bay containing hundreds of islands, attracted attention. It is said that many pirate vessels hid in the safe waters around the islands in the old days, and the same waters now are favoured by yachtsmen. Over a century ago John Wister, a wealthy stove manufacturer from Philadelphia, decided on a vacation in Nova Scotia.

This was in the old horse-and-buggy days. The family arrived by boat, landed at Yarmouth and took the coach for a tour of the province. From Halifax they drove to Chester, where they were so attracted by the scenery and delightful summer climate that Mr. Wister purchased property and established a summer home. He soon induced others to come, and the coming was all that was necessary, for one after another of these visitors bought ground and erected summer homes, bought sailing vessels and spent their summers in recreation and relaxation. Soon after the turn of the century the summer population became larger than that of the winter season. The Wister girls, who came with their father in the long ago, became women and married, then they continued coming to Chester, and now own their homes in the town and are foremost in all the good work that goes on.

We saw the large Hackmatack Inn that during the war years was a rest home for Norwegian seamen, but it was now filled with tourists, and then we drove back to the main highway and wondered if any photographer had ever succeeded in obtaining an adequate picture of Chester. It is so perched on a hill, with so many different slopes, and with so many little coves about, that one tries to look in every direction at once. We stopped at a filling station, and the attendant offered his opinion that we would find more high-priced cars in Chester than in any other Nova Scotia town twice its size. "In summer, I mean," he qualified. "Owned by summer visitors."

He seemed interested in our undertaking of finding out all we could about the country, and asked if we knew the story of Horseshoe Cove. We admitted that we did not, and he quickly led the way to his house. "My grandfather plowed ground at the Cove and he has the whole story," he said. "It was up on the La Have river, and the place wasn't found until ten years after Lunenburg was settled. Then one of the settlers happened on a clearing of about forty acres, with a long, low wooden house in the centre, built in a T fashion. There was a blockhouse, loop-holed for muskets, and with a swivel gun on the upper floor. A big bell hung from the rafters.

"Well, the settler went to Halifax and got a grant of a thousand acres that took in the Cove, then he moved out there and lived in the low house. The story was that he dug up or found some money, for he dressed in a fine double-breasted coat of blue Saxon cloth, and a pair of black breeches with silver knee buckles. He and his boys cut firewood and took it to Halifax in a shallop he owned. Then some Indians came to the clearing and asked him not to cut any more of the maples in a grove they were near, as it was an old Indian cemetery. There was no more cutting there that fall, but the Indians never came back and, in October, 1777, the settler and his boys cut another load of wood there and went to Halifax. When they returned a terrible sight awaited them. The wife of the settler and the three children who stayed with her had been murdered by the Indians and hacked to pieces, while every article of furniture in the house had been broken.

"The settler raced to Lunenburg and told his tale. Men with muskets joined him in the chase. They tracked the killers to their encampment and captured six of them. Then they brought them back to the maple grove and hanged them there, as punishment for their crime, and to warn other Indians of swift justice. The two boys would not live in the Cove again, but built a cabin in Lunenburg and obtained work there. The father stayed with them, but he had become a strange silent person, refusing to talk with anyone or to move about. One cold night he was missing, and when daylight came was tracked back to the Cove where he was found, frozen to death, lying on the grave of his wife.

"For six years after no one went near the Cove, then a stranger, Captain John Smith, came and purchased the grant from the settlers' sons. Smith was a tall, fine-looking man who could speak several languages. He soon learned to talk with the Indians and they became his friends. He had two servants from the West Indies, both rather small in stature. They wore gold earrings and bright red sashes, wore charms on a string about their necks. In 1795 a runaway boy found lodging with Smith and was well treated, but two months later he went to Lunenburg and told that Smith had murdered a pedlar who came there, and had disposed of the body. He said an officer from Halifax had been a guest there at the time. They had sat up, talking, until very late at night. Towards morning the boy had been wakened by noises and had peered out to see the stranger and Smith carrying a man's body that had been stripped of clothing. In the morning when he was having his breakfast Cato, the man servant, told him that the pedlar had left early in the morning. The boy did not believe the story. He slipped outside and found tracks leading to the river, and there a hole had been cut in the ice. He needed no further evidence. Then the officer had gone and shortly after Smith had accused the boy of stealing a silver cup, so the boy had run away.

"Smith was arrested, and Cato, who stuck to his story about the pedlar leaving early in the morning. Smith could not tell a coherent story, so great was his anger at the boy he had harboured, and a jury brought in the verdict of "guilty." Smith was sentenced to be hanged, and was placed in the

jail while the gallows were being erected. There was a violent
thunder storm, and during its height a man came yelling into
the tavern, saying he had been seized by a demon and almost
strangled by his own neck cloth. Then the demon had lashed
him with a whip, and he had the marks to show.

"His story was so lurid that the people in the tavern
decided a devil was abroad, helping Smith. So they took
a rope and went to the jail, determined to do the hanging
themselves, at a willow tree. But there was no Smith. He
had vanished.

"No word of Smith was received by anyone, but many
declared that his black people were in league with the devil.
Then the officer from Halifax returned, and went to the
Cove. An Indian guide led him up river to where Smith
was hiding in a camp he had made for moose hunting. Smith
said he had escaped easily by raising a plank in the jail floor
and worming outside under the rotting sills. The officer
talked with Smith all afternoon and stayed with him the
night, but Smith declared he was innocent of any crime and
would say nothing except that the night the boy declared
the murder had happened a fur buyer had come and it was
late before they had come to terms. Then Smith and the
buyer had wrapped all the pelts in a large moose skin, turned
inside out, and had carried them outside to the buyer's
sled. The pedlar had left, as the servant said.

"The officer believed Smith's story, especially as he had
the name of the fur buyer and could check with him. He
started back down river and on his way made a gruesome
discovery at a bend in the river where low bushes and weeds
held a body badly decomposed. Nearby was the remains of a
black bear. The pedlar still gripped the pistol with which
he had shot the bear, but his head had been crushed by the
infuriated animal before it was dead. The pedlar's pack
was there and in it was the missing silver cup. The officer
went on to Lunenburg and there told of his find, but when
they returned to locate Smith and declare him innocent they
found the great old house in flames. He had sent Cato and

Cato's mate away to Halifax, and had burned the dwelling.
He was never seen again in Nova Scotia."

We thanked the man for his story and scanned the old
writing on the manuscript he had, noticed another paper he
had and saw it was an old deed. But it concerned an area
inland and we explained that we could not leave Highway
3. "There'll be somebody along some day who will," he said.
"The best history of this country hasn't been written because
you fellows stay on the main roads."

We drove into Hubbards, named after an early settler,
and found it a pleasant shore resort with many cottages of
summer residents. The man at the store told us of the beauty
of a drive out around Blandford, and then became enthused
about Peggy's Cove, which, he said, we might reach from
French Village Station ahead. It was a bumpy road for the
time being, but was to be improved. Then thousands of
people would be going there to see a wilderness of mighty
boulders with the Atlantic pounding on shore with sheer
violence that amazed one. Some were almost big as a house,
he said, and the lighthouse was on a ledge of gray rock, and
not a grave could be dug there or a cellar. Sea and surf and
onshore wind! There was the little breakwater and sheltered
spots where wood for the stoves was piled, and rock ledges
right and left and forward and ever the hammering of the
sea. Artists and poets, our informant said, never get enough
of Peggy's Cove.

There were beaches with wide sand and strong surf for
miles along the way—Queensland and Cleveland and Black
Point. Then the road switched inland among bush barrens
and boulders and in and out of small villages until after a
snaky series of turns we saw "No Parking" signs and knew
we were riding into Halifax City. We came down a long hill,
twisting and curving, to traffic lights and a broad vista of the
famous Northwest Arm on our right, and Simpson's huge
store on our left. A swing around as the lights changed put
us on Quinpool Road which we followed along the Arm,
seeing boats and canoes and yachts, bathing houses and

yachting clubs. Far down on our right we could see the Memorial Tower, commemorating Representative Government.

Curving residential streets ran along the Arm, and at two homes near once lived men who became premiers of Canada —Sir Charles Tupper and Sir Robert L. Borden. On we drove and along the road until we were at the Willow Tree, where tradition says the first suicide in Halifax, a carpenter, was buried in a shallow grave and a stake driven through the body. Before us was the Common, used for horse racing in the old days, and today as a playground for children, summer and winter. In the old days, too, it was used for plowing matches, when there would be tents up everywhere to serve as canteens, with side-shows galore, fortune tellers and silhouette makers. In the canteens they served a drink known then as "shrub," made of rum, peppermint and ainseed. To our right was Queen Elizabeth High School, modern and large, and the new Camp Hill Hospital. We followed the coaches and then drove up on Citadel Hill, parking where we had a full view of the old Town Clock.

Citadel Hill rises in the centre of Halifax, 271 feet above the harbour, and the rest of the city is draped over lesser hills, looking up to the squat, gray-walled citadel that was never attacked. When Colonel Edward Cornwallis and his thirteen loaded transports came to found Halifax by royal order the hill was fifty feet higher and almost cone-shaped, composed largely of boulder-clay. We sat in the car and visualized the ships in the harbour, with boats going back and forth and pig-tailed sailors helping unload supplies on a rude pier of logs, while on the hillside sweating fellows from London's docks and alleys toiled with axes, beavering off trees and struggling with the construction of humble shelters. Small wonder that Cornwallis, watching, had such grave fears of the future, and purchased so much framed lumber from Boston. The Indians hovered about, and Rangers had to be imported and placed in position at the head of Bedford Basin to keep the redmen in check. Nine blockhouses were erected on the peninsula flanked by the harbour and Northwest Arm, and stockades helped give a sense of security. Batteries on the water front were not completed until 1755. They were erected twelve feet above highwater mark, were 240 feet long and sixty-five feet wide. The parapet was seven feet high, of logs and framed timbers filled with gravel and stone and sand. Over nine thousand logs twenty-five feet long were used in the construction of one battery, but twenty guns were mounted.

Cornwallis and his men landed on June 21, 1749, and by April the next year the frame for a church had come from New England. The building was named St. Paul's, and the first service was held in it on the 2nd day of September, 1750. It is the oldest Protestant Church in Canada, is in active use and is visited by thousands. Services in Micmac have been read there, and in the church a Micmac chief has prayed for the welfare of King George the Third. The first organ was taken from a captured Spanish ship and was said to have a solid mahogany frame. The only heating at first was by means of small foot stoves carried in by worshippers, these being small iron boxes filled with charcoal or wooden boxes containing hot bricks. Lord William Campbell presented two stoves to the church in 1773, but none were installed until 1796, when they smoked so badly that a blacksmith was called, who found no pipe provided.

The *Gentlemen's Magazine,* of London, published some new verse in 1750, a poem that pictured the new settlement in glowing terms. The first verse began:

> Let's away to New Scotland where Plenty sits queen,
> O'er as happy a country as ever was seen:
> And blesses her subjects, both little and great,
> With each a good house and a pretty estate.

Halifax lived from hand to mouth between wars, but when war was on prosperity touched the town and made everyone happy. It was touch and go for survival after 1750 until a force came to make ready for an attack on Louisbourg, and spent most of the summer in the town, raising cabbages on the Common and spending money for supplies. No attack took place, and the next year another force came with more money. The Pontac Inn had been built and was the favourite place of entertainment, so General Wolfe had a dinner there at which he entertained forty-seven friends. The cost was ninety-eight pounds, for 120 bottles of wine were consumed, to say nothing of twenty-five bottles of brandy. Such prosperity existed after two years of spending by visiting forces that a workhouse was proposed in 1758, a structure fifty feet long, with only four small windows to a side. Why waste good money on glass for paupers? Three fireplaces were considered adequate to heat both floors of the building, and the main feature was a whipping post in the centre. Later this institution was called a House of Correction, and a coloured constable in a uniform of scarlet with gold sash and feathered cap handled the lash with great efficiency.

The next excitement that stirred Halifax was the American Revolution, when thousands of soldiers and refugees swarmed into the town and set rents and all prices soaring to fantastic heights. The refugees from the American colonies took shelter where they could find it. Hundreds lived in leaky wind-blown tents on the Common, getting water from the brook there and eating anything they could obtain. It was said that not a cat or dog was to be found in the town a few months after the refugees had arrived. Some people lived in cellars or in attics, even in stables or under overturned carts. Three and four families huddled together in one upper room, paying more rent than a full house would have brought in normal times. Ships brought families with fine belongings, silver and linen, and soon the residents of the town had taken such possessions in payment for food and lodging.

Seized ships auctioned in the harbour meant more money for Halifax, and soon a new prosperity was known. The refugees were taken elsewhere for settlement, and the town began to develop a social set. Hair dressers came and set up in business, wig makers and tailors, and there were several new coffee houses. Hunters and fishermen brought in the best the forest and sea yielded, and there were banquets on every occasion of note. A favourite chowder served at the inns consisted of cod, haddock, onions, sea biscuit, butter and pepper, boiled with milk. Moose meat and partridges were sold from door to door at any time of the year, as were trout and salmon, lobsters and cod.

On October 26, 1787, H.R.H. Prince William Henry arrived with several warships and was royally received. A carpet was laid from the King's Wharf to the Inn at which he stayed, and a band rendered fitting music as he arrived. Every house and shop in Halifax was ablaze with lights that night, and a great ball was given at which the Prince made himself very friendly with Mrs. Wentworth, wife of the Surveyor-General of the woods of Nova Scotia. The Prince had a gay time. He visited many of the young ladies of the town, in turn, but paid most of his respects to Mrs. Wentworth, a beautiful woman, an American, and a cousin of Wentworth's. She had married him fourteen days after her first husband died. Soon the Prince was at the Wentworth home most of his time, while Wentworth had to take himself off on business. Dinners were served at midnight, and it was the custom to drink at least six or seven toasts. A Captain Dyott was selected by the Prince as his companion, and in his diary Dyott relates much of what went on during that gay period in Halifax history. He wrote of dinner on the ship, when Madeira from the East Indies was served in quantity, of dining at three in the afternoon until five, then drinking until eight, when coffee was served. The Prince breakfasted entirely on cold turkey. His barge crew wore velvet caps embroidered with the King's Arms. The coxwain's cap was of gold and cost fifty guineas. Dyott wrote:

The Commissioners gave a Ball in honour of His Royal Highness. He dressed at Mrs. Wentworth's and went in her carriage, but not with her as the ladies of Halifax are a little scrupulous of their virtue and think it in danger if they were to visit Mrs. Wentworth. For my part I think her the best-bred woman in the province. His Royal Highness, Major Vessey and myself and six pretty women danced the Country Bumpkins for nearly an hour. He dances vastly well and is very fond of it.

There was another great affair at which twenty-three bumper toasts were given without a halt. Just twenty dined and sixty-three bottles of wine were consumed. The Prince had high notions of doing something a bit out of the ordinary and conceived the idea of having the biggest salute ever heard in the country fired in his honour. After a toast he ordered that every gun in every ship in port be made ready to fire at a given signal. Another toast, and he ordered every gun in every blockhouse and fort loaded and ready to fire at a signal. One more toast, and he ordered every soldier to be routed from bed in the barracks to load muskets ready for the big salute. Then a lackey whispered to the master of ceremonies that if the Prince's drink were mixed he would pass out. So another toast was proposed, the Prince's drink was mixed and the grand salute was never fired.

A daughter of the Admiral died and there is description of the funeral. All the pall-bearers wore white trousers, white shirts with love ribbons around the left arm, black velvet caps with white ribbons tied around them, and gloves. The coffin was covered with white cloth, and all mourners wore white hat bands and white scarves.

The Prince returned to Halifax in 1788, was present at a dinner given by the town at which twenty-eight bumper toasts were drunk. On September 1st he gave a dinner on his ship, with so many courses that it lasted three hours. Then an elegant dessert and champagne was served. Four days later he gave a ball on his ship, the deck being covered with canvas, lined with white colours and blue festoons. The Surveyor-General was to become Sir John Wentworth, Governor of Nova Scotia, and the romance of the Prince and Mrs. Wentworth might have helped with the promotion. They drove about in the Wentworth carriage and cared not who knew their affection for each other. So Wentworth took himself a great deal to his farm at Preston, and when the Maroons came he stationed many in that district and had Maroon Hall erected. There was a lovely girl among the Maroons and Wentworth, perhaps starved for affection, fell in love with her. He had a barge built at the King's Wharf with a platform in the centre on which a sofa was placed. Four rowers took the craft up and down Northwest Arm in the evenings while a musician aft played sweet serenades and Wentworth sat with his dusky belle on the sofa. Long years after the barge was sold to a lobster fisherman. The Prince became a King and sent for his old flame. The Wentworths went to England and Lady Wentworth never returned, while Wentworth died a lonely old man, almost unnoticed, in Halifax.

Then came the Duke of Kent and his French lady to stimulate society and gossip that had dulled after the departure of the Prince. The Duke moved out to Prince's Lodge and had it landscaped and flowers planted, and there great balls were held. He insisted on strict discipline in his regiments, however, held parades at five in the morning, and was present himself to see that none were absent. Drums beat and guns were fired at eight in the evening as a signal for all to retire. He created the greatest stir when he gave orders that the members of his regiment be clean shaven. It was an era of whiskers, and great pride was taken in the longest and widest beards that could be grown. So proud were some of the men of their whiskers that they risked all in disobedience of the order and a corporal's guard was named to seize and strap down and shave those who had not removed their beards. All was shine and polish on Sunday mornings when church parades were held. In the afternoon there would be bands playing around the town and taverns did a great business. The Duke was very popular during his time in Halifax, and did much to improve the town.

In June, 1796, a large number of Maroons arrived from Jamaica, and were established in the town and at Preston. They were fine big men who were not afraid of work, and it was they who took the top off of Citadel Hill and built new fortifications. They cleared land at Preston, and worked at many places, but the cold of the winter was too much for them. They had officers to govern them, and these wore gaudy uniforms. The Duke was greatly impressed with their work. When Citadel Hill was finished there was a celebration. At that time not much was needed to declare a holiday, and we find that during that year no fewer than twenty-eight public holidays were celebrated. Each of the Maroon officers had the privilege of having more than one wife, a colonel rating four, his majors three, and the others two each. The guns on Citadel Hill were fired that day in honour of one of the Majors, whose three wives had that day given birth to three sons.

At the turn of the century the press gangs were the bane of the town. Warrants were usually given for twenty-four hours, and every able-bodied man not engaged in governmental duties was liable to be taken. Desperate battles were common, and the women joined in to help friends and husbands. In October, 1805, an organized resistance to the press gang of that time resulted in one man being killed and several seriously injured. Thereafter few warrants for such actions were issued, though by July, 1812, desertions had become so frequent that proclamations were posted in Halifax offering the King's Pardon to all who would return to their ships.

The War of 1812-1815 brought a prosperity to Halifax that created problems for its citizens. Ships captured on the high seas were brought in almost daily, and as many as twelve were auctioned in a single afternoon. Fees for such auctions netted Richard John Uniacke, the Solicitor-General, fifty thousand pounds sterling. There was such an accumulation of prize goods in the town that permission was asked to sell some to the American market. Merchants dare not keep all their gold in one place. Apprentices had to sleep over the money chest in the shop, and at the house the money was kept in a strong box that was stored in the master's bedroom.

There were racing horses and fine carriages. Dancing and parties filled the evenings. Afternoon teas and dinners were attended by husbands as well as wives, many business men not returning to office or shop after three in the day. The lower class had their own share of the prosperity, ready money from drunken sailors and soldiers who patrolled the streets and haunted the brothels. Fighting in the street was such a common occurrence that many citizens were forced to carry stout canes for self defence. Depraved women of the toughest character were everywhere on the upper streets near Citadel Hill, bare-headed and bare-footed, blowsy slatterns shouting evil songs and hurling lewd remarks at every passerby. Letters in the paper of the day had small effect. As long as there were not too many murders, and robbery was not too prevalent, the police of the time were content to let other matters alone.

The problem of coloured people appeared again. British men of war brought to Halifax slaves who had taken refuge on them while they were in American ports. Soon they numbered several hundred, and they had to be fed and clothed until quarters were found for them at Preston and at Hammonds Plains. When British forces seized Castine, Maine, a large quantity of blue and yellow uniforms were taken, and now these were issued to the coloured men located at Preston. The York Rangers were being disbanded, and their green and red uniforms were distributed among the coloured males who had settled at Hammonds Plains. On market days these folk came to Halifax selling berries and wildflowers. Soon there was trouble between those who wore different colours, and there were several pitched battles before the uniforms were worn past identification, the "Rangers" having small love for those wearing the blue and yellow.

There had been a ferry from Halifax to Dartmouth from 1750 on, first a succession of row boats and then a clumsy craft with a lugsail and four oars. Its operator blew a conch shell on arrival and would not leave until he had a full load, his crossing taking a full thirty minutes. This type of ferry passed from the scene in 1816, being supplanted by a team-boat—two boats united by a platform with a paddle wheel between. The deck was surmounted by a roundhouse which contained a large cog-wheel resting in a horizontal position. Eight horses were harnessed to iron stanchions which came from the wheels, and as they plodded around and round in a circle they turned the wheel, which moved the paddle. Only twenty minutes were required for a crossing, and the large deck supplied room for cattle, carriages and horses. A mast was placed on the round house to hoist a square sail when the wind was fair, which helped greatly with the crossing. Afterward a topsail was added. As traffic continued to increase several "grinders" were put in service, small paddle boats, having paddles at each side which were turned by two men operating a large crank. This was strenuous work and often drunks sentenced to jail worked out their time on the seats of the "grinders."

A winter of deep snow and severe cold ended the war years, and smallpox once more raged in the town though now the people were ready enough to accept vaccination. Those so inoculated had to abstain from meats, spices, butter, wine, highly seasoned foods, to avoid severe exercises, violent passions and warm rooms. Sly ones were peddling with great success a bottled mixture that was called "Salt of Health," and it was said to cure ulcers, jaundice, the King's Evil, hectic fever, consumption and boils. It consisted of powdered jalop and one ounce of cream of tartar placed in a half gallon of barley water sweetened with brown sugar. Word of Waterloo caused a great town illumination and celebrating that lasted two days, with half the populace drunk and the other half feasting. Records showing the number of cattle, sheep, pigs and poultry being brought to the Halifax market at the time prove how well the majority of the people were living. The town had enjoyed about sixty-five years of existence, and forty-four years of that period were war years.

There was the easy money to be spent, and so some of

the merchants banded together and purchased cheaply a considerable area of ground along the Musquodoboit River. This they had cleared by hired gangs, and then small neat frame houses were erected, stables built and the little farms offered to families who would go and live there. If a large settlement could thus be started, reasoned these merchants, there would be buyers for their goods in the years to come. It was an investment against hard times in the future. There was something wrong with the plan, however; they had not reckoned on human nature. Families quickly applied for the homes, and were moved there. They were to receive one year's rations, seed grain, farming implements and freedom from taxes. During the year of free rations the families stayed together, having a real good time and doing very little work. The merchants complained, and during the second year one family after another drifted away, leaving the cultivated acres to grow up in weeds. No other families could be induced to take their place unless the free rations were included and the merchants, once bitten, were twice shy. Soon the entire place was abandoned. Winter came and the Indians moved into the houses. When the frost settled about they calmly tore down the stables and out-buildings for fuel. Later on they removed partitions in the houses, and when the third year rolled around there was little left but frame skeletons and stone chimneys.

A different venture was tried on the highways. The first coach line was established between Halifax and Windsor. The roads were rugged trails, but the stage coaches were strongly built, cumbersome vehicles with three seats inside and plenty of room at the top for baggage. Six horses were used to drag the coach through mire and mud, with frequent relays along the way, and the service ran well until the snow set in. Halifax was made a free port, more schools were established, and Dalhousie University had its beginning in an humble building on Grand Parade. The citizens became interested in gardens and fruit growing, the first steamships arrived in port, and Charles Dickens came to pay his visit to Province

House, then the pride of all Haligonians. Then came its one hundredth anniversary, and there was not too much in the way of excitement, the biggest movement of the day being the families that travelled out to visit Downs Zoo in Dutch Village, carrying their lunches in large baskets and having a merry time meeting with neighbours. An afternoon spent gazing at parrots and monkeys and moose and raccoons seemed very satisfactory, and long after the dusk had settled down tired folk were crossing the Arm by ferry or trudging home-ward by way of the Commons.

But 1949 was a distinctly different year, and on Citadel Hill an entertainment feature was the Theatre under the Stars. A stage had been brought from Hamilton, Ontario, where it had served during the staging of a beauty contest, and the seats under the stars were canvas chairs. Visitors strolled up the hill in the afternoon to gaze out over the harbour, and were lured back in the evening by the prospect of sitting in such a romantic and historic spot while being amused and given fun-coated doses of Halifax history, for the musical play was entitled *Halifax—1749*, and based on the arrival of Cornwallis to found the town.

Now we stood in the afternoon sun and looked in all directions. Those looking to distance behold a glorious scene. The city occupies a peninsula, its shore-line to the east forming the main harbour which, lying north and south five miles long and very broad, is one of the finest in the world. At the head of the harbour, Bedford Basin is entered through the Narrows. On the west is Northwest Arm, a beautiful sheet of water, the rendezvous for those who love aquatic sports. To the south the eye looks upon the open Atlantic reaching gray-green into the haze of distance.

The fortifications on the Hill are the fourth in a series of construction, and they were long ago quite obsolete. Heavy muzzle-loading cannon lie embedded in the earth of the ramparts. There are nine-ton granite blocks in the massive walls that rise abruptly from a deep moat, a ditch that could be raked by rifle fire from narrow shooting slots in both walls.

The cogged windlass and heavy drawbridge over the moat make one think of the novels of Sir Walter Scott.

We gazed out over the harbour at the two islands everyone notices at once and asks about, the nearer one being George's Island, where Cornwallis landed some of his supplies and where prisoners were often kept, once a heavily fortified position. The farther one is McNab's Island. Some type of craft is on the go any time you glance over the harbour, and in war days careful police are on Citadel Hill making sure no cameras are being used. It was a thrilling sight to watch a convoy passing out to sea by way of the Narrows and harbour, the grey guardians slipping along as if they were already on the alert.

"Look down the Hill and see the tall flag pole on Grand Parade," we said to a stranger who had begun to ask us questions. "That's the Nova Scotia flag, but that pole is British Columbia fir and was presented to the city in 1947 by the Canadian Pacific Railway." We pointed out ancient City Hall, at one end of the Parade, and veteran St. Paul's Church at the other, and explained that the first buildings of the town were erected between the Grand Parade and the sea, mainly because the first crude wharf was there, used by the thousands of troops and sailors who came ashore during the first decade of the existence of Halifax.

It was a wrong move we had made, from a practical point of view, for the visitor was from Ohio, and had his wife along, both of them desperately anxious to see all they could of the old city before leaving on the morning train. So we gave them an hour or so, taking them down hill to see Province House on Hollis Street, a fine example of Georgian architecture, and displaying two ancient lamps from Waterloo Bridge at the main entrance. A memorial to heroes of the South African War was to our right, and a statue of Joseph Howe to the left. We took our visitors in to the red chamber of the old Legislative Council and let them see the long oaken table around which Cornwallis and his men sat to form a new and stronger government for Nova Scotia. We showed them the

Library, that was once a court room, and told them the story of Joseph Howe pleading his cause for the freedom of the press there in 1835.

There was not time enough to show our visitors all the plaques to be found at various points around Halifax, but we led them to the plate recording that Canada's first post office was nearby, and to another marking the quarters of Sir John Moore when he was in the town in 1779. They seemed interested, too, in our account of the easiest bank robbery ever to take place in the city. Barnum's Circus had come and the parade was something wonderful. The entire populace turned out to watch it go down Hollis Street, and the populace included the staff of the Bank of Nova Scotia which was established there. An enterprising thief, hoping for such an opportunity, went inside and cleaned out the cash on hand, over twenty-one thousand dollars, and made good his escape. He was not one given to superstition, that is sure, for just a few steps away is the old market square where the hangings took place, and drunks were pinioned in the stocks. On market days its sidewalks were covered with displays of vegetables, poultry, berries, lobsters and baskets offered for sale by a conglomeration of merry coloured folk, solemn Micmac ladies and gay Acadians.

Another plaque marks the printing place of Canada's first newspaper, but our folks from Ohio were more interested in going out to see the Richmond area, scene of the 1917 explosion. It was the one thing they knew about Halifax. So we took them out, showing them the Shipyards as we went, where more than seven thousand repair jobs on all sorts of naval craft were made during World War II. Then we sat on the hill near Fort Needham and they gazed at the Narrows where the steamer *Imo* had been coming toward the Harbour just before nine in the morning on the 6th of December. The *Mont Blanc,* carrying picric acid and TNT, did some clumsy passing and was grazed by the other ship, and the accident started a dangerous blaze for bursting drums of benzol had sprayed other chemicals. The crew of the *Mont Blanc* took

to boats and rowed for life to the Dartmouth side, reached
land and, running as they had never run before, saved their
lives. A gallant officer from a ship near led a small party to
the deck of the *Mont Blanc* and tried courageously to put out
the fire. An alarm had been sent in and a new fire engine
came tearing up the street along the water front. All who
lived near were at their windows, watching, and school
children were gathering at school doors. Suddenly there was
a frightful explosion that shook the entire city. The concus-
sion created sent a tidal wave that swamped all small boats
at their landings and almost bared the floor of the Narrows.
The *Imo* was driven high on the Dartmouth shore. The
Mont Blanc simply vanished, as did the volunteer fire-fighters
on deck. Her anchor landed three miles away. A gun on the
ship's deck landed at Albro Lake. Every building on the west
slope of Richmond collapsed like a stack of cards, and many
of them burst into flame. Eighteen hundred people died in
that split second of explosion. Thousands were homeless, and
many of them had lost their eyesight. Trapped ones called
for help. Dying ones groaned in the wreckage. All was utter
confusion. There was no telephone service left. No one knew
exactly what had happened. And after the survivors had
worked the day without rest, carrying the wounded to the
hospitals and schools, any place they could be sheltered, a
great snowstorm raged, driving drifts into houses and buildings where every window pane had been shattered. Doors and
boards and bedding and boxes were used to try to keep
back the snow and cold from indoors.

We came back from the new Richmond to Government
House, for we wanted our American visitors to see the old
place in all its beauty. Workmen laboured for six months
to prepare it for the 1949 celebrations, the first complete
renovation since it was constructed one hundred and forty-
eight years ago. The hanging staircase was restored to its
original appearance and beauty, as were the many fireplaces.
Crystal and gilt chandeliers of special design were erected,
three large ones in the ballroom, which is finished in white.

The entrance hall is lighted by old lanterns that hold clever duplications of candles. On the wall four tablets bear the names of seventy-five governors of Nova Scotia.

The Lieutenant-Governor's office at the left rear of the hall has the original Wentworth desk with a top that removes from four supporting sections containing the drawers. There is an old scarlet fire screen. The ante-room at the rear right has extraordinary wallpaper imported from France, and the original pattern is said to be 5,000 years old, from a design of cherry branches and blossoms used by the Chinese to line ancient tea chests. Here and elsewhere through the House can be seen old "pie crust" small tables, dating from Wentworth's occupancy. The drawing-room and dining-room are in robin egg blue. Huge mirrors have gold leaf frames that took an expert six months to regild. Crimson Italian brocade drapes the windows. There are fenders of Italian workmanships at the fireplaces, of Adams design. The large state table of mahogany has its surrounding chairs brightened by Roman stripe satin seats in yellow, red, green and cream. A modern electric kitchen has been installed in the basement, and new drains laid under the building to eliminate flooding which plagued the place for a century. The royal suite on the second floor is finished in a special blue, as is the Governor's suite. His dressing-room is in pink and his sitting-room is done in a grape colour. It pleased us immensely to note the awe that flooded the features of our visitors as they concluded their tour of Government House, and we felt we had done enough so we simply told them about three famous old individuals of Halifax, and let them go.

The three persons were Finlay Cameron, Philip Marchington and Dr. Sullivan. The last named professed a great aversion for anyone of Baptist persuasion, and spent much time and money in preparing his own grave. It was constructed so as to be perfectly waterproof, with a drainage system good enough, he thought, to endure until the last trumpet is sounded. Philip Marchington was a notable citizen who mixed with religious matters and built a church for himself. When his wife died suddenly he was so grieved that he had a glass top placed on her coffin and did not allow her grave to be filled in. This permitted him to go each afternoon to the cemetery to gaze at her. There is no record of when this performance ceased, but the legend around Halifax is that one afternoon some young sports of the town, observing a coloured lady much the worse for liquor, took her to the grave and deposited her in the coffin, first removing the late Mrs. Marchington to a spot outside the wall. When the mourner arrived he gazed in the dusk and got down on his knees, unable to believe that the departed one had so changed in appearance. He knocked some gravel below in his moving, whereupon the coloured lady stirred, stared about her, saw the gaping man, and said: "I'se cold. You gotta git me out of here!" The story is that the widower fled the yard and never returned.

Finlay Cameron was a staunch Presbyterian first, a tailor second, and got his name before the public by refusing to so much as thread a needle on the Sabbath when an irate colonel of one of His Majesty's best regiments wanted a tunic mended on one Sunday morning. For his daring to refuse such authority Cameron was taken before a magistrate and sentenced to twenty lashes on the bare back at Grand Parade. His small shop was on Hollis Street, and when he opened for business the only sign outside his door was a small wooden apple. Fruit-hungry citizens flocked inside, only to be told the place was a tailor shop. "But that's an apple, ain't it?" they queried. "It is," acknowledged Cameron, "and where would the tailor business be if it hadn't been for the apple?"

The would-be customers argued that his sign was misleading, and so Cameron had a friend prepare a large board that almost filled his shop wall, and there it hung for forty years. On it were two verses:

When Adam walked in Eden with a lady by his side,
He had a rosy future and his conscience for his guide.
The fairest flowers on earth were his, and every kind of fruit,

Except the ripe red apple, which was banned for man or
 brute
Till Eve, the lady with him, said she would take a chance—
And the apple is the emblem of the oldest known romance.

They blamed the snake for showing Eve that lovely apple
 tree,
What Adam thought was never said about his bride-to-be.
No doubt he knew his missing rib would ever be man's loss,
While Eve made apple cider, apple pies and apple sauce.
But this we know, it was Eve's bite that brought us skirts
 and pants,
And the apple is the emblem of the oldest known romance.

7

The Eastern Shore

Mysterious Margaret Floyer. Five admirals. The big
trout. Goldenville. Sherbrooke. Canso—fortified in 1729.
Grant's Hotel at Guysboro. The Strait of Canso, and the
ferry.

WE exchanged names and addresses with our friends in the
usual tourist style, bade them bon voyage and drove to the
Dartmouth ferry. Passing over on the big modern boat that
moves so quietly and efficiently, we thought of the stage
coaches, and the day of their glory. No one dreamed, then,
of trying to get on the ferry until the stage coach had driven
on board. They had great drivers in the old days, men of
fine appearance and grand voice. There was much flourish in
all they did, and Hiram Hyde was the man who drove for
years the coach between Halifax and Truro. Each morning
he drove to the ferry and on board with six handsome
greys that were the talk of the town. They were always
groomed to perfection. The coach was magnificent, painted a
royal blue, with the undergear and wheels done in lemon
chrome and black striping. The greys were only driven as
far as Portebello House, a few miles, then changed for less
showy animals. Great Percherons and Clydes weighing sixteen
and eighteen hundred pounds were used, and on the Windsor
run were two black stallions that weighed a ton each.

There was need of such horses, for the roads could be very
heavy, and Hyde wrote a letter of protest to the Government
on May 16, 1844, saying:

The mail coach sank into mud so deep that the axle

dragged earth in front of it, and the driver was obliged to unload the mail and raise the coach with levers to get along. The mail from Pictou did not arrive at Dartmouth until the ferry had ceased for the night, so had to wait and cross over in the morning as the road around the Basin is not passable. When I contracted for the conveyance of mails the roads were middling good, and it was understood they were to be made perfectly good, instead of which they have gone to ruin and repair. I commenced with forty-two horses. I now have seventy-five as good horses as can be furnished in the province and with the increased force cannot get the mails through in as short a time as in 1842.

Dartmouth is a busy town. We thought of its three prized stories, the Quaker whalers, Margaret Floyer and the Shubenacadie Canal. There are many others, of course, beginning with an attack by the Indians on the first sawmill in the town, scalpings and pursuits.

The whaling industry was in full swing at the beginning of the American Revolution, over 150 ships being engaged in the business, and London was their big market. Whale oil for lighting and carding and lubrication was indispensable, while whale bone for corsets and umbrellas brought nearly £1,000 per ton. The whalers knew that the Revolution had probably ruined their market, so they communicated with the Governor of Nova Scotia and intimated that they would like to establish a permanent base in the province. This seemed a fine offer, and the answer was that a free site would be provided for wharves, shipyards, factories and homes. The whalers accepted the proposition, and over £1,500 was paid to the owners of unoccupied buildings and vacant lots in Dartmouth. Then the town layout was changed to a more regular style as it was felt that with the stimulation of the whaling industry Dartmouth would grow to considerable size. A good feature of the enterprise was the fact that the whalers were Quakers.

Ten vessels arrived with the first lot of the Society of Friends in 1784, bringing small boats and equipment, household furniture and the frames of their homes in Nantucket, which had been taken down for moving. Boards and planks and the doors and windows were brought, so the houses could seen be re-assembled. Twenty families came with the first contingent and soon Dartmouth was a busy place. Houses were erected as quickly as possible, and within three months the whalers had brought in cargoes that realized over £2,500 It would seem that only prosperity lay ahead, and Governor Parr of Nova Scotia gave generous aid. Only English buyers were against the Dartmouth-nurtured Nantucket whalers. They wanted the fleet on their own grounds, and their pressure was so great that in 1792 the move was made, the community moving to Milford Haven, Wales, leaving property in Dartmouth valued at more than £4,500. Their village became a "deserted" one, but it was not long an abandoned site, for Loyalists drifted into the town and occupied every dwelling. The "thee" and "thou" were forgotten, and the owners never returned to claim rent or price for the homes they left behind them.

The story of Margaret Floyer has remained a topic for discussion in Dartmouth for a century and a half. In 1780 Lieutenant Wm. Floyer of the 60th Foot Regiment came from England to Dartmouth and built a home there for himself and his sister, Margaret. It was a pretty cottage and they lived entirely to themselves, never making friends with others in the neighbourhood. They cultivated flowers extensively, and during the winter months occupied themselves with reading, owning a considerable library and being very fond of books. Finally, after some years of quiet life together, the pair divided, Lieutenant Floyer being called to his regiment in the West Indies. He never returned. But Margaret Floyer received money regularly from an address in England. In 1793 St. Pierre was captured by a British force. The governor of the island was a Royalist, and he refused to return to France while Napoleon was Emperor. So he was granted permission to live on parole in Nova Scotia, and he selected Dartmouth as his temporary home, met with Margaret Floyer and asked if he might live with her. His request was granted, and Monsieur Danseville built a long stone cottage to replace the small wooden one that was of hasty construction. He, too, had a great love of flowers, and worked summer long in the garden with Miss Floyer. She had become fond of children, and would go to any home when called if there were illness, proving herself a most efficient nurse. She seemed sad and patient as one year after another went by without her brother returning or any letter being sent her. The years slipped by until it was 1814, and Napoleon had been routed. So Danseville took his old uniform out of his trunk, put it on and walked up and down the streets of Dartmouth all the afternoon, shouting "Vive la France." Then he made his farewells in the town and sailed for home. Margaret lived alone after that, busy with her flowers and books, until one day she did not appear. People investigated and found her unconscious. They did what they could, but she died without talking about herself. The address in England was used, and an account of Miss Floyer's death was forwarded. The only reply was money enough to cover all funeral expenses. Lieutenant Floyer never came to Nova Scotia. The cottage fell into disrepair and was finally taken over by someone. Rumour long had it that the couple were not brother and sister, but none ever explained the mysterious source of money that kept Margaret in fairly good circumstances for so many years.

James Gordon Bennett was a Dartmouth schoolteacher who began writing pieces for Halifax papers and any publications who would accept his offerings. His work became more and more acceptable, and he moved to New York City, where he became founder and publisher of the *New York Herald*. We met Helen Creighton in Dartmouth, and her home is one of the historic houses of the town, overlooking the site of the first sawmill and other landing places. She is one of the workers who are preserving the flavour of Nova Scotia for generations to come. Her first book, *Ballads and Songs of Nova Scotia*, won such favour that she is now commissioned to gather by record every folk song of the province. Some of the broadside ballads tell of wrecks in the vicinity of Dartmouth. One deals with the wreck of the *Atlantic* in March, 1873, when 535 persons were drowned or died of exposure as the ship struck on rocks near Prospect. The ballad begins:

> Dear friends, come listen to the tale,
> The loss which we deplore,
> Of the gallant ship, *Atlantic,* lost
> On Nova Scotia's shore.

There is a chain of lakes leading from Dartmouth to the Shubenacadie River, and this route was long used by the Micmac Indians in journeying from Halifax to the Basin of Minas. As far back as 1824 a governor of Nova Scotia suggested that a canal might be constructed that would be a great aid to shipping. Engineers of London were consulted, and a survey was made in 1825, reporting that a passage with a depth of eight feet could be constructed for £53,344. The Nova Scotia Government granted £15,000, and shares were sold. First canal ground was broken between Lake Charles and Lake Micmac on July 25, 1826, the ceremony being performed by Lord Dalhousie, Governor-General of Canada, at a spot called Port Wallis. The Governor of Nova Scotia, officers of the army and navy, with band and artillery, public officials and clergy attended. The vice-regal party with naval escort and band rode in carriages the three miles from the town, but the rest marched to stirring music and greatly enjoyed the day as throngs of citizens were already there, waiting, at 9 a.m. Shore and roadsides were decorated with flags and bunting. Every boat in the lake was covered with streamers. There were speeches and music and a grand salute was fired. Then refreshments were served. The officer in charge of the naval escort was Lieutenant Wallis, and the place where the sod was broken was named after him. Funds for the canal were increased by the sale of stock in England. A chartered vessel went to Scotland in 1827 and brought back forty skilled stone masons and their families. They worked three years on locks and dams, and as the years went by the cost of construction increased. A freshet swept away a lot of masonry and a mortgage was foreclosed by the British Government on June 11, 1851. In 1853 the Ireland Navigation Company purchased the project, and eight years later a steam vessel of sixty tons, the *Avery*, made the first trip through the canal. The next year the property was sold by the sheriff to a Lake and Rivers Navigation Company. Then came a burst of activity as several steamers, towing barges, made many trips, conveying lumber and cordwood and building materials to Halifax, and taking back supplies for farming and gold mining. In 1870 a Dartmouth man purchased the proposition and substituted an inclined plane at the Dartmouth end in place of two locks, which produced the deep rock cutting that is now bridged at the town's Portland Street. Approximately £100,000 had been spent on the Shubenacadie Canal, but only small profits had been realized, and the incoming railways were enemies of the scheme. So when a railway bridge was constructed at Enfield so low that a steamer could not pass under no great sympathy was expressed for those then operating the Canal. It was the end. The barges were tied up to rot. The locks became fishing pools. Anglers camped along the way and picnic parties used the nearest locations. The Micmacs had long treasured a legend of an enormous sea serpent in Lake William, fourth of the Dartmouth Lakes, claiming it lived in a bottomless hole on the eastern side, and at times of the spring and autumn moons would emerge and thresh the lake waters to foam in mad attempts to escape. Fearsome tales were told of its appearance while construction of the Canal took place, but it disappointed thousands who watched eagerly at the proper seasons for a glimpse of the monster, and today the legend is largely forgotten. The old locks are still favourites with those on picnics, and for a century the Dartmouth lakes have supplied ice for the domestic and shipping needs of Halifax.

At Lake Banook, on our left as we continued our way, we saw preparations being made for the Annual Dartmouth Natal Day Regatta, held the first Wednesday in August.

Westphal was. but a few houses with nothing of especial interest, but J. P. Martin, Dartmouth's historian, had told us to look for a plaque mounted there. We were on the point of giving up our search when a man emerged from a barnyard and inquired our need. Then he stood and chuckled. "A danged fool run into the post with his car and broke the thing," he said. "I've got it in the house. Come and see— if you want."

We wanted, and we read the inscription: "The Birthplace of Two Admirals of the Royal Navy, Philip Westphal, 1782-1880, and Sir George A. Westphal, 1785-1875, who were many times wounded in action, the latter having been wounded on the *Victory* at Trafalgar." It made us think of impressive ceremonies that had been held at H.M.C. Dockyard to honour five great naval heroes of Halifax who had risen to the rank of Admiral in the Royal Navy. Five plaques, bearing their names and inscriptions of their naval records, were unveiled at the new Maritime Museum there by Rear Admiral R. V. Symonds-Taylor, Commander-in-Chief of the American and West Indies Squadron, Royal Navy. Commodore A. M. Hope, O.B.E., commanding R.C.N. Barracks and Chairman of the Museum, presided over the ceremony and introduced the Admiral and the special speaker, Prof. D. C. Harvey, Provincial Archivist and Nova Scotia's representative on the Historic Sites and Monuments Board of Canada.

The five Nova Scotian admirals who were born within "sight and sound of Halifax harbour," were: Sir Provo William Parry Wallis, K.C.B., G.C.B., the Haligonian who rose to become admiral of the British fleet and who as a lieutenant brought the *Chesapeake* into Halifax harbour as a prize; Sir Edward Belcher, K.C.B., native Haligonian, who led early naval exploring expeditions to the Arctic, Pacific and Africa, and who became an admiral in the Royal Navy; George Edward Watts, C.B., who served in the Napoleonic wars and the War of 1812, and rose to the rank of Vice-Admiral; Sir George Augustus Westphal, native of Preston, on the eastern shore of Halifax harbour, and his brother Philip.

Our route was Highway 7, and we were still skirting the coast of the province as we had done all the way save driving across Cumberland hills from Amherst to Parrsboro, and making a deep V down from Truro to Rockingham and back to Windsor. This Highway 7 was the last main road established on the mainland of the province, and was first called the "Harvey Road," records saying it was "paved with a long series of petitions, the majority of which were read with indifference." This for the reason that throughout the first century of British settlement all efforts at road making had been eastward through the centre of the peninsula, with trails branching southward to the various coves and harbours along the Eastern Shore.

Over eight miles from Dartmouth is the site of the famous old "Stag Hotel," which was well-known in the old days. Legend has it that an officer-poet who stopped there composed some lines for the signboard that hung for years by the corner of the old inn. It is now in the provincial museum. The lines are:

> The Stag Hotel is kept by William Dear,
> Outside the house looks somewhat queer.
> Only look in, and there's no fear
> But you'll find inside the best of cheer.
> Brandy, whiskey, hop, spruce, ginger beer;
> Clean beds, and food for horses here.
> Round about, both far and near,
> Are streams for trout and woods for deer.
> To suit the public taste, 'tis clear—
> Bill Dear will labour, so will his dearest dear.

There were homes of coloured people along the way, and we remembered that many Maroons lived in the area at one time. This was Preston, named after an officer who during a riot in Boston in 1770, ordered a guard to fire into a body of rioters. He was acquitted after a trial, then removed to Nova Scotia to keep him out of harm's way. Over three hundred

Loyalists settled the place in the beginning, but only remained there while government allowances lasted. After that came French prisoners who occupied the log houses and planted many flowers. Governor Wentworth had his farm at Preston, though we could not see anything marking the spot, and he used Maroon labour for three years. We saw a road leading left to the site of Maroon Hall, where much land was purchased for them and a large building erected as a residence for the superintendent. Afterward this Maroon Hall, containing ten large rooms and a well in the cellar, was purchased by a Lieutenant Katzmann. He gave many large parties there, spending lavishly on music and liquor and decorations. Then he had financial troubles and soon found that his social friends were fickle. One trouble followed another and ended in his becoming insane. Finally he was chained to the floor in one of the large rooms of the Hall, and there he died, unattended save by a former servant who had no other place to live.

Our way led along rough and rocky land well suited to bush growth. There were occasional glimpses of the sea, with a few homes now and then, some with boards bearing crude lettering stating that there were "Minnows for Sale." Turn succeeded turn, with woods and brook and bush and lake and woods again, then a vista of the sea until at last we were in Musquodoboit Harbour, a little village in a pretty situation, far away from the hurry and worry of town or city life. A few stores, a church, a school, the inevitable cemetery, a modern filling station, and we were in the woods again, slowing instinctively as a porcupine crossed the road ahead of us, or when a rabbit hopped across the ditch. In one hundred miles on that highway we saw three deer, several ruffed grouse, rabbits, porcupine and a very bedraggled muskrat.

The further we drove the more we became impressed with the feeling that we were "away from it all." Salmon River Bridge was simply a bridge over an outlet to the sea, and there was but an ordinary-looking inn beside it, yet there was such a hint of vast hinterland to be reached by waterways, such a suggestion of privacy on lake or in the woods, that we stopped and had lunch. Sandy Myers was the proprietor, and Mrs. Myers an excellent cook and hostess. The price was moderate but the meal was as good as any at twice the price in the city, and to talk with Sandy is to feel you know the woods, that you "have breathed the faith of fir trees, slept with naught but sky o'erhead, waked at dawn with proud possession of the day that reached ahead." For many years he had camps at lakes of the interior and his guides took there parties of city anglers who spent days whipping the pools and regaining the vigour the wilderness can impart.

It was hard to tear away from Sandy, for I had known him in other years, had gone to his beloved lakes and fished them with fine companions. I recalled easily the day I had left the others when we landed on a small island for noon lunch, and poked my way through underbrush to the far end of the place where we had heard a mysterious splashing as we rowed past. My carefulness was rewarded. Down the bank at water's edge was a loon on her nest. Some sixth sense warned her after I had watched a time. She rolled ridiculously over the slight barrier of sticks and leaves that formed the side of her nest and was gone in the water like a diving muskrat. There was a day, too, when on another lake we had heard a fearful yowling and rowed near enough to an island to see a long gaunt wildcat, starved to skin and bone, racing around the edges of the beach, looking for a chance to leap into our craft. It had become stranded there, no doubt, when the ice had melted suddenly in the spring and hated or feared to try the swim to mainland. We rowed on, and it howled like a lost soul until we were gone from view.

Sign posts told us where we were at intervals—Ship Harbour Lake, Murphy Cove, Pleasant Harbour, Tangier, Pope's Harbour and Spry Harbour. Untouched by railways, this shore stretches for 200 miles, completely unspoiled, scarcely tamed by man. There are lighthouses looming above the tree tops in the most unexpected places. Long lagoons where blue heron gaze haughtily at passersby. There are rocky little inlets with deep water close to shore, scarcely changed since they were used as pirate havens. There were islands in clusters or alone. Sometimes we scarcely saw a gull. Then we would round a point and they would be sitting on rock ledges in long strings of social groups.

This district has always been great moose country, and it was a moose hunter who was being guided up the Tangier River zone who found the first gold in Nova Scotia. That was in September, 1758, and a little early for good hunting, but the man, L'Estrange, was an army officer, and it may have been his leave would not allow him any other time. He talked about the gold he had seen, and two years later another man persuaded the guide to travel with him until they had found the gold spot. He took out several hundred dollars' worth of nuggets, and the gold rush was on. One month later the Halifax paper reported that there were four hundred watchers and diggers at Tangier, and by the next year two hundred claims had been taken. The deepest shaft sunk was only forty-five feet deep, and the best nugget found that year brought three hundred dollars only, but gold hunting was in the blood, and for the next decade hunters and prospectors roamed all areas, watching for glints in every rock ledge they sighted.

Near Pope's Harbour a man with a floppy hat was driving a stake to brace his fence, and inside the pasture were three cows wearing "pokes." They had stopped their feeding as if to watch the man, and we stopped to ask some mileage question on the hope that he might be willing to talk. Our hope was well founded. He rubbed a stiff-haired hand across his mouth and declared the day was too hot to work but that his evil-minded cows would break out of bounds if he did not mend fences at least once daily.

"I ain't no idee what breed's in them," he admitted, "but I do know they ain't ordinary. That yellowest one can cast her eye along this here fence and tell any place a slab's begun to go. Then she'll feed near it half the day if I'm in sight and never touch it. But let me go to dinner and she's out on the road afore I've peeled a tater. Them pokes hinders her a mite, but they don't stop her."

We remarked that there was fine scenery along the Shore, and that there must be some fine fishing. He admitted there was enough scenery to satisfy the average person, and that fishing was good in both salt and fresh water. With that he leaned against the new post as if to test its strength, and remained leaning. "A mile along here," he said, "is where Jim Heeper lives, but he ain't there now. He's sawin' down the other side of Ship Harbour. I reckon you're wantin' to know about his trout?"

"No," we said. "Who is Jim Heeper?"

The man straightened and looked incredulous. "I thought every livin' soul around Halifax knowed about Jim Heeper's trout. They used to drive clear out here on Sundays to see it."

"Was it a big one?" we ventured.

"Big!" The man came and leaned against the car door, and odors of fish and woods and stale and fresh perspiration came with him. "Only way to make you understand is to tell all of it. Jim's a mill man, see, and away from home a lot. He's got a big family, too, mostly boys. Well, 'round about six year ago he was home over Sunday and went to the brook to git a bucket of water. When he was back to the house he was 'mazed to see he had a trout in the pail. He called the kids to look, and they begged him to put it in a tub they had. Jim's easy-goin' and fond of his family, so he emptied the bucket into the tub, trout and all, got more water, and all day them youngsters fetched worms and grasshoppers to feed the trout, and jest watched it. They hadn't any toys to mention, and no pup, so they got mortal fond of that fish. Jim said that if they wrestled around and upset the tub once, they did it a dozen times that first week. The trout flopped around the ground until they put it back again. When they weren't botherin' with it they pushed the tub under the porch and left it there. One day there come a heavy shower and the kids run indoors. But the trout got excited and jumped clean out of the tub. When they come out after the rain stopped here was the fish worked into a bunch of grass and good as ever. Come winter the trout had grown inches and Jim didn't know what to do with it. Finally he took a barrel and put it in the cellar, then filled it with water. He put the trout in it and his wife said she'd put in feed now and then. Like some other kind of chores, it was forgot plenty, and near spring when Jim come home one time and went to look there wasn't a drop of water hardly in the barrel. But the trout was still livin' and seemed healthy."

We had some oranges in the car, and as the man paused and looked at the cows edging over toward the fence we gave our entertainer some of the fruit. He stuffed the oranges into a large pocket and resumed his tale.

"That spring when the trout was outside it kept jumpin' from the tub half the time. Sometimes it'd be out an hour afore they'd find it, but it always seemed to git under grass or in shade of some kind. Stories about it spread, and on Sundays people come to see it, for it was growin' immense. All that summer the kids fed it, and Jim told me it would go well over three pounds when he put it in the cellar. When they put the trout out in the spring it wouldn't stay in the tub at all, and after a time they didn't bother with it. There were no cats or dogs to make a risk, and it was real surprisin' the way that fish could squirm around the woodpile and git in out of the sun. It eat near anything, and would stay around for hours if the kids dug for worms. Then came the real excitement. There was a piece in the paper offerin' fifty dollars for the biggest trout in the Eastern Shore district. That was a lot of money to Jim's family, and they set to feedin' their pet more'n ever until it was like you could see its growth one week to another. Time hayin' was over and grasshoppers plenty it was so big and fat it couldn't go in the tub, and nobody every thought of puttin' it there. One rainy day I went over that way and here were Jim's kids goin' along tater rows knockin' tater bugs off with a stick, and that danged trout wrigglin' along and eatin' them bugs fast as they dropped. I cal'late it would go over six pounds on any scales, but Jim come out and said the kids was goin' to kick up horrible if he took the trout for the prize. A week later Jim was cuttin' first grain on his back lot and noticed how thick the grasshoppers were there, so when he went back after dinner he jest picked up the trout to take it along. Crossin' the brook on his way, the trout give lurch and went out of his hands. It dropped clean down into the deep hole by the bridge—and was drowned afore Jim could git it out."

Our man looked away mournfully. He added that it was good clear weather we were havin', and if I wanted to check his story to call in on Jim's wife.

We thanked him and drove along, murmuring: "Full many a rose is born to blush unseen and waste its fragrance on the desert air." Here was a master story teller wasting his time on Highway 7.

What scenery along that road! For many miles the highway is tangent to deep bays or cuts across wooded headlands. We saw capes that looked dark in the distance as if their lining were turned inside out, and a white lighthouse sprouted from a spruce-ridden ridge. There seemed to be a break in the acre after acre of unfenced property when we came to West River Sheet Harbour and saw the pulp mill and stores. But soon we were out again where there were more spaces than settlements and we crossed Moser River. The next name was odd—Necum Teuch, but soon after we saw Ecum Secum Bridge, and a stream tumbling over little cascades into a placid inlet.

We liked Marie Joseph, a fishing village out on the wide sweep of the bay, and Liscomb, then we were at Goldenville, one of the oldest gold mining centres in the province. The story is that a woman in search of wild flowers rambled around and found a bright bit of quartz that attracted her. She carried it home and had it for some time, showing it to friends. One day a traveller who chanced to call saw the quartz, and asked eager questions. The woman willingly guided him to the spot, and the man, seeing what was there, became very tactful. He displayed no great interest and soon went on, talking of other things. Then he returned secretly and dug out quantities of the quartz. Soon he was selling it, and then watchers followed him and found the place. Claims were staked and a gold rush began which established Goldenville. One party gained $400 in one day by breaking up quartz. Millions of dollars' worth of gold have been taken from the district.

Sherbrooke is a small place with a delightful situation beside the St. Mary's River, one of the better salmon streams of Nova Scotia. We stayed there the night, enjoying the simple accommodation we found, and going out in the evening to watch anglers whipping a pool with amazing dexterity. Then we strolled up and down the hamlet, seeing people gathered in chatting groups by almost every front door, trucks coming and going with young folk piled in any which way, shouting and whistling at every one in sight. A cat stalked a robin on a lawn near the post office, and two dogs did some growling at each other by the church steps. There was no other entertainment.

Our hostess surprised us by inviting us in for some cocoa and cookies as we were on the point of retiring. Two ladies were in the sitting-room, and we were accepted as friends of the family. Soon we were being bombarded with information about Sherbrooke, and every effort was being made to impress us with its importance in our history. There had been a small French fort there back as far as 1662, defended by brass cannon, and it held off all comers until 1669, when a British force captured the place. After that many skirmishes took place between British and French forces that used the place in turn as a trading post or strong point, and it was finally named in honour of a lieutenant-governor, General Sir John Coape Sherbrooke. Then the ladies switched from history to fishing, and before they were through we wished we had salmon rods and plenty of leisure, for they not only told us of big catches of salmon at the different pools, but had photographs to back up their accounts.

When retiring we studied the map, and in the morning drove along Highway 7 as far as Melrose, then turned right and drove easterly to Cross Roads Country Harbour and down to the shore again. We saw the salt water until we reached Stormont, settled in 1783 by a Carolina Regiment, then we crossed a neck of land to Isaac's Harbour and went down along the shore to Goldboro and Seal Harbour. Off shore we saw the Harbour Island where the ill-fated *Saladin* stranded after her captain and part of the crew had been murdered on the high seas by mutineers. The rascals were taken to Halifax by a British vessel, and there tried in the big room of Province House that is now the library. Soon they were dangling from the gallows, and the papers of the day carried some sentimental verse about their passing.

Coddle Harbour—New Harbour—Larry's River—Port Felix. Little places, little boats, lobster factories, co-operative stores. We were very glad that we had adhered to our intention of driving completely around Nova Scotia without retracing much mileage, and though it had been a secondary dirt road after leaving Melrose we could not wish for better adventure. Here we were off the beaten track. Here we saw how a proportion of our Nova Scotians lived. It is a region where pedigree doesn't matter, and the people are weathered human souls. Where families have learned from generation to generation to make a little go a long way. Where there are rough exteriors but kind hearts and true. Where there are those who lack money and education and background, and good luck, but who are the salt of the earth.

We talked to a dozen or more people in the various little coves, yet could get no story different from that of their neighbours, but the more we talked the more we realized that it is these shore fishermen with their motorboats and dories who are the backbone of the fishing industry. They live by the sea because it is their choice, and their income is subject to the luck of the market. The glorious scenery all about them they take as a matter of course, not even realizing the picturesque beauty of bare rock guarding tiny piers dipping stilted feet into the salt tide, small wharves piled with lobster traps and fishing gear. The wooden homes of the fishermen are weathered sea-gray in colour, with windows looking widely out to sea and doors constructed to stand the strain of winter storms. At break of dawn, and often before, the weather is the main topic of conversation. Tides and storms and winds are never-ending problems. Add to them the uncertainty attached to the gathering of the harvest of the sea, and its market, and you will understand that the fisher folk in these outport places have small time for events that make the daily headlines; they are more interested in their handlines.

Many of the homes in the long series of coves we had passed now house fourth and fifth generations of those who have won a living from the sea. As young lads the men baited trawls; as adults they rose before dawn for the first tide, spent five or six hours on the water, then returned to dispose of their catch and to make ready trawls for the next morning. Day in and day out, in fair and foul weather, they plied their calling. Now, as oldsters, these men sit about the tiny wharves on sunny days and talk about the year of the big storm or the spring of fat herring. They hand down stories that have moulded their lives and, on occasion, make trips into the nearest towns.

It is natural to think that when war came the younger men of these coves would volunteer for service in the Navy. Some of them did, but the bulk of them chose the Army and the Air Force, just as lads from the farms of the interior rushed to recruiting officers who were handing out bell-bottomed trousers.

Fishermen as a rule take their politics too seriously to be swayed by orators at election time. These hardy Nova Scotians are born to their parties, just as they are born to their religion. Standings at Cove polls vary little in a century, as long as births and deaths remain at normal levels. The little Cove churches, generally sited where they will serve as a landmark, are filled with the same numbers that attended when they were built.

Motorboats made a great change in the Nova Scotia fisherman's existence. The daily drudge with the oars was discouraging when the water was rough, and a day at sea was hours longer before the motors came. But the dory is and always will be a Cove necessity. Youngsters learn to use the oars by the time they are ten-year-olds, and errands up and down along are cheaply done with a dory. It is a common sight, too, to see an oldster rowing up the Cove and around the point to visit an old crony, pulling easily with the tide and finishing each stroke with an inimitable fisherman's tug.

There are few coves in Nova Scotia where the fishermen do not farm to some degree. As a rule the land is poor along the South and Eastern Shores, but inland a bit of good earth begins, and if the patches are inclined to be stony the fisherman will not be defeated. Stony land requires patience, and he has all the patience in the world. Born by the sea, he accepts the weather without grousing, even when hampering fogs drift in, filling every cranny of wharf and cottage.

Summer has really begun for the fisher folk when the wives and children go berry picking, when strawberry pie becomes a part of the regular menu. Then the hay patches are ripe for the scythe, nets and boats are abandoned for a day, and the cheerful raspings of stone on steel ring along from field to field. Women and boys with rake and fork make a picnic of piling up the new hay, and it is taken in as barrow loads or on little carts hauled by a horse or a lone ox. The hay ensures a winter's feed for the cow, and milk is a precious product along the coves.

Soon after haying the raspberries are ripe, and then the blueberries. None go to waste in the fishing areas. A generation ago few fishermen of Nova Scotia could swim. Today the majority can, and the car must be given credit for the change.

Here and there one is owned in the villages, and in the evenings the young folk go to beaches where summer visitors are bathing. Soon they, too, became good swimmers. The inlander, of course, thinks they all should be water rats. He will say that they can jump in from the wharf any old time. Then the inlander has a look from the wharf—and sees a bank of fish heads, sees their opaque blue eyes regarding him with melancholy indifference. He shudders as he turns away, and has no more to say about swimming from the wharf.

All these things we learned as we talked an hour with folk at one of the Coves. Their common courtesy did the heart good. They invited us in for a cup of tea, and as we sat in the little parlour with crayon enlargements of grandfather and his good wife gazing down at us, the proud little lady of the house called in her daughter, a youngster of ten or eleven, serious back of her freckles and possessed of considerable poise. "Dulcie is grand on reciting," announced the mother. "Dulcie—you give 'em a piece."

Dulcie's blonde pig-tails switched back and forward as she made a bow learned in the school house, and then she began. We had expected "The Wreck of the Hesperus" or "The Slave's Dream," but she gave up Masefield, "I must go down to the sea again," and many a time I have heard performers on city platforms not do half as well. The setting may have aroused our emotions until our judgment erred, but I doubt it. She "had the gift," and some day will be heard by many people in much larger places than her home Cove.

July 30th was a big day at English Harbour in the Tor Bay district. A tablet was unveiled there with due ceremony. Prof. D. C. Harvey, Nova Scotia Archivist and a member of the Historic Sites and Monuments Board of Canada, was chairman. The fishermen from the area were there, but as we parked by the spot and looked around the little harbour described by Lescarbot three and a half centuries ago, we wondered if the import of the plaque had registered with these folk. The plaque is attached to a massive granite rock by the roadside directly facing the sea, and the inscription reads:

CAPTAIN SAVALETTE
Pioneer of "dry" fishery in Nova Scotia.

Among the islands of this bay Captain Savalette carried on the "sedentary" fisheries for forty-two years prior to 1607, when he entertained both Champlain and Lescarbot on their way from Port Royal to Canso.

It is hard to visualize the rugged old captain looking up from his labours as Champlain came ashore, and calmly telling him that he was having his forty-second summer in the little port. It makes one wonder how many other Savalettes there might have been in that 16th century.

We drove into Canso, feeling somewhat awed to realize that we were on the most easterly tip of the North American continent. It is not an impressive little town, however, and one needs to know the history of the place really to appreciate the situation. There are no records to tell us who the first white men were to go ashore at Canso, but there is little doubt but that it was back in the 15th or 16th centuries if not before then. Fish were to be had in plenty, but the fishermen, having come so far, must needs go on land to contrive boat stages, drying sheds and flakes for his catch of cod. Spaniard or Portuguese, Frenchman or Englishman, no one knows, but some of these were there long before Columbus crossed the ocean, and down through the years there has always been someone to create an outpost of Canso.

There is the story of a shipwreck among Canso Islands away back in 1629, when a gale drove a French vessel onto uncharted reefs. Two of four priests on board, and eight of twenty sailors, succeeded in making their way ashore, and were afterwards rescued by a stray fishing vessel. Before leaving they had buried many of their mates as the bodies drifted ashore, the first of a long series of graves that have been dug in and around Canso.

On the school grounds we found a cairn erected by the

Historic Sites and Monuments Board. The inscription on the tablet read:

First developed as an important fishing station by the French in the 16th century. Fortified by the British in 1729. Scene of several combats between them and the French and Indians. Captured by Duvivier in 1744. Rendezvous of the expedition of Pepperell and Warren against Louisbourg in 1745.

In 1688 the French thought of making Canso the capital of Nova Scotia, or Acadia as they called it then. In 1700 those who knew it urged the French government that "Canseau is a place esteemed by many as of greater commercial and military importance than Port Royal." After the final capture of Port Royal by the British in 1710 the mainland of Nova Scotia was supposed to be a British possession, but the French, strongly posted at Louisbourg, could not refrain from fishing at Canso, and were still there in 1719, so that Governor Phillips of Nova Scotia insisted that a fort be built at Canso. He wrote under date of September 27, 1720: "Canseau is the first which we think ought to be possessed and defended in regard to the great advantage which accrues from the fishery and the number of British subjects which would resort there if sure protection can be obtained. Two hundred men to raise the fort, and one hundred to be left there in Garrison after the fort is built, we humbly conceive to be a necessity."

He was too late, and too little was sent to help him. The French, aided by the Indians, attacked Canso and carried away goods to the value of twenty thousand pounds sterling. They attacked again the next year, killing five men, a woman and a child. In 1722 the Indians made a great show of wanting peace and were received with ceremony at Canso by the governor. Then the redmen set out to capture British fishing vessels and were successful to such degree that they had eighteen taken before the governor was properly aroused. He then armed two vessels with experienced fighters and set out after the redskins. Within three weeks he had retaken every vessel, killing a goodly number of the Indians in the doing,

among them four outstanding chiefs who had been greeted
with such ceremony in the spring.

The fighting went on and on. Often there were two or
three thousand men in and around Canso. There is record
of seventy sloops laden with whale putting into Canso on
one September day in 1733. There are legends of pirates,
tales of the strength of the blockhouse built by the efforts
of the fishermen on poor fishing days, of the sudden attack
that captured blockhouse and homes and ships and all, of
the great bonfire made by the attackers in which every last
dwelling and dory were fired, and every man, woman and
child carried off as prisoners of the French.

It was rebuilt again, and then came more war and rumours
of wars, and, finally, the American Revolution, bringing
privateers and warships in pursuit. In 1776 the notorious
Paul Jones sailed in and destroyed fifteen ships at Canso, as
well as much property in the town. Small wonder that when
the first Loyalists arrived there they found only five families.
Men needed nerves of iron and the courage of a lion to live
in such an exposed port. Wars and raids and battles and
gales and wrecks and fires—Canso has had them all. We stood
and gazed out to sea, at the islands, at the people hurrying
about their various duties between garage and store and
wharf, and wondered what it must be like to live there in
winter. It is hard to think of another place along the Atlantic
where one can more easily visualize the heroism that attended
such settlements. No one knows Nova Scotia completely until
he has visited Canso.

Now we turned our way northward and drove up along
the Shore of Chedabucto Bay to Guysborough, putting up
for the night at Grant's Hotel, a cozy little inn with meals
that linger in the memory. The drive was interesting, for
the seascapes are bold and varied, and there is a sense of
loneliness that grips one as the road winds around a part
where no dwelling can be seen and the gulls wheel overhead
and cry mournfully. Then there are homes clustered about
a general store as chickens around a mother hen, with a

church or school near, and the children wave and call out as if glad to know there are other people in the world. Twice we stopped and chatted with folks in the little places, nice friendly folks, anxious to please but having no story to relate. One oldster, winking ponderously, told us he had been to New York when he was young, and we had no doubt but that the visit had grown hugely in his memory.

Guysborough is very old. In 1682 Bergier, an early French adventurer, noting the good earth there, planted wheat and barley and rye. On September 21st he reaped the harvest and took the produce to France for exhibition, having beans and peas from his garden as well. His report of the wonderful New World caused quite a stir in Paris, and he was encouraged to go on with his settlement. He had a wooden fort which he called "Saint Louis," consisting of two buildings sixty feet in length, providing quarters for thirty-three persons. He had four cannon mounted on a platform of logs and felt secure against all comers. Four years later 150 persons were living around the fort in rude log dwellings, and more land had been cleared, crops of flax and hemp gathered. But all was lost when a British force came in 1690 and captured the place.

The victors did not stay and gradually some French drifted in and the settlement had new growth when, in 1713, another force came marching overland and once more took the fort, burning it to the ground. The records of crops grown is understood better when it is pointed out that back in 1636 Denys had a trading post there, thirty acres under cultivation and a company of 120 men.

For decades there was no more than an occasional fisherman at Chedabucto Bay, and the forest was reclaiming the land when down on the South Shore a new settlement named "Guysborough" was burned and, the ground being stony, there was no talk of rebuilding. Instead, the people were moved to Chedabucto Bay, and there they quickly took over the clearings left by the French, cutting away the young bush and planting crops. It was an irony that another fire burned several of their log dwellings, but they had seen rich earth and logs were cheap, so the homes were built once more and the village grew. It was not large, for in the party were those who were restless and they had moved on, but enough were there by 1812 to have the government deem it necessary to erect a fort to defend the place. The outlines of the old structure are still visible and until recently old cannon were rusting by what had been earthworks. But now the point of land on which the stronghold stood is a fair place for a picnic, and one will travel far to find a fairer spot than Chedabucto Bay. There is a sense of dreaminess hard to describe, but real enough, in Guysborough. There is a peacefulness that soothes the restless, a calmness that quiets the nervous, a beauty that reaches under the most hardened exterior. We talked with summer visitors who were strolling about the Bay shore.

"There isn't much to do here," we observed.

"Do!" They echoed. "Who wants to do anything? We've been here a week and we're still just soaking in Guysborough atmosphere. We're never coming any other place for a holiday."

John A. Morrison is a friendly Scot who has written the history of Guysborough as a hobby, and he is simply bursting with stories of the county and its coves. His account of the hotel intrigued us. Among those disbanded soldiers who came in 1784 was an officer, Captain William Grant, who received a grant of 900 acres within the township. He became a prominent citizen, married a Miss Ann Fertile and raised a family of four fine sons. Meanwhile a John Dennis and his wife came from England and settled in Guysborough. Dennis purchased a lot of land and built a home and shop fronting on Main Street. He was the father of five lovely daughters. There is romance in the air of Guysborough, and so it was but a matter of time before the four Grant sons were married to four of the Dennis daughters, and when John Dennis died he left his property to his daughter Ann, wife of John Grant.

A hotel or inn was needed in those days, so John and

his wife moved the store around to serve as a dining-room, and opened his place as the "Grant Hotel." It prospered, and when a new Methodist parsonage was being built John bought the old one and moved it to the back of his house, where it became an ell of extra bedrooms. John and his wife died in ripe old age and left their hotel to a second John Grant, and his sister, Annie. When they were gone a niece, Nellie Grant, carried on, and the gracious old hotel was in Grant hands until 1941. We talked with the present proprietor and found she had been connected with the hotel for fourteen years. "I just couldn't bear to leave it," she said. "It's so old and so full of stories. A whole book could be written just about what has happened in this old place."

One of her guests was a retired cultured man who might live wherever he wished to go, but he prefers to stay in Grant's Hotel. The reason—brown trout. The species has thrived in Guysborough County, and they come down to salt water at the mouth of the river. There they can be taken by an expert fly fisherman on the turn of the tide, and the fishing is good, for only a few have the patience to wait the right time and select the right fly. We saw the retired man coming back in the dusk from his evening's go at the brownies, and he was carrying a beauty. "Great luck you've had," we observed.

He stopped and gave us a quiet survey. "This fish," he stated, "won't go over five pounds. Do you call that luck? I don't. I want nine and ten-pounders." We thought he was spoofing, but found he was not. He really gets the big ones.

In the morning we drove on fine paved road again, up to Monastery, on Highway 4, through a district that ships many carloads of Christmas trees to the American market. There were homes scattered along the way, and we saw women and children about the yards, turning to watch a car go by, unhurried in all they did, even the children seeming to lack animation. It could have been the weather, for it was hot and sultry, but we felt it was the influence of dreamy Guysborough, reaching that far.

Soon we were back alongside the sea, and the name of

the village was Havre Boucher. Away back in 1759 a ship came into the little port, and the captain was a jovial fellow who liked visiting the few settlers in the place and toasting himself by their fires. They cautioned him that it was late in the year for ships to be in and out of harbours, but he laughed at them—and rose one morning to find his vessel frozen solidly in the ice. There was no method of transportation for him. He had to stay the winter with the people, sharing their food and labours, and when he sailed away in the spring he was so well liked that the people named the place after him.

We soared up a long grade and down around a cove and then up hill again, like a long roller coaster, seeing a sign board—Auld's Cove. Ahead, on our left, we could see the outline of Cape Breton Island and remembered that the first ferry ran between Auld's Cove and McMillan's Point, on the Island. Up and up we went over the high rump of Cape Porcupine and then down into Mulgrave, a railway terminus of the C.N.R. The Strait of Canso looked narrow as we drove down grade toward the ferry, and as we sat on the wharf in line with other waiting cars we saw men pointing to where drillings were going on for foundations for a bridge to link the Island with the mainland. There is no older story around that end of Nova Scotia than the promises of politicians to have a bridge or tunnel constructed. Two men were using hammer and saw in some minor repairs on the wharf and we talked with them, asking questions about Mulgrave. They praised it highly, and pointed hopefully to where the drillings were going on. They gave us a fine story about a church that was built in the village back in 1848 by one carpenter who had thirty sailors to help him. The entire job was finished in three days, and the church seated two hundred people.

"It'd take six months anyhow, the way men work today," concluded our informant. "Times have changed. I don't know where it's goin' to end."

8

Colourful Cape Breton

Port Hood bathing. Photographed for a dollar. Sunrise Valley. Beautiful Ingonish. The girl who came back. "Sainte Anne—Settled 1629." Rev. McLeod and his "Ark." The Gaelic Mod and Highland Gathering. Ghosts.

WE waited in line with other cars. It was warm and everyone bought ice cream from the canteen alongside, then stood outside the cars to eat it, watching the ferry come plowing over from Port Hawkesbury. The cars rolled off and up the little grade and then we were going on board. There was no waiting. Once loaded, there was a little toot from the engine room, and we were away. The air was grand out in the Strait but we were hardly settled to enjoy the view from the top deck before the ferry was squaring away to meet the Island wharf. Port Hawkesbury faced us with a fine new Information Bureau, a faded relief map of the Island, a garage and church. We stopped at the Bureau and went in to talk with Mrs. Hilda Gillis, in charge, an attractive little woman who has talked with thousands of visitors to Cape Breton Island until she has an uncanny knack of knowing what they want before they tell her. We listened to her telling those ahead of us in the building about the Cabot Trail, the Bras d'Or Lakes, the Gaelic Mod, Keltic Lodge, Louisbourg National Historic Park, Cape Breton Highlands National Park, hooked rugs, where the Cape Breton giant is buried, and where the best salmon fishing could be had in midsummer. "And as she talked, still more the wonder grew— that one small head could hold all that she knew."

One by one she answered them, and so concisely that there was no prolonged argument. They had a quick look at her map, and then they were off, shifting gears as they mounted the steep little rise into the town's main street.

"After the years I've been here," said Mrs. Gillis, "nothing surprises me, unless it's the fact that there are so many nice people in the world. You'd think to read the papers that a third of the population were not to be trusted, but the tourists are, on the whole, the finest on earth. And ideas! I had a woman yesterday from Idaho who had driven here because she had read there was a Lone Shieling in Cape Breton, and she had always wondered how it came there. She thought they were some natural rock formation peculiar only to Scotland. It's funny, too, what ten minutes on a ferry does to people. It makes them feel they're away from the mainland. In a different country. There's quite a bit of road work going on here this summer, but they don't notice it. The scenery gets them. They stop all over the place, and will stay in the queerest spots. I'm so glad it's been a fine summer. Give them a fine day and a stranger just worries over not having given himself enough time on the Island, but when it rains and the mist comes down over the hill, they don't want to drive."

The oldtimers of Port Hawkesbury still talk about the circus that came there on August 22, 1870, arriving by steamer. The whole countryside was there, for a balloon was to be sent up first as an attraction. The tents opened at 10 a.m., and the admission was high for those times—fifty cents per person. A sturdy Cape Bretoner handed a ten dollar bill to the ticket seller and received fifty cents change. He shouted for the rest of his money but was ordered to move along. No Highlander would do such a thing, and so the ticket seller blew a whistle. In rushed a tough lad with an iron bar and with it he felled the man who had been short-changed.

It was a big mistake for the circus men. Others rushed in, but the Cape Breton blood was up, and one Angus Gillis knocked three of them down before they could strike at him. The ticket seller drew his revolver and fired, wounding a man. The pistol was knocked from his hand and a battle royal began. The crowd seized the side of the tent and tore it away, overturning cages and wrecking everything. Monkeys ran all over the place, some reaching the rooftops of nearby houses. Clowns and horseback riders scurried hither and yon, seeking safety. Cages of lions and tigers were overturned. Camels and elephants walked the streets as they willed, free of keepers. One man was killed and several were severely hurt before order was restored, and the circus folk were happy to get back to their boat with the majority of their animals. Some wagons were broken beyond repair and two monkeys were never caught, but created fear and confusion among farm wives of the neighbourhood until they were shot.

We turned left and drove northward on Highway 19 that skirts the western side of the Island, for just as we did on the peninsula, we were simply going around the outside, and clockwise, as traffic does on the Trail. So we still had the sea with us as we went through Port Hastings and then saw nothing but Scottish names for sixty miles. First there was Craigmore and then Campbell, and soon the Judique—a number of them, said by the Scots to be a French word, and by the French called a mongrel Gaelic. There were small shops here and there and an occasional garage, but there was the impression of space and no crowding for any. As we stopped to get gas a trio of weathered oldsters sunning themselves at the back of a cart gave us a nod and announced that if we'd been along an hour sooner we would have seen a large bear.

"Aye," said the oldest-looking. "Weigh four hundred easy but dead." He chuckled as he watched our faces. "Them's the only kind you'll see up here. But they been takin' our sheep, and Malcolm John found two of his half-eaten over by his back pasture. So he jist took his rifle last night and set down in the bush. Purty soon mister bear comes out to have his supper, and Malcolm John didn't miss. That's three he's shot this last year or so. Bears is the devil with our sheep."

The next place of size was Port Hood, and off shore we

could see Port Hood Island, largely covered with trees. It was from that island the French took most of the stone with which they built the great fortress of Louisbourg. We were going north all the time, and yet as we parked to look around we saw a dozen young folk coming from the beach in bathing suits.

"Is the water warm up here?" we asked.

"You bet," said a blonde pertly. "Around seventy today. Best there is up in this country. We've been in every day this week."

"Are you visitors?"

"I'll say. Four of us are from Wisconsin. Two's from New Hampshire."

"First trip?"

"Second for me. Third for some of them. And we're coming next year. You a reporter?"

"Not at all. Just on vacation. Sorry we haven't any film in our camera."

The blonde shrugged and sauntered on, and they walked in file on grass toward a large house on a hill.

"What we need," said a voice out of nowhere, "is a big hotel here."

We looked around. A short little man with a pencil back of one ear was beside us. "Up here we've the best bathing in the world. The best climate. Lots of room. Boats for fishing or to visit the island over there. Scenery. Places to hike. Just give a hotel and it'd be full all summer."

We murmured that it looked a fine place.

"This was a town," came the rejoiner. "Good coal mines. Then they begun to flood and nobody woke up in time to stop it. A fellow's been tryin' to git goin' agin, but the sea stopped him. There's all kinds of coal here, if you can keep the sea out."

The short man went on, waving his hands and talking until we could not longer understand what he said. The long pencil stayed on its perch back of his ear, and we wondered why it was there.

Highway 19 does some plain and fancy curving before it takes you into Inverness, and the town is not inspiring in any sense of the word. It's a typical mining community, with a core of company houses snugged too tightly together, as alike as peas in a pod, while around them, in a looser fringe, are the homes of independent residents who built according to their choice. The location of Inverness, however, is superb. It sprawls on a gentle hillside overlooking the sea. Waves lap lazily along a sandy beach and from the top of the hill where a striking double-steepled church dominates the scene, one can view a fine vista of sea and hill and beach and trail that makes him forget the monotony of the bare streets of the town. Hardy Scots from the islands of Skye and Rhun founded Inverness, and the first grants given extended inland a mile and a half from the shore line. The MacIsaacs and MacLeans were first, and then came some MacLeods from Dunvegan. There was little to encourage them, but they were folks of fine courage, and so they stayed and eventually the mines were opened and two thousand people were in the town.

Inland again we followed Highway 19, and soon were at Margaree Forks and gazing at one of the most famous salmon streams in eastern America, then on we went looking wistfully backward at the salmon pools and knowing that just a wee bit further inland was the beautiful Margaree Valley, beloved by artists and photographers, dotted with elms and so situated that the sunsets are beyond description, lingering on the pools and then gradually drawing last colours through silhouettes of tall elms until the beauty of it all is etched in the memory.

Soon we were at Margaree Harbour and having a delightful lunch at Duck Cove Inn. Around us in the dining-room we heard the salmon fishing discussed, and there was much being said against the net fishermen coming too close to the mouth of the river. We only listened with half an ear for it was a glorious day and there was a clearness in the air that was amazing. We didn't want to linger too long indoors, and soon we were on the road again, and surprised to note that since the Forks we had been on the Cabot Trail.

Belle Cote—Terre Noire—Friar's Head—St. Joseph Du Moine. For over twenty miles we drove through Acadian settlements where all speak the Acadian language of their forefathers and retain many Acadian characteristics of a century ago. There are little villages where lobster pots adorn the tiny piers and dories are moored in friendly families. Box-like homes that stand in random places about the coves are almost foreign in appearance. We had been told at Margaree Harbour that there were not many hotels up along the Trail, but that no one ever need go hungry, as a Cape Bretoner is always ready to open his house to a guest. Lobsters fresh from the sea grace many tables throughout the season, and there are no better cooks where lobsters are concerned than these Acadian women of the north. They are also clever with handcraft, and we saw fine hooked rugs hanging on fences with "For Sale" signs tacked to the post. Rugs on the floor and patchwork quilts on the beds would lend warmth to any home, no matter how humble, and also provide some needed colour. Most of the houses do not gleam with white paint. Instead, their shingles and clapboards have been rubbed down by sou-easters and given a thorough polishing by the summer's sun.

Our Trail wound in and around Grand Etang in fascinating fashion. At times we felt we would finish up in some one's back yard. Then we were out on the road again and soon driving up the long main street of Cheticamp, where we put up for the night at the Acadian Inn, and enjoyed a wonderful dinner. Mrs. Aucoin is an artist with food, and as fine a hostess as ever graced a hotel. We strolled about the streets in the evening, hearing French spoken on every hand, and admired the huge church that overlooks the entire shore. When the moon rose its beams glinted on the metal roof of the church and turned it to silver. Loading equipment for gypsum is a feature of the place, and next in industry is rug-making. Rugs from Cheticamp are in American homes from

Maine to Florida, and some huge ones costing hundreds of dollars have been made to order by a dozen or so women working together on the project.

Our bedroom was at the back of the Inn, and when we looked out it seemed as if we were on a ship, for lapping waves were below the window. There are no trains in the north of Cape Breton, and there is little traffic. At ten o'clock Cheticamp retired and there was only the murmuring of the sea, and cool sea air. We slept more soundly than we had in a week and arose refreshed. Small wonder that Mrs. Aucoin says she never knows when an overnight guest is going to leave. Often they stay a week, and let their reservation for some other place go by the board.

It was another beautiful morning, and soon we were crossing Little River above Cheticamp and viewing a striking picture—the shore line from Cheticamp to the hills. Fishermen-farmers live there in trim little homes that have been handed down from generation to generation until it is said that no stranger has settled in the district in half a century. The Acadian women do many chores about the farm as the men tend their nets or crops, and we paused by one field where a lame man was weeding his garden. He put knuckles to his forehead in a fine salute and asked if there were any news.

"Last week my radio goes bad," he said in quaint English. "I am lost with it so, and in the shop they say it is a week to fix it. So everything will happen and me, I don't know it. My woman don't care, but me, I do."

He talked on without needing much prompting, telling us he was the fourth generation on his farm and not one in the family had been lost at sea, which was something of a record. During the summer they fished for cod and mackerel, and had fair luck. In the fall they fished haddock. Sometimes, not often enough, they had a few salmon in their nets and gained a good price for them. The sea meant much. It was a provider of food, a means of transportation, and it also gave them fertilizer for the land. He used seaweed and dogfish and manure in equal quantities and had big crops of whatever he planted.

As he talked his wife came from the house and leaned against the fence beside him, listening. She was deeply wrinkled and was minus most of her teeth so that the tip of her chin was not far from her nose. She had a bright kerchief wrapped about her head, and she was calmly smoking a short black pipe. Her husband was talking about sheep when a car with a New York license came in view. It rolled along slowly, and stopped. A fussy little man in a striped shirt and white flannels got out and came over. He talked fast, like a brush salesman. He was taking pictures, he said, and his wife had noticed madame by the fence. Would she, for a dollar or so, consent to be photographed.

Everyone looked at madam. She sucked on the pipe and squinted her eyes, then nodded agreement. Fine, Be-e-eautiful. Now would she please get in the car, back of the wheel. No, madam did not like cars. She preferred to have the picture taken by the fence. But no, there was a reason. Three dollars if she would but sit in the car one minute. Some new American bills appeared, and madam's black eyes were sharp. She walked over and stood beside the car. That would do, please. Ten minutes later the man had got her in the car, and back of the wheel. He had her grasp the wheel firmly. He tilted her head slightly, tugged the kerchief over one ear, had her shut her mouth tightly on the pipe. Beside her sat the New Yorker's wife, a fat woman, and she put her hands up as if to shut out what she saw. The picture was taken. It looked as if madam were driving recklessly toward a cliff or blockade and nothing on earth would stop her.

The camera had scarcely clicked before madam was on the ground. She accepted her three dollars and whipped back inside the fence. Then another car shot into view. We could hear it as well as see it. It belonged to the days when tops were raised as protection against rain, and by main strength. Now the top was gone, but the brass finish on the radiator shone. As it chugged nearer we saw that a twin to madam was driving, and her expression was one of do or die. Beside her sat a wizened little man with his hat pulled low, and his hand gripped the top of the door beside.

"There goes Marie," said the lame man admiringly. "She can drive like the devil, in the ditch or out."

He was just speaking to us. The New Yorker was in his car in wild pursuit, his wife holding the camera.

Cape Breton Highlands National Park is entered a few miles beyond Cheticamp, and the scenery from then on is simply superb, with the highway serving as a grandstand seat for the motorist. There are expansive views of the sea and coast on one side, and to the right rugged mountain wilderness reaches down to the highway. We began to climb hundreds of feet of narrow reddish riband, and when we were up a distance glanced back from a spiral turn to the majestic beauty of the scene below us. Turn after turn was made, always climbing and at last it did not seem possible, looking down, that we had climbed so high. Then we were on the summit and seemingly away from civilization.

A doe and fawn appeared on the road ahead of us. We slowed to bare rolling, and the fawn turned, came a distance toward us as we stopped. The doe watched us closely, her large eyes filled with inquiry. Then she turned and trotted into the bush and the fawn, bewildered, turned and chased after her. It was the perfect touch to the morning.

It seemed no time at all until we were descending, in second gear, from the summit of Mt. MacKenzie, going down 1,260 feet in a series of zig-zag turns, each bringing a different breath-taking view to the fore. Three boats out at sea looking mere specks on the water, and gulls flew in slow circling between us and the road below. But at last we were down, and rolling into Pleasant Bay where we stopped to view the stumps and blackened places that showed in spite of all the greenery, telling of the devastating forest fire that practically wiped out the settlement a year ago. There was a gas pump by a house, and a boy in the sunshine. We asked him what lay beyond.

"Red River Valley," he said. "You heard the song?"

"Don't get smart, Georgie," called a woman. She had been there all the time, but we hadn't noticed her, sitting in the shade around the corner of the house, ready to man the pump if we needed fuel. "Nice day," she remarked.

We agreed, and began conversation. She gave us a graphic description of the fire, and pointed to different sites that had been denuded of buildings, and showed us where the boats had been that took off the people. Everything happened up there in Pleasant Bay, she said. Ship wreck and freezing and fires. She told us about the winter when ice forms for fifty miles out and for days on end no one travels more than from one house to another. She talked of a cannon and anchor found in a cove, of rusted cannon balls and a sword, proving that soldiers had once landed at the Bay. Fishing was good enough, she said, but there was not much brought in by the sea as in the old days. We queried her on that matter, and she explained by telling of the year kegs of rum came floating in to the beach, of a year when cases of dress goods were rescued, and hung on fences and bushes for three miles up the settlement; of a year when cases of butter were salvaged, barrels of flour and caddies of tea. Then she sighed and said she must get dinner ready, and be sure we had a look at the Lone Shieling.

We had the look, and it reminded us of Scottish pictures. A car from New Hampshire was there, and a trio of ladies were eating lunch inside the building so we did not loiter long. Anyway who could wait when there was such a road ahead and along as that leading overland from Pleasant Valley. It was up a little and down a little on soft earth that made no sound against the car wheels, and the silence was broken only by an occasional bird call. High trees almost met overhead and delicate shafts of golden light poured through tiny openings. A deer stood ten feet from us in soft moss and leaf-mould and only raised its head a trifle as we rolled past. A ruffed grouse and a flock of half-grown chicks scuttled from the wheel rut ahead. A rabbit leaped clear and wheeled about to watch us, its snout moving strangely. Blue jays flitted silently across a glade. So lovely was that drive to the hill that we looked for a spot to turn about and do it over again.

The climb over North Mountain is a long one, and there is a sea of tree tops to look over on one side, and sheer rock reaching upward on the other. A thick stone wall serves as a guard rail over the mountain and the descent is a long one. We passed a car from Delaware, and the couple in it, oldish folk, were simply sitting, parked, gazing over the great ravine of forest as if they would be a long time drinking it in. At long last we were down again in another low spot—Sunrise Valley—and passing alder thickets and evergreen groves. As we arrived at a turning a house stood at right angles, and there was garden reaching down to the road. In the centre of that garden was a deer, nibbling away at forbidden greens. Smoke issued from the house chimney, but it was apparent that no one had looked out of the kitchen window for some time. The deer had quick glance at us, then went on eating.

Soon we were on a rising that gave us a magnificent view. No photograph taken does justice to Sunrise Valley, its supreme sweep of field and stream and hillside. Far away, almost in a haze, is Aspy Bay, and the hill tops seem to grow higher in the distance and to blend in the haze. We had glimpses of the Aspy River, saw a place near a bridge where countless ages of rushing water have washed the coppery river bed so clean that its reflection in the sunlight had the appearance of gold.

Through the Valley the farms are fertile and well protected. The homes are quite small, to ensure easy heating through the long winter. The barns are large, to hold hay and grain enough to feed stock through the cold months, when storms rage and the valley is filled with snow. Soon we saw a sign pointing to Dingwall, but we kept to the Trail and edged around a corner into Neil's Harbour, a quaint little fishing town with rough-and-tumble appearance, fishing smacks, pounding surf, weathered fences and buildings and the tingling smell of the sea. We parked and talked with some fishermen who were standing about in long boots and under shirts.

"This place ain't nothin'," said one. "You should go have a look at Hungry Cove." He pointed. "It's about a mile yonder. They call it New Haven now."

"Picturesque" is the only word to describe New Haven. It's off the beaten track, and its thirty-odd homes cling precariously to steep slopes which almost surround the Cove. The rugged highlands jut out to the very ocean itself. A stream without a name cascades down and must be a torrent in the spring. There is no gradual shelving of land, where man could build himself a village, but the homes hug the hillside wherever a few square feet can be gouged out of solid rock to form a footing for a foundation. So it is that the chief charm of New Haven, like that of Neil's Harbour, is that the rugged landscape does not permit any set pattern of streets or lanes, but forces the houses into a striking irregularity of position, unique enough to be startling. Paths lead from one house to another. Every child and dog going around seems to brace its feet instinctively at each downward step, and there is the sound of the sea eternally in the ear.

From Neil's Harbour there is not much along the Trail but scrub bush and rock and loneliness and swamp and barren, not until you reach Ingonish, and then you feel you have arrived in another country. We drove to The Point for lunch, and feasted on home cooked food for which Cape Breton is famous, then strolled toward the shore and feasted our eyes on the beauty that belongs to Ingonish, the long stretch of beach, the little inlets and piers, the winding road and cottages at all angles. There is North and South Ingonish, and Ingonish Beach. The name is said to be of Portuguese origin, and tradition has it that the Portuguese knew the place and had a fishing settlement there as early as 1521. Whether true or not, it is known that the French had a thriving village there in the 17th century, and that in 1740 no fewer than fifty-four fishing vessels were operating from the port. When the British force came to capture Louisbourg a number of frigates were sent to demolish any French settlements. They found Ingonish and destroyed every building.

Over one hundred years later, in 1849, a bell was dug up on the sand beach. Its inscription reads: "Pour la paroisse de Miganiche, j'ai été nominés par Jean Decarette et par Francois Urail, parrainet marrane La Fosse Huet de St. Malo m'a faite l'an 1729." Other relics of the French period have been uncovered. This eastern part of Cape Breton was once the feeding ground of untold numbers of moose and caribou. In 1789 buyers in the ports offered ten shillings each for every hide brought in, and so great was the slaughter that ships passing the coast could smell the odours from decaying carcasses. Word was passed to the military, and soldiers were sent to the Ingonish area to control the killers. They were too late in arriving. Over nine thousand carcasses were found, and within a short time not another caribou was seen on the Island.

A promontory running out between North and South Ingonish is called Middle Head. Between it and South Ingonish Harbour there is an excellent sand beach, and in this locality the headquarters of the Park are located. One of the finest golf courses in North America is there, also a fresh water lake between the beach and mainland. Tennis courts and an athletic field add to the natural attractions of the place. The sheer beauty of the spot is beyond description, and there is some peculiar charm and atmosphere to the area that distinguishes it from all other holiday resorts on the continent. A few hours drive will put one in Sydney, yet there is a feeling of remoteness from the rest of the world, a tranquillity that provides an escape from the strain of modern life. We drove under birches up a lane to Keltic Lodge on Middle Head, and felt it a real journey's end for the discriminating traveller. The view from the main lodge verandah is simply magnificent. A ladder leads down a rugged cliff to Pebbly Cove. The cottages of the Lodge lead down the slope. In all directions are gorgeous vistas of hill and sea and sky. Each year artists work there, trying to catch the changing lights on the great surf-drenched rocks, on the harbour and sand beach, and on the great sleeping bear in the distance, blueberry blue against the skyline—Cape Smoky, sheer one thousand feet up from the sea, with mists hovering halfway up, giving the bluff its name.

Two cars were parked by the foot of the hill leading up to Smoky's crest, and both bore American license plates. A woman was standing by the roadside, and as we came in sight she flagged us to stop. "What happens here?" she asked. "We can put the car in neutral and roll uphill."

"Right," we said. "And you can do that in at least two other places in Nova Scotia. They call them 'magnetic hills,' but there is no magnet. It's simply an optical illusion."

We left them after a time, first one and another testing the grade. The setting is perfect. It does seem as if the car rolls uphill.

There is not the slightest danger for the motorist on the Cabot Trail at any point, if the car is in good working order. But there are few who drive over Smoky and begin the descent without feeling a tightening inside and a few butterflies around the stomach. The long sweeping turns look down on each other, and the sea seems so threatening as you glimpse it. But the effect is marvellous. I doubt that any person can drive the Trail and truly say his or her emotions were not vastly stirred by the experience. The grandeur of the scenery is awe-inspiring. The turns are exciting, the constant change is stimulating.

From Smoky onward the Trail changes. After seeing so many little villages with fascinating disarrays of boats, boat houses, fish flakes, lobster pots and gear, it seemed strange to drive through lonely wooded stretches, crossing occasional brooks and seeing many gates, or gate-less, lanes leading to humble homes centered in clearings won from the domineering forest. A girl stood by one post. She had a bit of cake in her hand and was coaxing a chipmunk toward her. The little fellow kept approaching nearer and nearer, almost flicking his tail off, and finally nipped some frosting from her fingers. The taste of the goody was too much. In a moment the chipmunk was gobbling fast, quite unafraid.

"Not many houses along here," we remarked. "We saw some back at Wreck Cove, but very few since."

"There's Skir Dhu and Briton Cove," she said quietly, so as not to disturb the chipmunk, "but the houses along aren't many."

"Do you live here?"

It was rather a bold question, but she appeared to think it natural. "I did," she said. "Then an uncle came from the States, and when they were leaving I jumped in the car and wouldn't get out. I was fifteen, and I carried on so they thought I would have a fit. So they let me go. I got a job and I worked hard so I wouldn't have to come back. That was eleven years ago. I come back now each summer to see my folks, but I wouldn't live here again for anything. It's too quiet. A big noise would be easier to stand. One house along here has a worn place across the front room like a cross, from window to window. The woman who lived there come from a town. She kept walking from one window to another for five years. Then they had to take her away. It's better now, though, since the cars come through, and plenty along here own either a car or truck. So they take folks to meetings and parties."

She talked about squirrels she had tamed, and of walking miles to exchange newspapers or catalogues in the winter, and then she went to greet a dour-looking woman who came through a woods path as silently as a ghost. So we drove on.

There were other small settlements along the road, and then we came to a fork in the highway. We could go to Baddeck by either route, and we wanted to see all we could for the beautiful waters of St. Ann Bay were ahead, so we drove to our left to the Englishtown ferry and were taken across a very narrow but turbulent bit of water that' boiled and eddied and showed such strength of current that the small two-car ferry—onto which you drive and then back off—was swept past the landing place and had to make a wide circuit to come in again.

In the little cemetery to our left we saw the grave of Angus MacAskill, the famous Cape Breton giant, who died in 1863. He was a remarkably well-proportioned man, standing seven feet nine inches in height and weighing 425 pounds. But he was more noted for his strength than for his size, and tales of his prowess abound in the St. Ann district. Big Angus travelled extensively, making public appearances, and gained considerable money. Then he came home and was a fine citizen of the community.

We walked out of the cemetery and up a small grade to a cairn bearing the following inscription: "Sainte Anne. Settled, 1629, by Captain Charles Daniel, and site of an early Jesuit Mission. Selected, 1713, as a naval base and one of the principal places in Isle Royale, named Port Dauphin and strongly fortified. Its importance declined with the choice, 1719, of Louisbourg as the Capital." The visitor standing there can visualize little of the happenings recorded three centuries ago. Captain Daniel put in there to construct a small log fort, and as he worked fishermen happened by and told him of a Scottish expedition erecting another fort farther along the coast. This was a project of the Baronets of Nova Scotia, and there was peace between France and England. Captain Daniel cared naught for that. He captured the Scottish post by a surprise attack, took all the stores and brought the prisoners back to St. Ann and made them finish the building of his own stronghold. Then he sailed for Europe, landed the unimportant prisoners on an English shore and carried the Scottish baronet to France, holding him there three years as a sort of prank. When finally the poor man was in Britain again he reported his usage in detail, but those were stormy times, and his pleas for a refund of capital were ignored. The garrison left at St. Ann became bored with each other in the wilderness spot and trouble arose. Finally the officers quarreled and one shot the other dead, then vanished in the forest.

The first Jesuit Mission on Cape Breton Island was founded there, and it was the Jesuit fathers who named the spot "Sainte Anne," in honour of Queen Anne of Austria, mother of King Louis XIV. Their crude little chapel was the first in America to bear the name, St. Ann, now borne by sixty-three different church edifices in various parts of the continent. Fort Dauphin was well constructed, and some traces of the old masonry can be seen. From 1650 onward an extensive mercantile business was conducted at St. Ann by Simon Denys, and it was a fairly prosperous colony for nearly a century.

The ferryman was rather bewildered when we re-crossed and drove back on the road by which we had come, and we heard him telling his helper that a lot of money was wasted by people who did not know where they were going. We went back to the fork in the highway and entered the district of South Gut St. Ann. It is so steeped in Scottish history that even outsiders linger there as if they wish to catch some echoes of the past. The central figure in the story was Norman McLeod, a hardy Scot from Sutherlandshire, born in 1780, a man who had a good education for his time. In fact he was a gold medal winner in moral philosophy, but differed with the Church when he entered upon his theological studies. Scottish tempers flared and McLeod was forced to turn to teaching school for a living, while feeling ran so high against him that the pastor of the district would not allow another minister to baptize McLeod's first-born. His troubles seemed minor ones, however, when the fateful Sutherland evictions began taking place, and McLeod was among the hundreds of homeless Scottish folk who came to Nova Scotia to find a home they could call their own.

The lot he was with settled in Pictou County and there, with no one to stop him, McLeod preached the gospel in his own fashion, made his own rules, ran his own church, and so well did he succeed that his name and fame reached far places, bringing him an invitation to take a fine church in Ohio. The prospects held out were enticing, but McLeod hated to part with his congregation, so he did the best thing possible—offered to take every person along with him. The good folk were so fond of him that they readily agreed to the arrangement and broad axes hewed timbers for a sturdy ship that the ones outside the congregation named "The Ark." Rev. Norman McLeod did not resent the term, and so the Ark was painted with the three crude letters. It seemed a cheap way to transport the flock from Pictou to an American port, but when they were out to sea a great storm was encountered and the Highlanders steered for the nearest refuge they could find. Chance took them into St. Ann Bay, and there they were safely anchored as darkness fell. When morning came the sun shone and they thronged the deck to gaze on a scene so like Scotland that they wanted to go no further. McLeod took the ship to the head of the Bay, took two square miles of fine land on a shelf-like slope for himself, and had his people settle around him.

Strong arms cleared the slopes about and homes were erected, a church built. Crops were good. There were fish in plenty in the Bay. The settlement prospered. McLeod had his troubles, but he ruled with an iron hand, and the majority loved the iron. For thirty-one years all went well, and then the failure of a potato crop stirred the old man to longing for a new land, though he had had a second church built at St. Ann, a huge box-like affair that would hold about fifteen hundred people. McLeod's son sailed away with a cargo to sell in Glasgow, and eight years went by before his father received word that the lad was in Australia, and liking it fine, so well that he wanted the whole of St. Ann's folk to come and join him. The Rev. Norman was seventy-two by this time, but he seethed with action, had his men cutting timbers to build ships for the voyage before any protest was raised. He persuaded them to plant crops and have plenty of provisions made ready for the journey.

The first ship ready was the *Margaret*, of 236 tons, but it had to lay in the stocks for a year until enough money could be raised to purchase the necessary rigging. The *Margaret* sailed from St. Ann Bay on October 28, 1851, and made a voyage of 12,000 miles without mishap. In the next seven years six more ships were built, and as fast as they were ready there were passengers in plenty to go aboard. Nearly all the people wanted to follow McLeod. He had not found Australia to his liking, however, and had sailed to New Zealand, where he and his people were kindly treated and given extensive grants of land. The last ships sailing went direct to New Zealand, and all made homes in the new land. McLeod died in his eighty-seventh year, and tales of his sermons and actions are still household possessions in and around St. Ann Bay district.

We were especially anxious to reach the spot chosen by McLeod, for it is now the site of the only Gaelic College in America, and there each July the Gaelic Mod and Highland Gathering is held. We were just in time. A sloping hillside forms a natural amphitheatre, and the dark-blue water of St. Ann Bay thrusts in like a wedge down at the foot of the slope. Across the water the shimmering green of St. Ann hills makes an immense backdrop for the Mod stage. There was colour everywhere. Splashes of red where Mounties were stationed. Kilt and plaid and bonnet in all directions. All the tartans of the clans. Over all, dominating the area, was the music of bagpipes. A band played near the stage. On every fringe of the hillside lone pipers were practising. A fine new brick building was a "Craft Centre." American visitors in the crowd were eager to buy neckties, scarves, all manner of handcraft articles that were for sale. We saw a "Giant MacAskill Museum," displaying implements used by Scottish pioneers. Then the pipe band led a parade of dancers down to the great outdoor stage and fifty Highland lassies danced in a massed Highland Fling. The applause that followed echoed and re-echoed from the far hills over the water.

The bowl-like slope of the natural theatre is perfect. Engineers could not improve on its formation. The seats are planks arranged in rows and spiked to timbers running up and down the slope. The plan provides accommodation for a great number, but the seated one is not entirely comfortable. A public address system makes it possible for every person in the area to hear every speaker clearly. Over two thousand Cape Breton Highlanders sat on those seats or stood about to watch the dancers and hear the pipes and Gaelic singers. They came from glens and valleys around the beautiful Bras d'Or Lakes, from all the Baddeck district; from along the rugged eastern coast of the island. It was their great week of the year. Many of them date happenings from "before the Mod" or "after the Mod." When the pipers played there were five-year-olds dancing like elves in little corners outside the seating space, and we saw many oldsters of more than fourscore years sporting their bit of tartan. Mingled with the crowd were the visitors with cameras and thousands of feet of colour film were being shot in the bright sunlight.

There was everything to entertain. Dancing, singing, piping, fiddling, sports and speeches. An old-timer mounted the platform and showed the crowd how to pick them up and put them down in a step-dancing competition. He knew how, for he had been dancing for sixty-three years in competitions. One enormous Highlander roamed around with yards of tartan he had purchased to make himself a dressing-gown. He stood nearly seven feet tall and weighed 338 pounds. Then, mid-afternoon, you could feel the emotions growing tense. When the "Road to the Isles" was played a sigh of content was visible. It rippled through the audience. But the greatest moment was when a Scottish lassie sang an old song of the Hebrides. There was a silence after that could be felt. Not a listener stirred while she was singing and down many weathered cheeks tears slipped without check as the voice rose and fell, thrilling and softening in turn to the Highland mood of the song.

We drove twelve miles on paved road to Baddeck, and were lucky to have accommodation at the Baddeck Hotel, for every inn and hotel was jammed to capacity and hundreds were in rooms let by the people of the little town and countryside. It was evening, and Baddeck was like something one might see in a dream. The lake was a silver surface. Yachts that had raced during the afternoon were moored by the wharf and their spars were like pickets on a tall fence. People strolled up and down the main street, or grouped by gates and shop fronts to talk about the Mod. There was no other subject. We inspected the place in front of the court house and read its inscription:

Commemorating the work of the Aerial Experimental Association which resulted in the first flight within the British Empire made by J. A. D. McCurdy, at Baddeck, Nova Scotia, on February 23, 1909. The Aerial Experimental Association was founded at Baddeck by Dr. Graham Bell. The other members were F. W. Baldwin, whose first successful flight was made at Hammondsport on March 12, 1908, G. H. Curtis, J. A. D. McCurdy and Thomas E. Selfridge. Their contributions to aeronautical science are gratefully acknowledged. Erected by the Canadian Flying Clubs Association.

C. W. K. McCurdy is the genial Municipal Clerk at Baddeck. He ushered us into his office and showed us relics he has gathered during an interesting lifetime, and the chief item for us was a small cannon of an unusual type which was found under a mound of earth in the north of the island near the spot where Cabot made his landing. It is quite possible that the cannon was left there by members of that expedition. We strolled back to the hotel and sat with others on the wide verandah. A piper going past was invited to play. He strode up and down and gave us a selection of Scottish airs so entrancing that a young girl rushed up and began dancing as if the music were in her toes and beyond her control. Then someone started singing, and the dusk gave us more and more singers until the full volume of melody rang out over the lake, grand old Scottish songs, lilted with a fervour that left them in our memory.

In the morning Baddeck was full of colour. The gardens were full of bloom. The tartans were everywhere. We gazed our fill and remembered C. Dudley Warner's book—*Baddeck and That Sort of Thing*. Then we drove to the top of Beinn

Bhreagh (Gaelic for "Beautiful Hill"), a long winding climb that goes past the grand home of the editor of *National Geographic Magazine,* and to a hill crest where one looks down on Baddeck as if it were a tiny toy village, and the lake stretches in sheer blue beauty as far as the eye can see. We stopped in a glade and went by a path to a large boulder marking the last resting place of Alexander Graham Bell and Mrs. Bell. The famous inventor of the telephone spent many years at Baddeck and loved the place above all others. It was his wish to be buried there, and we have never seen a more lovely location.

Down hill again, and to Ross Ferry but a short distance from Baddeck, and there we left the Cabot Trail and followed Highway 5 to Sydney through the Big Bras d'Or and Little Bras d'Or districts, the two Bras d'Ors are streams of salt water connecting the Lakes with the Atlantic Ocean. After crossing the Little Bras' d'Or the highway traverses Boularderie Island, once granted to a distinguished French soldier, Chevalier de Boularderie, in reward for valiant service at the defence of Port Royal in 1707. Descriptions of the fine farm buildings he erected and of the grain and vegetable crops he produced are found in records of the island. We drove through Sydney Mines, a mining town, then North Sydney, where the boats leave for Newfoundland, and where a plaque on a cable building reads: "Cape Breton Newfoundland Cable. This tablet commemorates the successful laying in 1856 of a submarine telegraph cable between Cape Breton and Newfoundland as part of a plan for speedier ocean communication which later developed into the Atlantic Cable."

Any visitor blessed with average eyesight will know as soon as he enters the broad straight streets of Sydney, squarely set to the harbour as if on parade, that he is in a city as dignified and flavoured with military memories as a retired sergeant-major. He'll forget this military aspect, though, as soon as he meets the citizens, for they are a genuine, friendly people, proud of Sydney and proud of their island, but never stiff about any traditions.

They have every reason for their pride. Sydney was founded by the leading United Empire Loyalists from New York State, headed by Hon. Abraham Cuyler, a former mayor of Albany. The Harbour had been known to European sailing masters for at least four centuries, ever since the first Europeans crossed the Atlantic. It is the front door of Canada, just as Cape Breton is the oldest French name in American geography. The Spaniards were at Sydney first, and so the place was called Spanish Bay for many years. The first person there was a Loyalist who grounded his boat at Battery Point in May, 1784, felled a few trees and built himself a home on the banks of Muggah's Creek. He had the entire town to himself, not a tax to pay nor a by-law to interfere; but his reign was short-lived.

That year the northern part of Nova Scotia was set apart and named the province of New Brunswick, and soon Cape Breton had a similar separation, largely through the influence of Lord Sydney, the Colonial Secretary. Major J. F. W. DesBarres was appointed its Lieutenant-Governor. He was a Huguenot, born in Switzerland and educated as an engineer. He had served with distinction under Wolfe at the second siege of Louisbourg, and again at the taking of Quebec. For ten years he had been making a survey of the coast of Nova Scotia, and Spanish Bay was his immediate choice as a site for the capital.

He spent the winter at Louisbourg with the ex-mayor of Albany and four hundred Loyalists from New York State. In May, 1785, they moved to the Bay, and a beautiful site was chosen on the peninsula which juts into one of the largest and best harbours in the world. Everyone was given a task. The town was laid out with military precision, and fortunately DesBarres insisted on streets of a width unknown at that time. Unlike the beginning of most North American settlements, the town builders worked for the government in clearing a general site, then the lots were granted fairly to those who had accomplished the work. Everything was done according to an elaborate plan. Barracks were constructed for six companies of the 33rd Regiment, and "Spanish Bay" was changed to "Sydney" in honour of the Colonial Secretary.

On September 1, 1785, DesBarres formally declared the new capital established, and invited more citizens. His invitation was accepted by nearly four thousand New Englanders, and not all of them were Loyalists. DesBarres had promised provisions, building materials and implements to all comers; but those who held the purse strings at Halifax thought him too free-handed, and sent curtailing instructions to the colonel in command of the garrison, who had charge of the food supplies. Winter came and many citizens were refused rations. DesBarres gave orders, but they were not obeyed. He had the backing of the people, but was too much the soldier to incite violence. A vessel loaded with provisions was fast in the ice at Arichat. He sent men to buy both ship and supplies, and it was chopped free of the ice and sailed to Louisbourg. Then, to foil any military interference, the cargo was taken overland on sleds, twenty miles, and so the people were fed.

DesBarres sent the bill to Halifax and it was marked "no funds." It ended in his being recalled, but he had the confidence of the people, and before leaving was presented with an address signed by every citizen of consequence in Sydney. Down through the years his memory has been cherished, and he is remembered as a wise builder, the man who first realized the worth of Cape Breton's coal mines, one who was diplomatic in a tight corner and ever considerate and humane with his people. He lived to be 103, admired by all who knew him.

The next few years were hectic ones for the new capital, but it was a husky infant and the nearby coal mines spelled its survival, though it had to weather the eccentricities of divers governors who came and went in bewildering fashion —colonels and brigadiers, retired army officers utterly unfitted for their duties. Some did not serve a year, and the story is told of one irascible old fellow who had a fine garden in bloom when his recall was presented and he was informed that his successor was waiting on board a vessel in the harbour. Enraged, the recalled one spread straw over his flowers and burned all, declaring it would be his "or nobody's."

St. George's Church, erected the year after Sydney was founded and used as a garrison chapel, remains in service, a quaint and kindly veteran warmly loved by all adherents. The old deed to the property given when the parish ceased to be a garrison chapel is still retained and bears the great seal of Cape Breton, which probably cannot be duplicated today on any other document. St. George's was the centre of attraction those early Sundays when the soldiers marched in fine parade and all the civic dignitaries made up a solemn procession.

On weekdays the place of interest was "Washing Brook." The well water of the town was hard, while Cape Breton summers enjoyed too much sunshine to keep the rain barrels filled, so the settler wives were glad to find that the brook on the east of the peninsula was of marvellously soft water. On wash days fires were built along the banks and garments of all descriptions adorned the birch and bracken, while the ladies formed a social centre in which news and spicy gossip flowed as easily as the brook. Many a gallant major was troubled with burning ears, and the male population in general gazed with trepidation toward the brookside on days when flannel, calico and cotton billowed in the breeze.

In 1820 the Island was joined with Nova Scotia again, and the procession of peppery military incumbents ceased. For sixty-nine years Sydney was a garrison town, and many colourful regiments came and went, though none enjoyed the popularity of the 42nd Black Watch, which was twice stationed there, and whose plaids, kilts and skirling pipes added to all festivities. Its members were of such sterling character that throughout their year of occupation not a member was charged with a civil offence. After the soldiers had gone Sydney became more mellow, a leisurely Victorian town filled with gentle dignity. Then came the awakening.

Steel!

Capital had suddenly realized the excellent situation of Sydney for the development of a great steel industry. Iron ore in quality and quantity without exception on this continent within sixty miles by water haulage, coal at its door, and every mineral with the exception of one or two minor factors in the manufacture of steel, within twenty-five miles! Capital had looked, too, at the map of the world, and seen that Sydney is nearer Great Britain than any other port on the continent, and 600 miles nearer Rio de Janeiro than New York City!

Within a night Victorian Sydney was enveloped by a cosmopolitan growth which had come as a result of the largest steel plant in Canada, and in the evenings dumped slag painted crimson sunsets on a skyline dotted with fine brick structures. It had become a city of commerce, industry and culture. Its harbour filled with varied shipping, and at last the old site that DesBarres laid out with such care was filled to overflowing. But had he lived to see he would have been content, for the great mills, blast furnaces and chemical works are established to the eastward of his broad streets and the city proper, so that prevailing winds carrying all smoke and odour from their vicinity.

Under the new prosperity Sydney became a genial city. The old-timers have great tales to tell. One deals with the time Prince William Henry came there, and there was such a gay holiday that when the officials became sober they wanted to name the harbour "Prince William Henry's Sound," and it was so called on a few official documents before the name was forgotten.

John Meloney, a United Empire Loyalist, was Sydney's first settler. He arrived in June, 1784, landed at Battery Point and made a clearing there. Afterward he took up land east of the Creek and there built the first house in Sydney, a log cabin. He planted some apple trees, and one of them bore fruit until 1899, when it had to be removed to make room for additions to the Steel Plant. Meloney wanted a cow so went to Louisbourg and bought one, placed it on a schooner and had it transported to his farm at Sydney. Soon after the cow was missing one night, and after an extensive search was found twenty-five miles along the coast, making its way back to Louisbourg. The spot was named Cow Bay, and only recently was changed to Port Morien.

It was easy to secure one type of story in Sydney, that of buildings being haunted. One place was pointed out as being owned by a doctor. A soldier in the garrison committed suicide and the doctor secured the body which he proceeded to dissect in his rooms. Word of what he was doing became circulated around and friends of the dead soldier were making plans to raid the place when the doctor hastily buried the remains in the back yard of his residence. There, for years after, the ghost of the dead man would parade—with both arms severed at the shoulders. Another house is said to be built with parts of a gallows. The story goes that three persons were to be hanged, but no material could be found with which to construct gallows quickly, so the timbers of a half-finished house were taken and used, then returned to the owner. When the house was completed the occupants had uneasy nights as the droppings of the "trap" of the scaffold could be plainly heard, and the words of the priest giving last comfort to the doomed ones.

Another old house at the north end was used as a sort of prison when the regular place was overcrowded. Years after it was sold and the new owner discovered several skeletons in the cellar. He was so upset by his gruesome find that he moved the building over a new cellar and filled in the old one, now a part of the lawn beside the house. There the ghosts dance often on dark wintry nights.

We left Sydney by Highway 4, a fine paved road, and went through Big Pond Centre and Hay Cove. The waters of the Bras d'Or Lake was on our right, and the shore rose steeply in places. At Soldier's Cove we paused to buy drinks at a canteen by the wayside, for an elderly man wearing moccasins had attracted our attention. We asked him if there were anything unusual to see in that part of the country.

He pointed outward toward the lake, and told us about Chapel Island, speaking in a slow husky voice, but obviously proud that we had questioned him. The Island, he said, had a very old Indian shrine, dating back to November, 1792, when two full-blooded Micmac chiefs obtained permission to build a chapel on the island for the exercise of divine worship. "I can remember seeing the processions over there when I was a boy," the old man continued. "The Indians would come from all over the Island and there would be several priests, and everyone wore full regalia so that it was really an impressive sight. I was a young school teacher then, and I thought the Indians were as good as the whites. But I never see these days Indian girls half as nice looking as the girls back fifty years ago."

We suggested his age might have something to do with it, but he shrugged that theory to one side. "I'm eighty-five and clear-sighted as ever I was, and what I see I see. I had training in that upon St. Paul's Island off Aspy Bay. Spent four years there when I were a youngster, and never forgot a day of that time. The place is haunted."

"Haunted?" We could tell that he firmly believed what he said.

"One morning in broad daylight I met a stranger who was soaking wet to the knees. I asked him where he'd landed, and he said over on the west side, and was there any building near. His wife was lying on the beach with a broken leg. I ran and got a helper and we went down to the beach with a blanket and pair of poles. But there wasn't a soul in sight, and not a track on the sand. I went back to where I'd been standing and couldn't find a trace of dripped water or anything. The man I'd had rush down with me declared it was a ghost and that others had met the same stranger. It made me feel queer, and after that I was watchful. The next June I was at the same spot on some errand when the same fellow came around a rock and began asking the same question. I went hot and cold all over, watching his expression, and some scratches he had on his hands and wrists. Then

I went close and said 'If you'll take my hand I'll show you where we are.' I was within a step of him when a cold air struck me full force, like from a freezer, and he vanished. After that I told them I was through on the island and I've never been on it since."

He sat quietly for a time and we waited. "You come from Sydney?" he asked.

We said we had.

"Then you should have heard the truest ghost story in America," he said. "It is one thing Sydney has left of the military days, for the town was a garrison town from 1785 to 1854, and some of the buildings erected in 1833 are still there. On October 15, 1785, two officers, Captain Sherbrooke and Lieutenant Wynyard, were sitting in Wynyards' apartment, studying. It was four o'clock in the afternoon and perfectly light. One door from the apartment opened into Wynyard's bedroom, the other into a passage. Sherbrooke heard some one come along the passage. He glanced up, and there stood a tall young man looking extremely wretched and ill. He was dressed in light clothing, strange for the climate. Sherbrooke nodded welcome and nudged Wynyard to greet his guest. But Wynyard, after a first look, almost collapsed on his chair, and sat helpless to move or speak as the visitor walked on into the bedroom. Then Wynyard gasped that the stranger was his brother. 'See what's wrong with him, then,' said Sherbrooke, and he led the way into the bedroom. But no one was there. A search was made of the building, and the story told. No one could explain the mystery, but a brother officer suggested that Wynyard make a note of the exact hour and date, then write to his brother who was an officer in the Guards in India. This was done, but no mail was received from India until the 6th of June. Then came word that Wynyard's brother had died in India at the exact time the ghost had been seen in the apartment. Sherbrooke afterward became Lieutenant-Governor of Nova Scotia and never tired of telling the story."

We thanked the old man for his information, and asked

if he would have a cup of tea with us. He agreed courteously and said that he had once drunk tea with a premier of Nova Scotia, then left without telling us his name.

St. Peter's did not appear so much of a place when we arrived at it, but we knew it was one of the historic places of Cape Breton. The notable Nicholas Denys tells about it in his diary, for he had an important fishing and fur-trading post there in the early part of the 17th century, which he protected with a small fort. By 1636 he had over eighty acres cleared and cultivated, and was doing a fine trade with the Indians. The little colony prospered until 1653 when a French marauder came and captured the place, robbing Denys of a year's catch of fur. Denys went to Paris, saw the right persons and had St. Peter's restored to him, but that did not bring back his pelts. However he kept on trading and gradually made good his losses, when along came another villain in the piece, named La Giraudière, and once more Denys had to stand the expense of a trip to the homeland to have his rights restored. There was no great difficulty with the officials, but when Denys was back and had things in shape again a greater catastrophe overtook him. All his buildings with all his stores and crops and furs and provisions for the future were burned in a fire that raged until not a timber was left standing in the entire habitation, a loss Denys relates, amounting to at least 25,000 francs. It was the end for him there. He had no money with which to rebuild and he went up along the coast of New Brunswick to find a new home free from the misfortune that had dogged him at St. Peter's.

His clearings attracted others, however, and soon there were new homes and fish stages, and by 1737 the French had erected a strong post on the ruins of Denys' old fort. Eight years later Col. Moulton came with an English force, captured the place and burned the buildings together with four schooners that were at anchor there. Then he sailed away and the French came from the forest where they had hidden and began re-building. Others joined them, and in 1751 a fine highway was made between St. Peter's and Louisbourg by Count de Raymond. The Home Government of France was greatly aroused when it learned of the accomplishment, declaring that the road gave the British a perfect means of attack on the French stronghold, and de Raymond was moved from office. In 1793 Lt.-Col. Moore came to St. Peter's and built a strongpoint which he named Fort Granville, and mounted eight cannon there. There are still traces of its foundation at St. Peter's.

St. Peter's Canal cuts an isthmus half a mile in width, and has one lock 300 feet long, forty-eight feet wide and eighteen feet deep at low water. This Canal connects the Bras d'Or Lakes with St. Peter's Bay, and saves seventy-five miles for vessels wanting to enter the Bras d'Or from the south-west. We saw a cairn near the Canal and read the inscription: "St. Peter's. Site of Denys' port and trading post, built in 1650. Selected in 1713 as one of the three principal ports in Isle Royale, named Port Toulouse, and fortified by works at Point Jerome. Destroyed by Pepperrell's troops, 1745, re-occupied by the French 1748, evacuated 1758." The second inscription was: "St. Peter's Canal. Connecting St. Peter's Bay with the Bras d'Or Lakes, it follows substantially the portage of the old French trading days and materially shortens the distance to the eastern coasts of Cape Breton. First surveyed in 1825. Construction commenced in 1854, but suspended 1856; renewed 1865 and completed 1869, enlarged 1875-1881; 1912-1917."

Grand Anse was our next stop along the way, and there we saw a road branching off to the left to Isle Madame, reached by a bridge over Lennox Passage, and settled by descendants of Acadians who came there centuries ago. At the filling station the attendant told us that many artists went to Arichat on the island each year to sketch the quaint shore scenery. Soon we were back at Port Hawkesbury again and crossing over to the mainland of Nova Scotia.

9

Along Northumberland Strait

The Antigonish Casket. Broadway. The shy man.
Donald and Malcom and Sandy. The New Year's banquet
at The Rock. Green Hill Lookoff. Pictou and the Lobster Carnival. Tatamagouche. Pugwash and the Preacher.

COMING back to the mainland on the ferry made us feel
that we had been to the uttermost parts of the earth. Cape
Breton does that to one. There is a sense of remoteness up
along the Trail and in the Ingonish area that makes the
visitor feel at long last he has escaped the hurly-burly of
modern life and can have decent quiet and rest and peacefulness. Sound seems to travel softly and in dreamy fashion.
There is no hurry anywhere. People walk and talk with
deliberation, and impress you as being genuine. Silent vows
are all the same on that ferry. "Some time I'm coming back
to Cape Breton."

From the ferry landing we had to retrace our mileage, but
it was only a short time before we were away on Highway 4
and passing through villages new to us—Tracadie and Bayfield.
There were some superb views of the water, and cosy little
farms. Then we passed an unusually fine cabin colony at
South River and soon were crossing a bridge and turning
left into the town of Antigonish.

The Royal George Hotel is an old-timer, roomy, with high
ceilings, a sort of lazy place, quiet and worn and, perhaps, a
little tired, but our room was clean and the bed restful. We
liked the old place, and when we walked around the town in
the evening we liked it, too. We bought a copy of the town's

paper, as the name is intriguing—*The Antigonish Casket*. It is largely a church paper, Roman Catholic, but we found some interesting items, so much so that we talked with a local shopkeeper and wangled a dozen back copies from him. Two items in the paper we liked very much. First, the tales by Don Deadline, and secondly the fine sketches by Eileen Cameron Henry. We had read some good poetry by Mrs. Henry and also some excellent prose and knew her ability, but we had not known of Don Deadline, and our queries only brought the information that "Don" is very feminine. In her column was the tale of a day picking raspberries on the mountain when, tired and hot, the group of children dropped in on Kittach Ronald Angus and her brother Donald in hope of caraway cookies and tea. The tale goes:

They lived in a snug little house in the clearing. The branches of the trees almost brushed the back door and the brook sang its way a yard or so from the kitchen window. An old maid and an old bachelor, simple and innocent, they were as unworldly as two sparrows, and so guileless that they made even us children feel old and wise in comparison. They were refreshing themselves with afternoon tea when we filed in. We dropped in a tired row and gazed hopefully at the old brown teapot. Kittach arose clucking like a fussy little hen. She set out chairs. She made a dash at the teapot and refilled it from the steaming kettle and the caddy with gold dragons, on the kitchen dresser. She trotted to the cellar for a fresh pat of butter and thick cream.

We sighed contentedly and gazed around. We loved this cozy little kitchen. The shining stove was low and long with a barrel-shaped oven resting on top of a pipe-like projection. It did not need the inscription "Little Gem" in raised letters across the front damper to inform us of the excellent pies and cakes and cookies that funny little oven could turn out. There was a built-in dresser with open shelves to the ceiling. Two large flowered platters, one blue, one brown, were at home on the top shelf with the corresponding plates and tureens below. The other shelves were given over to Kittach's tea-set which started out to be purple and ended by being pale blue—flowing blue—our Ma called it, and the butter dish on the exact middle of the dresser top was a blue hen sitting on a nest. The shelf above the stove was dressed in a scalloped paper frill, and the lamps standing there were trimmed and filled to the brim and polished like diamonds. We peeped into the bedroom off the kitchen and saw Kittach's feather bed, fluffed as high as the curly posts and covered with a red-and-white patchwork quilt.

The tea was ready and we fell to like wolves. There was fresh bread made from darkish country flour, with a brown crackling crust and woolly insides; crab-apple preserves, a pat of butter stamped with an acorn, hunks of tangy country cheese and Kittach's famous caraway cookies. Donald, looking like Santa Claus with his long white hair and whiskers, rosy cheeks and twinkling eyes, bombarded us with questions, which we merely answered "yes" or "no" between mouthfuls.

"Is your Da home the day or did he went to the village? Did ye start the hay on the mash yet? Did ye kill a sheep? Is your Ma as good as ever at the oat cake? What is your Da paying for butter?"

"Shet your mouth, Donald, and let the poor things eat," ordered Kittach.

The sun was beginning to cast long shadows and we groaned and reached for our buckets. From the reeds at the head of the lake a loon called heartbreakingly. Rain to morrow, we thought, and suddenly longed for mother and home, and deep sweet sleep. "Goodbye," we chanted, impatient to be gone, "and thank you a thousand times."

"Ach, it was no trouble at all," said Kittach. "It's nice of you to bother with two old things like us."

"Ho, hi," said Donald. "Here's Kittach herself was half a century yesterday."

We gazed in stupefaction. Half a century! What an enormous age. She was faded and thin, with straggling hair skewered in a knot on the top of her head. But one girl asked "Kittach, did you ever have a beau?"

Donald snorted in disgust, but Kittach tossed her head and simpered. "Well, onct when I was a girl I came home from a frolic with Hughie John Donald from back of the mountain, and he was that nice to me."

"Oh, Kittach, what did he do?"

Kittach twisted her apron, put her hand over her mouth and tittered. "He was that nice," she whispered, "I'm telling you, he lifted me over the brook when he was leaving and. . . ." She paused and eyed us doubtfully.

"Come on, Kittach," we pleaded.

"And when he was leaving," said Kittach proudly, "he pinched me twice."

It is our hope that some day Don Deadline will have all her Recollections published in book form, for they are the best we have read in many a day.

Antigonish is a fascinating town. It is dominated by St. Francis Xavier University and St. Ninian's Cathedral and you have the feeling that it is a cultured place, with people who appreciate the finer things of life and have the time to do so. No one hurries. There are trees everywhere, beautiful shade trees, and every man, woman and child seems to know the entire population. In the morning when we were astir on the street that had seemed so dreamy and quiet and romantic in the evening there was still no hurry, and at the various corners any person who came along was hailed by a dozen others, and children came together as by common consent and chatted as if they were one large family.

We had no trouble ourselves in getting into conversation with many of the people in the shops and on the sidewalks. We found them, one and all, very proud of their university and the fact that its Extension Department is largely responsible for the adult education programmes in Nova Scotia, the Credit Unions and the Co-operative Stores. They tell you about their Annual Highland Games, and we knew they must be colourful, for a dozen girls in bright tartan danced the Fling on a green simply to satisfy a visitor with a camera and plenty of colour film.

One of the really remarkable pioneers of Antigonish County was Jane Pushee, who came within a year of the founding of the first settlements when the town was being called "Dorchester" by a few. She was a small woman, but possessed of unbounded courage and energy. She was the mid-wife of the district and its doctor as well, having a vast knowledge of herbs and Indian remedies. She lived to be 103 years old, and is said to have brought 1,056 babies into the world. There were few bridges over the streams in the early days, and when freshets were on she had a dread of crossings, so used to huddle in a large clothes basket and be carried over by a couple of men. She also had a number of cats and a fine yellow dog, named "Sally," of which she was very fond. One day, legend has it, a call for Jane was sent by the usual settlement telegraph—one youngster running to the next cabin, then another relaying to the next—and by the time word reached Jane it was dusk. The two men who did the carrying had received the word as it was passed along, and they hurried over. There was the big basket by the door and Jane had covered herself with a blanket. They picked up their burden, crossed a stream by felled logs used as a bridge and soon were at the home where they thought Jane was needed. They deposited the basket and pulled back the blanket. There lay Sally with five very young pups.

Meanwhile, in that land of many Macdonalds, Jane had gone unerringly to the right place, but she sent a message, when she heard what had happened, written with charcoal on birch bark, a relic long preserved by her descendants. It read: "If anything happens to my Sally or her pups may the Lord have mercy on your souls."

We left Antigonish, and Highway 4 was one of the prettiest drives we had had on the mainland. We passed through James River and Barney's River and then gave ourselves to the full enjoyment of continual curves and easy winding grades through a series of valleys with hills on either side and lovely gardens and tidy homes. Over all there seemed to be an aura of peace and content and achievement, good land and good living. Then a sign by the road said "Broadway," and we stopped by the school to talk with a man who seemed to be inspecting the building. It was one of our lucky moves. We had talked with more than fifteen likely-looking citizens from Mulgrave to Barney's River, and not one of them had anything more to tell than the gossip of the day, how the election went in his district or the fact that there was to be a bridge across the Strait of Canso.

But this man was different. "I've been figgerin' on new stove pipe for the school," he said, displaying a small bit of cardboard covered with large figures. "It ain't three years since we put in new, but that's the way things you buy are today. It's near enough to discourage a man."

"Perhaps we're better off here than in Europe, at that," we suggested.

"Right enough," came instant agreement. He doffed his hat and revealed a bald cranium that had been exposed to the sun until it was a delicate pink. Then he recited in a solemn voice:

> My grandad, viewing earth's worn cogs,
> Said things were going to the dogs.
> My great-grandad, in silken togs,
> Said things were going to the dogs.
> Great-great-grandad, in house of logs,
> Said things were going to the dogs.
> His grandad, in Flemmish bogs,
> Said things were going to the dogs.
> There's just one thing I have to state—
> Those dogs have had an awful wait.

We praised his offering, and asked why the settlement was called "Broadway."

"I can't say," he remarked, putting his hat on and fingering his stubble chin. "In this here country there ain't no accounting for half what goes on. In the first place, it's Scotch as oatmeal, 'cept for a baker's dozen of us English that crept in somehow. I don't like to tell my name in this county, for folks won't look up to you 'less you're a Macdonald or MacNeil or Ross or Sinclair or the like. When you go in town look in a 'phone directory. You'll find three pages nothin' but Macdonalds, and it's a small town. They say some around here was started out for preachers, and come down to farming. There's been doctors raised here, and lawyers and engineeers and theatre fellows. One time we had eight bachelors along this road, and there was quite a talk about taxing them extry. Then people started calling them 'Willie Andersons,' and five of them got married the next year."

"Who was 'Willie Anderson'?'" we asked, remembering our friend in Lunenburg.

Our informant plucked a strong stalk of timothy and chewed on it as he talked in a slow pleasant drawl. "He was raised in Halifax by his pa and an uncle. His ma died when he was born, and there was no woman in the house after he was a year or so old. Fact is, none he could remember. So he got to be mighty bashful, and the time he was twenty he was so bothered that he made up his mind to leave the town. You see, he was quite a good-looking chap, and didn't drink or raise hell any way, and there weren't too many of them kind back a hundred and fifty years ago. A shipload come over to settle, and they were sent up here to Antigonish county. I've heard they were at South River, and again others say it was just back there in James River. Anyhow Willie went along with them, and the Government give him a grant of land same as the rest. But Willie didn't start to clear his. He set out to walking in the woods, looking and looking and looking. The rest was too busy to bother with him and he was halfway through to the next settlement before he found what he wanted—four trees growing so they'd make four perfect corner posts for his cabin. He limbed them, and squared them as high as the cabin corners would go, then cut his logs and built. He cleared ground and put in a crop and got along good. But his looking so far had taken him away from a spring or brook, so he went to Antigonish and bought a molasses puncheon and rolled it back to use as a rain barrel."

A car honked in the distance and our friend started, then looked sheepish.

"I thought that might be my wife. She took the truck to town for some hen feed. She does most of our trucking, and she's a good driver. Let's see, now, about Willie. Well, he got lonesome there with nobody to talk with, and so he used to go to the harbour or James River and work with a farmer or fisherman. The second summer he was working at haying when a fine-looking girl went through the trail to visit at the next settlement. It was pretty hot under the trees, and when she was passing Willie's cabin she glanced into the rain barrel and saw it was half full. She had seen Willie working with a farmer the day before so she thought she would have a quick bath in the rain barrel, and Willie would never know anything about it. She was splashing merrily when the cabin door opened and Willie looked out. She peeped over the edge of the barrel and they eyed each other until Willie knew who she was. He had had toothache the night before and had come home. Now this shy lad, who had never walked a yard with a girl in his life, suddenly got some inspiration, or something. Anyhow he shouts to her. 'I'll stay right here, I won't go in and shut the door, 'less you promise to marry me'." Well, the girl in the barrel liked the look of Willie. She knew he was a good worker, and he had a fair clearing and decent cabin. It was likely, too, him being so shy, he'd be easy to manage. So she hollered back. 'You go in and shut the door and I'll marry you.' There ain't much about them after that till about four years later. Then they moved out to the Harbour on account them four trees still growing had lifted the cabin more'n three feet above the ground."

We had never heard a better story teller, and we said so with sincerity.

"It's nothing but telling what I heard when I was a youngster," he said modestly. "I never had much schooling, but I've a good memory, and this place is full of stories, or used to be. Now there's two other good ones. One about a doctor that went around with two dogs hitched to his sled in winter. He had a medicine box nailed on it, and them dogs was called 'Shilly' and 'Shally.' I'll tell you why. The other story's about a woman blacksmith over at Lismore who made every nail in the old church there. Now there was a woman. . . ."

An elderly truck with more than one rattle accompanying its movements came toward us, and its horn honked vigorously.

"I've got to go," said our friend. "There's a woman won't wait on anybody."

He shuffled quickly around our car and we drove on,

wishing very much we had heard more about the doctor and his dogs.

The road continued to curve its way through beautiful countryside, winding in and out and down and around until we came to one sharp turn, then crossed a bridge, and in no time were on the outskirts of New Glasgow, a fine town built on the banks of the East River. On a map accompanying the historian Charlevoix's work the mouth of East River is marked as the site of a large Indian village. This was on the east side, and many Indian relics have been uncovered there by the plow and by those digging wells and cellars. The discovery of coal in Pictou County was largely responsible for the growth of the town, named after the city of Glasgow, Scotland, by James Carmichael, a settler who built the first house in the area.

Legend has it that among the first Scottish settlers were a number of bachelors, young men who cleared land and built stout cabins, but had no chance to do any courting as there were no young ladies within a hundred miles. Two summers after they had taken up land and were doing well rumour came from Halifax that a ship had arrived there having on board a number of Scottish lassies who had come to the new land in search of employment. Three of the bachelors at once started and followed the blazed trail through the woods to Truro, then went down the horse path to Halifax. As soon as they arrived they found that the information received was correct. Indeed, they soon saw several of the girls walking up and down the board walk of the town, gazing in shop windows and admiring all they saw. The three young men, Donald and Malcom and Sandy, trailed along until by chance Donald learned the name of the lassie he fancied. Then he set off alone and met her as she lingered by the Coffee House.

"Good day," he said, "and it's glad I am to meet you, Jeanie, for I was feared I'd miss you in so big a town. I'm Donald Fraser and I've a snug place outside Halifax. I'd like for ye to marry me."

"Marry ye!" ejaculated Jeanie. "Why I've never put eyes on ye before. How dare ye speak wi' me at all?"

"Now, lass don't ye take on," soothed Donald. "Maggie coom over wi' ye and she's to wed my friend Malcom. So I though ye might. . . ."

"Maggie Ross! To wed your friend, Malcom! What a lass! All the way over she were just like the rest o' us, hating the thought o' going to work wi' some crank, and wishing she could wed, but never a whisper of what she planned. We-lll, now, let's see." Jeanie did a bit of pondering. "I'll wed ye, Donald, providing ye do this for me. Never let on but I came to meet ye. I'll show her I'm as smart as a Ross ony day."

"That ye will," cried Donald triumphantly. "And now will ye point her out to me, for Malcom's been praising her so I want to see her for myself."

Jeanie quickly obliged and when Donald had chance he slipped away and told Malcom about Maggie Ross, who was as comely as Jeanie. Soon Malcom had made his proposal to Maggie, telling her that as Jeanie was to wed his chum he would like very much to have Maggie go to the same place as his bride. Maggie soon agreed, on one condition. That they would pretend that all the time she had come to meet him. Then she introduced him to a third lassie, and soon Sandy was proposing to her. The upshot of the matter was that the three couples were married the next morning in the court house by the magistrate for the sum of three shillings, and then, the men, carrying the brides' leather trunks, the newly-weds set off for the homes "just outside Halifax."

By noon they had reached Six Mile House, and were hot and ready to rest. After they had eaten the three brides refused to move until their husbands told them exactly how much further they had to go. It is to their credit that they took the truth as a joke on themselves and entered into the spirit of the project. For two nights they slept on beds of brush and moss beneath the stars, but the weather held fine and they reached their new homes in good health. The story of their romance has lived down through the years, and many descendants of the trio are in Pictou County today.

Men were really men in those days. Thomas Fraser and his family arrived in Halifax in August, 1784, and received a grant of 400 acres on the west side of East River. He built a log cabin and snugged it ready for the winter before the first frost came. He cut trees until he had plenty of firewood, and he obtained enough flour and oatmeal to provide food, but could get no potatoes in the area. When winter came on he made a sled to draw by hand, and when the first snow came he walked the trail to Truro, forty miles, and bought three bushels of the precious tubers. It was impossible for him to draw the load and make the distance in one day, so he slept in the woods, burying the potatoes in snow and leaves to keep them from freezing. A fire gave him company and warmth, and he did not start until the sun was well up in the morning, arriving home without losing a potato.

The first vessel built at New Glasgow was launched from Clue's Brook in 1826, a topsail schooner, *Isabel,* constructed by Charles Sutherland. After that many a ship was built on the banks of East River and the town prospered. Soon a fine stone inn was built, and it was opened to the public in 1829, and known as "The Rock." There were fine paintings each side of the entrance. Sir William Wallace, with his sword held ready, was on one side, and Lord Nelson gazed out to sea from the other side. There are many tales of the hospitality enjoyed in this famous inn, and none better than the one about a New Year's banquet given to the Scottish élite of the community. As the guests filed in one lusty Highlander who had not been invited made his appearance. He declared he was a Gordon, and deserved attention, and he had brought along his sword to back up his arguments. When a protest was made he slashed at the lighted candles with much vigour and before he could be overpowered one wild slash had almost removed the gown of the magistrate's wife, a stately dowager who did not take such an offence lightly. She insisted that the Gordon be placed in jail, and there he was taken.

After his departure, and due repairs to the gown, the dinner went on, and conversation turned to swords. Someone examined the fine blade that had done the slashing and found its edge keen as a razor. Thereupon the magistrate's wife suggested that it be handed to the prisoner in his cell, together with a bottle of whiskey. The magistrate flinched at the loss of a bottle, and furthermore he saw that the idea was to have the fellow, alone and drunk and desperate, do harm to himself with the sword. He made some weak protest, and then sent a constable with the whiskey and blade. The party lasted until morn and no one roused early to begin the new year. When the jailer finally made his inspection he was amazed to find that the brawny Gordon had actually hewed his way to freedom, cutting through the plank door. The bottle was on the floor, empty. A light snow that had fallen covered all tracks of the intruder and he was not seen again in New Glasgow.

We had lunch at the Norfolk Hotel, and were told that it was the American House in the old days. A fine photograph taken in the days of the coach showed a gallant band of ladies and gentlemen watching the departure of guests for Truro. Before that era the hotel was known as the Donald Forbes Hotel, and in those days was a landmark of the town. It has a one-way main street, parallel to railway and river, and considerable hustle in its affairs. Stellarton and Westville and Thorburn are towns within a few minutes drive, and all the district is thickly settled, giving New Glasgow plenty of traffic at all times. The town has a daily and a weekly newspaper, but the publication that creates the most talk on the street is *The Clarion,* that has grown from a church bulletin to the most powerful Negro newspaper in Canada today. Mrs. Currie M. Best is manager and editor, and in just three short years the growth has taken place. *The Clarion* carries social and personal items and news from all coloured communities in Nova Scotia and from several New Brunswick and other Canadian centres. Rapidly becoming known for its excellent women's page, the paper also contains a column written by J.

Calbert Best, son of Mrs. Best, and a graduate in journalism of King's College, now taking his master's degree at Dalhousie University.

We had followed Highway 4 from Sydney to New Glasgow, a grand paved road, and we left New Glasgow by that route but at Alma, six miles out, we turned right and followed Highway 6, also paved and a beautiful scenic drive that skirts the Northumberland Strait. To our left was a high hill and we could see a tower at the top. A sign pointed a climb to "Green Hill Look-off," and up we went. When we arrived at the parking place by a Museum we were amply rewarded for climbing the hill. The view is one of the finest panoramas in eastern Canada of ocean, island, hills, harbours and valleys. Fields below us were a patchwork of different colours. Roads were tan ribbons leading to little farming communities. The sea glistened darkly in the sunlight of the afternoon. From the tower we could look across the Strait and see the long blur of the shore of Prince Edward Island.

A Museum of Scottish relics of pioneer days is based beside the tower, and there one can spend hours. A centre piece is the old stage coach in which King Edward VII rode when he was the Prince of Wales. When the Rt. Hon. Ramsay MacDonald, Premier of Great Britain, spent a holiday in Nova Scotia he visited Green Hill and its Museum. There he poked and probed and examined to heart's content and was so impressed that he presented the Museum with an ancient Hand Grist Mill used in the 17th century. Our attention was caught by a huge pair of shoes, and the attendant told us they had been worn by Annie Swan, the Nova Scotia giantess. She stood eight feet two inches tall and weighed 425 pounds. Annie was born at New Annan, and weighed eighteen pounds at birth. When she was eleven years old she could no longer wear her mother's dresses, and by the time she was fourteen P. T. Barnum had heard about her and had sent his agent to try and hire Annie for his circus. Her parents would not hear of it until the agent offered to give Annie a good education, then agreement was made. Her parents went to New York with her, and her mother stayed there a long time. Annie learned to do needlework, and was a well-mannered and highly intelligent girl when she met Captain Bates, a giant who was nearly her own height. They were married and built a house suitable for giants, with furniture to match. They had two children but neither lived long, and Annie died at the age of thirty-six. She was one of a family of thirteen, many of her sisters and brothers dying young.

We coasted down hill again to the paved road and drove on to Pictou, famous as the greatest lobster centre in the world, and as the greatest exporter of brains in the country. Thousands go there each summer to attend the Annual Lobster Carnival. A schoolhouse we passed bore the name "Loch Broom," and we remembered that the district supposedly was settled first by Camerons who were relatives of the noted "Cameron of Lochiel." One of the first churches in Pictou County was built in this section, a log building forty feet long and twenty-five feet wide. The pews were slats supported by blocks, and a crude gallery for younger folk was reached by a ladder. The church was only used in summer as there was no means of heating it, and the first services were held in Gaelic. We parked and gazed at the site where the church was supposed to have been, and thought of the many bear stories that came out of the County, one saying that the good folk had to stay a bit longer in the meeting house, even after a two-hour sermon, as a flock of five bears were seen alongside the path to the cabins.

One of the first Camerons was attacked by a bear as he tried to scare it away from his sheep, and had a narrow escape. He climbed a tree and the bear came after him. He whittled a branch to a sharp point and thrust desperately, blinding the brute until it dropped to earth, crazy with pain and rage. Another citizen in a race up a tree had the heel torn off his shoe by the bear's teeth. A cabin was burned in a clearing but the stout stone chimney survived. A bear pursued a settler across a field and he took refuge up the chimney, climbing up the fireplace. The bear reared against the stones and the man, up above, loosened a large one and dropped it, striking bruin on the skull and stunning him. A larger stone also hit the target, and legend had it that the bear was killed by the stones dropped on its head.

We drove across a bridge and past an old stone house where handcraft was for sale, then were in Lyon's Brook, a pretty tree-lined village. The place is named after the Rev. James Lyons, a Philadelphia settler who came in 1767. The first schoolhouse in the County was built by the brook, and the first Sunday School in Nova Scotia was organized in the old log building. We stopped and chatted with two men who were painting a shed, but they had no story to tell, even of bears.

Highway 6 crossed a railway and then took a sharp turn left and right to enter Pictou town. The entrance is rather drab, but the residential part is prettily situated on the hillside and the view is grand. We ambled to a book store and were sold a copy of *Pictou Parade,* a book of stories about Pictou by Roland H. Sherwood. Soon we had met this author, who is a veteran telephone man, the head of the Carnival, author of a column in the *Pictou Advocate,* an amateur photographer, and, once, a runner of some fame. He told us that the countryside simply teems with stories of the past, that there are many diaries of early settlers at the Acadia University Library in Wolfville.

According to history, Pictou was founded in June, 1767, by six families from Pennsylvania and Maryland, sent by the Philadelphia Company which had received a grant of 200,000 acres in the County. The six families arrived on the brig, *Hope,* and while they were still on the vessel in the harbour a son was born to Mrs. Thos. Harris, the first male of British parentage born at Pictou. In 1769 Mrs. Harris gave birth to a daughter, the first female of British parentage born in Pictou. Two of the six families soon moved on, but four remained and were joined by twelve other families. Meanwhile there was urgent need for more settlers, and one John Ross was sent as an agent to Scotland, where he painted glowing verbal pictures of a land so rich and varied that sap, sugar and fuel could be had from the same tree. He offered a free passage, a farm lot and a year's provisions to every family that would move to Nova Scotia, and hired the *Hector,* an old Dutch ship in bad repair and a poor sailer. It sailed with thirty-three families on board, and twenty-five unmarried men.

It took the *Hector* eleven weeks to cross the ocean, and so miserable were conditions on the ship that eighteen persons died during the voyage. When the ship did arrive the land seemed solid forest to the water's edge and, to add more trouble, they glimpsed Indians along the shore. At first they were in dread, but a piper dressed in all his regalia and led the way with rousing Scottish airs, and the redmen gave no opposition. The town was built on the site of an ancient Indian village, and when it was a village of size its citizens had more trouble in getting a suitable name for it than all the rest of the places in Pictou County. First it was Coleraine. Then New Paisley. Some didn't like that, so it became Alexandria. The leading merchant objected, and it became Donegal. No, said all the women, fearing trouble, and overnight the name changed to Teignmouth. Too hard to say, objected several, and there was a change to Southampton. Too English, was the objection, and so came Walmsley. It is said children would wake and ask what is the name of this place today? In 1790 the name "Pictou" was adopted, and a solemn resolution made that not another change would be made.

Pictou County had grand stands of pine in all directions, and the early settlers found they could earn good money by felling, squaring and rafting timber to the harbour. As early as 1774 a shipload of squared timber was sent to England, and a few years later no fewer than fifty vessels loaded with timber at this port in a single summer. Then it was found profitable to build ships with the abundant good lumber, and craft of all type from ninety tons to nine hundred tons were launched from the harbour yards. August 17, 1833, was a big day in

Pictou. The *Royal William* left there for England and arrived at London twenty-five days later, marking the first transatlantic passage accomplished under steam.

The site of the first Pictou Academy, founded in 1818, and from which many prominent men graduated, may be seen, as well as the birthplace of Sir William Dawson, LL.D. A monument in Market Square commemorates the landing of the *Hector* pioneers. A cut stone monument bears the inscription: "Site of the first Pictou Academy, which was erected in 1818 and demolished in 1932. Under the leadership and example of Dr. Thomas McCulloch, it opened the door of opportunity to a hitherto neglected element of the population of the Maritime Provinces and gave many prominent men to Nova Scotia and the Dominion of Canada in journalism, literature, science, theology, education and government." A tablet placed by the Nova Scotia Historical Society reads: "This tablet commemorates Sir John William Dawson, F.R.S., 1820-1899, Geologist, Educated at Pictou Academy, Superintendent of Education of Nova Scotia, 1850, Principal of McGill University, 1855, first President of the Royal Society of Canada, 1882, President of the British Association, 1886."

It is legend that for half a century there was not a university of note in eastern America in which there was not at least one professor who had graduated from Pictou Academy. All the County was conscious of the institution and education was held in great respect. Many Reading Circles and Study Clubs were organized, and the first Debating Society in Nova Scotia was started in 1830, when the people of one community gathered at a home to argue as to which was the greatest—Anticipation or Realization. There were four to a side, and the schoolmaster headed the trio of judges. The good woman of the house, however, was very nervous of the outcome, as the usual jug of potent beverage was brought for the occasion. As the debate waxed hot she took every opportunity of pouring water in the jug. Finally the last speaker was finished and the decision was given in favour of Realization. Then the food was passed around, and, last but not least, the jug. One old-timer had several swallows, then he rose and solemnly moved that the decision of the judges be reversed. The Club flourished for three years, and when there was a shortage of men to argue the women joined in. Soon it was found they could hold their own with the best of the male orators. So it was planned that for the final meeting before Christmas there would be four men debating against four women, and in order that neither side would have any advantage, the subject was to be drawn from a hat on the evening of the debate. Some wag put a slip in the hat, and it was drawn. The subject was: Resolved that wives will join their husbands in heaven. The women objected so strenuously that the meeting broke up in disorder.

The West River Farming Society, founded in 1817, had a better career. Its motto was in rhyme:

Let this be held the farmer's creed;
For stock seek out the choicest breed;
In peace and plenty let them feed.
Your lands sow with the best of seed,
Let it not dung nor dressing want,
And then provisions won't be scant.

Each member paid one shilling and three-pence quarterly. The rules read: "If any member shall curse or swear or use any indecent language, or introduce any subject inconsistent with the business of the Society, he shall be fined by the President and a majority of the members present, in a sum not exceeding five shillings." In the year 1818 they staged the first plowing match held in Nova Scotia. The Society also gave prizes for best cattle, for best wheat and for "the person who should stump and plow fit for crop the greatest quantity of land never plowed before, not more than three stumps per acre left on the land, and all stones that materially obstruct the operating of plowing and harrowing to be removed, the quantity to be not less than two acres." In 1919 this veteran organization became the Pictou Agricultural Society.

At Lobster Carnival time in Pictou all the world's a lobster. You see them in every shop window, it seems. You can smell them everywhere, for throughout the day a dozen canteens that mushroomed into being overnight sell delicious lobsters, cooked any way you may desire. They are served that day in all the restaurants and in the hotel. For once in your life you can have all the lobsters you wish to eat, for the prices are very reasonable, and the portions large. The parade is led by Father Neptune in person, and a monster lobster is generally a feature. Babe Ruth came from New York to attend a Lobster Carnival in Pictou, and never had a better time in his life. He posed for pictures with Father Neptune, he ate bushels of lobster, and he watched the lobster boat races in the harbour with the greatest interest. The boats are raced by men who make their living by fishing, and know well what can be done with craft of the type they handle. The way they churn across the harbour in flying foam and spray thrills every inlander.

It is along the Pictou shore that Roy MacKenzie gathered many of his Nova Scotia Songs and Ballads. Possibly the Scottish blood in the descendants of the first pioneers had a liking for verse dealing with death and disaster, also for matters more or less romantic. Some of the old classics can be heard yet of a Sunday evening in the home of an old-timer who has a gift for singing and reciting. One of the favourites is "Captain Wedderburn's Courtship." The first verse begins:

> The Duke of Merchant's daughter walked out one
>   summer's day,
> She met a bold sea captain by chance along the way.
> He says "My pretty fair maid, if it wasn't for the law,
> I would have you in my bed this night by either stock
>   or wa."

There are many verses, dealing with the terms of the courtship, and the gallant bold sea captain was able to meet each demand, so that the last line of the last verse runs smoothly.

> So he and she lie in one bed and he lies next the wall.

We left Pictou with reluctance and soon were at Toney

River, which seemed to consist of ninety per cent. summer cottages. There is a wonderful sand beach stretching endlessly and there were bathers in all directions. Two MacLeods from the Island of Lewis settled the place in 1803, mainly because they had never seen better stands of white pine, and one first settler loaded three vessels with pine he cut as he made his clearings. Seven years after the first settlers came there were large sawmills at the mouth of the river, and vessels came to load with the sawn pine. Pitch pine of a superior growth dominated, and it was said that for miles every grown tree would yield a timber fourteen inches square.

Next along the way is River John, first known as Deception River, then John's River, finally River John. The bridge is in the centre of the community, and the first one was a crude affair of logs built by first settlers from Alsace, France. One of the tragic stories of pioneer days in Nova Scotia came from River John. The Patriquins were a leading family, and one of the children was a bright lad named John. He was only five years old, but eager to travel about the farm with his father. One morning a buyer purchased several steers from the boy's father and drove them several miles toward Tatamagouche. Little John asked if he might go along, but his father said the distance was too great. After the cattle were on the way, however, John escaped his mother's watchful eye and followed the route his father had taken. Some Indians who had been encamped near River John were moving to New Brunswick and they captured the boy and took him with them. Searchers found the tell-tale tracks and tried to overtake the party, but it scattered on reaching the forests of the north and the trail was lost.

Each summer for years after the mother would walk the woods where John had been captured, calling his name, hoping against hope that the Indians would relent and bring him back. But they never did. Thirty years after he returned, a hunter who lived with the Indians. He could speak English, but refused to admit his identity, though he looked much like his brothers. His parents were dead and he did not stay long in the community. Resisting all arguments and persuasion, he returned to life in the Micmac wigwams and on the hunting trail.

A truck was blocking the road completely when we drove into Tatamagouche. There were parked cars on either side and the truck had come out of a driveway at too sharp an angle to make a turn. In trying to back into the driveway again, it had crashed the plank bridge over the ditch and there it was, while a dozen persons looked on and offered varied advice. But no one spoke in anger or impatience, and the driver, a young man, acted as if he knew he was among friends.

"If you're in a hurry," said a voice by our car window, "just go up the street to your left, turn right, and you can come down into the town again."

It was a kind gentle voice and it belonged to a gentle-looking little man who wore a felt hat tipped jauntily to one side, a chin that needed shaving, and a brown paper parcel in his arms.

"If you're going that way," we invited, "get in and ride with us."

The invitation was accepted, and for the next hour the gentle man was our guide and historian. We learned that Tatamagouche is an Indian word meaning "the meeting of two waters," and that the waters are the French and Waugh's Rivers. The Acadians found it a pleasant countryside more than two centuries ago, cleared land and lived in content. But at the time of the Expulsion they were treated as were all others of their race. A detachment of New Englanders marched there, and their orders were to burn and destroy everything, from crops to boats at anchor. Captain Willard was the officer in charge, and he must have had an argument with his conscience for he stopped with an elderly couple who cooked many loaves of bread for him, and made him a fine dinner of chicken. Word was given that all the men of the place were to report at once to Fort Cumberland, and every house in the village was searched for arms. The next day the unfortunate male prisoners moved out, carrying with them all the food that could be taken, blankets and keepsakes.

Our historian showed us an excellent little book, *Acadian Tatamagouche and Fort Franklin,* by Frank H. Patterson, K.C., and I am certain that anyone interested in the village would treasure such material as is found on the pages of the volume. Mr. Patterson draws a true picture of the place at present: "In the countryside around are modern houses, spacious barns, orchards with ripening fruits, gardens bright in bloom, fields of maturing grain, of pastures and of growing crops, where the Acadians once cleared the forests, built their cabins and swung scythe and sickle in fields studded with stumps. Now motor-cars and trucks go racing over broad paved roads, where the Acadians on foot or with ox teams trudged along the rough trails through woods and over swamp and upland."

It is no doubt correct that the Micmacs had a large encampment at Tatamagouche for many centuries before the white man came to Nova Scotia, just as they had at Merigomish and Pictou and East River and a dozen places along the South Shore, for the red men made their camps where life was easiest, and at the mouths of the two rivers, the Bay and its creeks they could find plenty of lobsters, eels, trout, salmon and cod, while in the extensive mud flats were clams and oysters. In the fall and spring geese and duck were there in abundance. What better existence would a redskin ask? Our guide pointed out to us a bit of island ground said to be the ancient burial ground of the Micmacs, and told us that many arrow heads and Indian pottery had been picked up around Tatamagouche in days gone by.

Some time during the 18th century the Acadians came to the Bay and remained there. There were not many, but when their folk from the Basin of Minas began shipping cattle and produce overland to Tatamagouche thence to be carried by ships to Louisbourg, the place gained importance. The route reached across country from Tatamagouche to what is Belmont today on Highway 2, and soon it was well-known to both

Indian and Acadian. The notorious Abbé Le Loutre, who had his headquarters at Shubenacadie, came to Tatamagouche in 1738 and took the place under his charge. Some years later be built a French chapel there, and a house for transient priests. First settlers to Tatamagouche found the site when they arrived, and the Acadian burying ground with its wooden crosses still standing. It was purchased by a settler who respected the last resting place of those firstcomers, and to this day it has not been touched but is now a small wilderness of bush and brier.

First touch of war came to Tatamagouche in 1745, when one French officer, Marin, who had made an ineffectual raid against Annapolis Royal, came marching back with a view to helping the garrison at Louisbourg. He marched a motley force of French and Indians through the trails to Tatamagouche, and there spent three days making ready to go by water to the Cape Breton stronghold. He had with him as captive, a Captain Pote, who kept a diary of proceedings, and told a story of Marin embarking in a sloop, followed by the rest in canoes and shallops. Three British privateers that had been watching for French supply ships came upon the flotilla and dispersed it at once, but lack of wind and shallow waters prevented them from overtaking the enemy, and Frenchman and Indian took cover behind banks on shore and dared the soldiers to come after them. Pote tells the story quaintly:

Ye Shott came Exceeding near us. The Endians seeing this there was a Great Confusion amongst them. He was ye Best Man could get on shore first. We halled our Connews up behind a Sea Wall. Ye sloops stood near the shore and Fired Verey Briskly upon us.

The three British vessels had the enemy neatly trapped in the shallow creek from which they could not escape, so were forced to travel overland. Our guide showed us the plaque on a cut stone monument. It read: "Naval Encounter at Tatamagouche (15th June, 1745). In this harbour Capt.

David Donahue of New England, with three armed vessels, surprised Lieut. Paul Marin's allied force en route from Annapolis Royal to Louisbourg. He drove them ashore, disheartened the Canadian Indians and prevented the French and Micmacs from reaching Louisbourg before its fall."

Tatamagouche was next reported in history when a force came marching from Beauséjour in January of 1747, guided by treacherous Acadians, on their way to surprise Noble and his men in a midnight attack at Grand Pré. The force was entertained with the meagre resources of the natives, and then proceeded on their way to an attack they had not dared to make in open summer weather with the chances even. There is no doubt but what some of the stronger Acadians of Tatamagouche joined with the expedition.

Much has been written in sentimental vein about the Expulsion, and no one will deny that, viewed in a certain light, it was a cruel action. The average writer, however, seeing but one side of the picture, forgets the true situation. No British settling of a country belonging to Britain could take place while it was populated with thousands who not only encouraged the Indians to constant attack on British settlers but often went with them on such forays. And peaceful quiet Tatamagouche, enjoying late August with its tang of tide and late marsh odours, was full of knowledge of Indians in war paint driving British captives on the long trek to Quebec, of black-robed priests and political agents, of shallops and schooners creeping in furtively to take on supplies smuggled away from the authority of British garrisons at Annapolis and Windsor. They knew, too, of the fall of Béauséjour and must have realized that some measures of security would be taken before another winter had passed. Willard kept a diary of his work and his own story shows that he acted in the best interests of all concerned, preventing needless bloodshed and carrying out his orders as a soldier must. The women and children certainly had a poor time of it, and although ships were sent for them, the majority evaded capture and joined others on Prince Edward Island.

The settling of Prince Edward Island by the British made necessary a strong point at Tatamagouche, as it was on the direct route from Halifax to the Island. So in 1768 soldiers and engineers were sent there with supplies and building materials. Our guide showed us the site of the blockhouse, and its well. It was called Fort Francklin, after the Lieutenant-Governor of the province, and was garrisoned but a short time. Its protection, however, encouraged the operating of a ferry, a small decked boat that sailed back and forth between Tatamagouche and Prince Edward Island.

We were advised by our friend to eat at "Bay Acres," and found it a delightful spot, a lovely home on the corner of a high slope overlooking the sea. The dining-room was inviting and the food excellent. The hostess told us something of the history of the place, and it was interesting for in the old days ship-building went on down at the water's edge, there was a long wharf and a store for those who worked in the shipyard. Bay Acres is really three houses made into one, we were told, and one of its owners was a man who loved flowers. One hundred years ago a member of his family brought from Scotland a rhododendron that was highly prized. It thrived in Nova Scotia soil after the long vogage over, and when winter came a small house was built over it as protection against storm and chill. For forty-two years the house was erected over the shrub each fall, and then it was thought there was no need for further protection. Today the bush is taller than a man and bears magnificent bloom. Age has not troubled it at all.

We drove on past a sign pointing to Malagash, where there is a large salt mine, and then arrived at Wallace, where signs bothered us nearly as much as at the Pubnicos for there was Wallace, Wallace Bay, Wallace River, East Wallace, Wallace Grant, Wallace Station, Wallace Ridge, Wallace Bridge, North Wallace and Head of Wallace Bay. "We've three things to brag about here," said a man at a filling station. "First, Newcomb, then the quarry, and then fox berries. On the average it's the quarry that's talked about.

We've sent building stone to Halifax and Ottawa and Amherst and near half the big places in eastern Canada. It's in the Province House at Halifax, in the Victoria Museum at Ottawa and there's ten anyhow big buildings in the States that is mostly walled with Wallace stone. You go along there a piece and you'll see where Simon Newcomb was born. They tell about a big tree in which he used to sit when a boy and do his studying. Anyhow, go look at the stone monument to him."

We looked. The inscription read: "Marking the birthplace of Simon Newcomb, who, self-taught, in the face of adversity, became one the world's greatest scientists. Migrating to the United States at the age of eighteen, he devoted his life to astronomy. For his contributions to science he was awarded the Copley Medal of the Royal Society of London, made a foreign associate of the French Academy of Sciences, and honoured by many universities and learned societies throughout the world."

There is beautiful scenery, enchanting vistas of land and sea, all along Highway 6, or, as it is locally known, "The Sunrise Trail," and the miles between Wallace and Pugwash are really thrilling.

We had begun to tire of trying to find some person with a story to tell, but the luck we had had elsewhere kept edging us on, and when we drove into Pugwash and saw the ground made trim and decorative through the efforts of Charles Eaton we parked to feast our eyes on the scene and to ask questions of any who might pass by. In the short reach within our vision along the main street we could see car licenses from nine different States, and three from other Canadian provinces. Little groups walked back and forth from shore to drugstore, the tanned ones and the sun-burned ones, tall and short, stout and lean. The day was balmy; there was no other word for it—and so still that when a car came over the bridge the sound seemed to echo through the town.

An elderly man walking slowly came along the roadway, and we could see by his laboured breathing that he suffered from asthma. He let himself down in a seat with a sigh of relief, and we strolled over. "Very hot day," we commented.

"The kind I like," he returned, mopping his flushed features. "You new here?"

We explained that we were not tourists, but were in search of material to put in a book.

"Just the history of this place would fill a book," he observed. "There isn't any fort or the like of that, but there's plenty of story about the brickyard over the bridge and around the turn. You can see it if you walk past the drug store. There's all kinds of tales about ships that have been here, and smugglers, and lobster poachers. You go and see Charlie Hollis. He was the head fish warden here for years and years, played hockey till he was about fifty. He knows Pugwash."

We waited patiently as the old man did more mopping with his handkerchief.

"I haven't the breath to spare to tell you what you should know," he went on. "Best I can do is tell you two stories, then send you along to see Charlie. First story is about Hallowe'en when I was a youngster and the place was wild enough. We had a good preacher then, a Methodist, he was, and one to speak his mind. Well, when Hallowe'en come around the boys did the usual tricks of taking off barn doors and gates and rolling rain barrels down main street, and blocking chimneys and upsetting outhouses. About ten o'clock the fun had gone far enough, the constable decided, so he got half a dozen citizens to help him put a stop to things. They circled the town to make sure no more mischief was going on and when they went by the parsonage they saw the outhouse there had been over-turned. What they didn't know was that the preacher was in it—been there when the building was pushed over and it fell forward on the door, trapping him. He wasn't hurt too much and now he heard voices, and recognized them. The barber was one, and he said the preacher had it coming to him. He was far too drastic in his talk against liquor. The butcher agreed, and said he never thought the man could preach much anyhow. The constable said he was always being pestered to raid some stores where rum was sold, and he'd be glad when the preacher moved elsewhere. They all spoke their opinions strongly, and went away. Then three men who worked on the water front, and bought their rum at the stores mentioned, came along. They observed the wrecked building, and one said: 'The preacher's a good sort. He says what he thinks and he doesn't bend a knee to any of these so-and-so's in the stores.' The others agreed, and decided to restore the building to an upright position.

"Their amazement was great when they discovered the preacher, who at once invited them into the parsonage and made them a pot of tea and served a fine apple pie his wife had made before going visiting for the evening. After the lunch was finished he invited them to light their pipes and they sat around chatting until the good wife arrived home. She was not in the least alarmed at sight of the fellows, but got herself a cup and joined them. The next day the preacher walked into the barber shop and told the barber that a fair exchange of opinions should be a considerable help in a community. The barber, puzzled, agreed fully. 'Well,' said the preacher, 'I heard you give your opinion of me last night. And this is my opinion of you.' It was pretty straight truth, without sugar stirred in, but fair enough and without malice. The barber was too beaten for words, and his customers simply gaped in awe.

"Then the preacher moved on to the butcher's shop, and by the time he had finished there people were out on the sidewalk, watching where he'd go next. He caught up with the constable by the bridge, and that poor man was so mortified he was ready to jump in the water and drown himself. After that morning both storekeepers that was selling rum tried to get clear of their stock, and were caught doing it. On Sunday there weren't seats enough for half the crowd that tried to get into the church, but the preacher just flopped them by speaking about Pugwash being as good a town as a man could wish, now that there was no liquor being sold and everybody knew what the other fellow thought of him. That good man stayed on two extra years in Pugwash, and there never was a better in a pulpit here."

It must have been a rather crude way to gain information, we said.

"A good many things is crude," admitted the old man. "Even justice can be sort of crude, like with a certain fellow around here when I was young. We'll call him Sam, because that wasn't his name. The other man can be Pete, because that wasn't his name. Both were pretty slick traders and never let their conscience bother them if they could get something for nothing."

A lovely blonde wearing only a halter and shorts strolled by, and the old man gazed in eloquent silence, then sighed. "They have them cartoons in the paper about being born thirty years too soon," he commented. "That's only half the truth. It should read sixty." He continued to gaze until the blonde was gone from sight, then shrugged to free his head of other thoughts.

"When Sam was at his best cordwood was no more than five dollars here, and he had plenty of it a few miles west. He'd hire a young man to go in the woods with him and near work the youngster to death, for he was a good chopper. Then he'd let the wood dry all summer and haul it in during the fall, selling whatever he didn't need for himself. Pete, however, hadn't any wood lot. But he did have a good fish business and could buy all the fuel he needed. He was running a fish wagon down shore at the time and one night, coming home, thought of Sam's woodlot. It was only a step off the main road so in he went, for it was real dark, and he piled on a good load of the best dried wood. He was too cute to take it to his home, but he had an old fish shed around the turn from here, and he took it there. Next time he was out that way he took another load. In the meantime Sam, coming in with his lobster traps, had some boat trouble and landed near Pete's old shed. He wanted a board or stick and happened to look in and saw the wood there. It never

dawned on him it was his own. He just seen a good chance
to help himself. So the first dark night he took his boat there
and loaded it from the fish shed. Pete brought in more loads,
as it was getting on toward fall and he feared Sam might start
hauling. Sam kept going fairly often to the fish shed, and
he must have wondered a bit as the wood never seemed any
less."

The old man had a spell of wheezing, and it was some
time before he recovered. Then the blonde returned, and as
she passed from view once more there was another sigh.

"Nothing makes me feel older than seeing a pretty girl," observed the old man sadly. Then he went on with his story. "One
day Sam went back to his wood lot, and he saw at once that
he'd lost nearly half his wood. He said nothing, but come to
town, got his auger and some gunpowder. He went back to
the wood and bored holes in a few sticks, in different piles,
put in some gunpowder and plugged the holes. That night
he made two trips with his boat, so he'd have enough to
make up what had been stolen from him. He didn't try to
watch the wood lot, but bided his time, and didn't forget
Pete's shed. There was a row of moonlight nights, though,
and he daren't try to get any wood. Then Pete made trips
with his fish wagon three nights running, and Sam used the
boat near all one night. The next day he went and hauled
what was left in his lot, noticing the loaded sticks were
gone. Come the frost, the fires were put on. There wasn't
a week gone before there was a great uproar one night. An
explosion had torn Pete's furnace door clear and scattered
fire all over his cellar. The neighbours piled in with plenty
of water, for it was early evening, and they got the fire out.
Sam was there with the rest, and when the mess was past
danger he spoke his mind, telling about his losing wood and
his putting powder in the sticks. Just as he finished—bang!—
his own furnace exploded. The crowd all ran there. Except
Pete. He tore over with a lantern and looked into his fish
shed. Then he marched over to Sam's house, and when the
fire was out over there he spoke his mind about who had been

stealing wood from his fish shed. With that every man and boy in the place near bust with laughing. It cost both Sam and Pete more to fix their furnaces than if they'd both bought wood for the winter, and that was justice, crude or otherwise. Now you go along and see Charlie Hollis. I'm too tired to talk—and that blonde may come back."

We didn't try to find Charlie. It was such a nice day that we didn't want to talk or prowl about. We just drove along over the creaking bridge at ten miles an hour and then through the countryside, lovely with flowers, sweet-scented and still. There were little wooden lighthouses up in fields on both sides of the road, beacons that had to come inland for height, and soon we were at Port Philip where a deer leisurely crossed the road ahead of us and vanished in bushes not one hundred yards from summer cottages. Presently it emerged near one and we saw a young woman come out with a camera and take some photographs. The deer ambled about until some children started chasing it, when it ran back to the river and swam across. We watched it scale the far bank, and then we went to the store and had some ice cream. The man who served us was eager to talk, and told us of the troubles they had had in years gone by to get a bridge worth while. For a long time, when he was a boy, a ferry was used, and he had a clipping showing the old rates that were established at that time. A single horse was taken across for ten cents; two horses cost twenty-five cents. Sheep were two cents each, at owners' risk. Each person paid four cents, but going or returning from the church, which was across the river, was at half price on Sunday if you attended divine service.

We next saw Linden signs on a post office, and there were two old farms where we saw deer feeding in abandoned apple orchards. We counted six in one place, and when he stopped the car to watch them not one ran away. Next we were at Shinimicas, an Indian word for "shining water," and there saw an old mill that had been in service for many years. A side road bore a sign reading "Lake Kilarney," and it might lead to a charming spot, but we kept on our way, passing

through Amherst Head, then Truemanville. Trueman's Pond
was a shallow with black stumps sticking up like heads of
fearsome creatures, and when we stopped by the brook where
a boy was fishing he told of a man who had gone to sleep
at the wheel of his car and driven straight into the pond at
the only place where it was deep. The car wedged between
two stumps and the man drowned inside, unable to get free.

He seemed an intelligent lad, and when we plied him with
more questions he went to the nearest house and returned
with a treasured copy of the Amherst *News* of September,
1919, which had a page story of the Truemans. One Amos
Trueman, a Yorkshireman, had settled in the district about
1776, building a log cabin when he had three acres cleared,
then a barn which was logged up eight feet high, and covered
with poles and brush to keep out the cold. It was six years
before a cart trail was made through the forest, the nearest
neighbour was almost two miles away, and travelling was on
horseback. The Truemans prospered, cleared more and more
land, and multiplied until a century after their coming there
were some fifteen hundred of them living in the country,
one of them the President of Mount Allison University,
another a Professor in the Nova Scotia Agricultural College at
Truro.

Roads led left and right as we turned a sharp corner and
came in sight of Amherst, which we had left two weeks before.
There was a large round barn, reminding one of a spinning
top sunken into the soil, for it had a weather vane at the top.
Then we could see the broad marshes again, dotted with hay
barns, smell the sea and bared tide flats, and as we drove
into the town we felt as if we had travelled through a dozen
different countries, or one that was formed without a plan,
with settlements following the sea as they willed or as
convenience suggested. We knew no written words could
describe adequately the long lobster-claw peninsula, anchored
to the mainland by no more than a narrow strip of marshland,
for Nova Scotia has its own distinctive and inimitable character, a hundred different moods and more whisperings of

the past than any similar area on the continent. We had sensed the shattered dreams of countless little coves and harbours where wooden ships were the pride of the nineteenth century. We had heard countless Micmac names and stories that awoke to rustlings of moose hide moccasins moving along the well-worn slots of forest trails. We had savoured the romance of the Evangeline country, the scents of the apple orchards, the aura of old houses at Annapolis, the memories of old Port Royal, the Acadian cheerfulness of St. Mary's Bay Shore. Along the South Shore the battering Atlantic and weathered cottages of tiny sea havens had given us a glimpse of the salty strength of the province, and the half-wilderness of the Eastern Shore had been stimulating. Cape Breton Island had been sheer delight—grandeur, history, sheer beauty of lake and hill and intervale. Then the long red sand flats of Northumberland Strait, and stubby lighthouses shouldering farm fences and orchards, had spoken of a more sheltered life, yet just as remote from the hurry and worry of the modern world.

Those who get to know Nova Scotia best will understand why so many elderly persons have chosen the province for their retirement. There is an indefinable charm about the rugged headlands and quiet meadows that helps one believe that those who find Nova Scotia life sweetest are they who sip it slowly.

Often visitors make inquiries about sites on which they might build, and the dreamy ones roam shore lines planning where they will locate. "We're coming here when we retire," and, at the time, they speak with great sincerity.

Some few realize their aim, and each year their numbers are greater. We thought of those we had met and talked with about the future, and were glad we had made the trip. It helped us understand their feelings. It had given us, too, a stronger belief in that which has been said many times, that Nova Scotia is a place where beauty has had time to grow, where memories have gathered, giving depth and meaning to the lives of a people who always have leisure to be kind.

INDEX

Aldershot, 60
Alma, 275
Alton, 27
Amherst, 8 ff., 67, 213, 294
Amherst Head, 294
Annapolis River, 61, 81
Annapolis Royal, 34, 56, 62 ff., 75 ff., 79 ff., 86 ff., 90, 100, 103 f., 120, 285. *See* Port Royal.
Antigonish, 263 ff.
Arcadia, 121
Argyle, 122 f., 154
Aspy Bay, 242, 259
Auburn, 63
Auld's Cove, 231
Avonport, 54
Avon River, 46, 49 f.
Aylesford, 61 ff.

Baddeck, 251 ff.
Barney's River, 267
Barrington, 134, 136 ff., 143, 154
Bass River, 21 ff.
Bayfield, 263
Bear River, 98
Beaubassin, 3 f., 9
Beaver River, 111
Bedford, 31, 34
Bedford Basin, 31 ff.
Belle Cote, 237
Belmont, 26, 284
Big Pond Centre, 258
Birchtown, 148, 153
Black Point, 18, 188
Blandford, 188
Bloody Creek, 75
Bon Portage, 133
Bras d'Or, 253, 262
Brentwood, 27
Bridgetown, 70 ff.
Bridgewater, 171 f.
Briton Cove, 246
Broadway, 267 f.
Brookfield, 27, 30

Cabot Trail, 232, 234, 237, 245, 253, 263
Cambridge, 61
Cameron Lake, 44
Campbell, 234
Canso, 225 ff.
Cape Smoky, 245

Carsbrook, 20
Chapel Island, 259
Chebogue, 119 ff.
Chedabucto Bay, 227 ff.
Chegoggin, 134
Chester, 183 ff.
Cheticamp, 237 ff.
Chimney Rocks, 20
Church Point, 104, 107 ff., 114
Clare, 109, 114, 122, 128
Clark's Harbour, 145
Clementsport, 91 ff.
Cleveland, 188
Clyde, 134, 145 f.
Coddle Harbour, 221
Coldbrook, 61
Comeauville, 107
Cornwallis, 76
Cross Roads Country Harbour, 221

Dartmouth, 206 ff., 213
Debert Station, 26
Deep Brook, 94, 98
Digby, 96, 100 ff., 104
Dingwall, 242
Douglas, 49

East River, 284
Economy Hill, 20
Ecum Secum, 219
Ellershouse, 42 ff.
Elmsdale, 28
Enfield, 28, 211
English Harbour, 224
Englishtown, 247
Evangeline Beach, 54

Fall River, 31
Falmouth, 47, 53
Five Islands, 20
Fort Anne, 79, 87
Fort Edward, 47 f.
Fort Lawrence, 5 ff., 39
Fort Morris, 165
Fort Sackville, 34
French Village Station, 188
Friar's Head, 237

Gaspereau River, 54, 59
Glenholme, 25
Goldboro, 221
Goldenville, 219 f.

297